Murder, Mystery, and Mayhem
in the Rio Abajo

Edited by

Richard Melzer and John Taylor

A Valencia County Historical Society Publication

Library of Congress Cataloging-in-Publication Data

ISBN 978-1-936744-14-5

Cover illustration by Brent Jeffrey Thomas

To Tara Calico—

May your mystery be solved
so you can find peace at last in
the Rio Abajo.

Acknowledgements

The editors wish to acknowledge the unselfish contributions of the authors of the stories contained in *Murder, Mystery, and Mayhem in the Rio Abajo*, including Matt Baca, Oswald G. Baca, Sandy Battin, Jim Boeck, Don Bullis, Paul Harden, and John W. Pope. Major assistance was provided by many individuals, including Ana Anaya, S. Pauline Anaya, Becky Baca, Connie Baca, the late Joseph Philip Baca, the late Dave Candelaria, David Cargo, Regina Elkins, the late Bob Garley, Jamie Goldberg, Kenny Griego, Patty Guggino, Judy Márquez, Francis Torres Perotti, Kurt Sager, Ernestina Sánchez, Irene Sánchez, Raymond Sánchez, Esther Shir, Francisco Sisneros, Norbert Torres, Ramón Torres, Ronnie Torres, Martha Trujillo, LeAnn Weller, Bob White, the late Anne T. Williams, and all others mentioned as sources of information and images in the text.

We also wish to thank the editors of the *Valencia County News-Bulletin*, formerly Sandy Battin and now Clara García, as well as the paper's publisher, David Purdu, for publishing the Valencia County Historical Society's "La Historia del Rio Abajo" monthly series since 1998. Many of the chapters that appear in this anthology first appeared in "La Historia del Rio Abajo."

Finally, we wish to thank the faithful readers of "La Historia del Rio Abajo." Your enthusiasm for the series encouraged our authors to continue discovering intriguing new stories with the ultimate goal of one day collecting these tales in book form. Thank you, our neighbors, for your interest in all things mysterious in our Rio Abajo.

Contents

Introduction

A shot rings out on a dark night in Pinos Wells and a prominent rancher, businessman, and politician falls dead on the cabin floor—the assassin escapes into the New Mexico night. Eight years later a body identifiable only by distinctive scapular medallions and silk underwear is found lying in a trench filled with toxic sheep dipping solution—did he fall, or was he pushed? Later, a stone covered with mysterious hieroglyphs is found west of Los Lunas. Is it a clever college prank or evidence of ancient travelers to the Land of Enchantment?

These are but a few of the incidents of murder, mystery, and mayhem that make the Rio Abajo such a treasure trove of intriguing history for local residents and historians alike. The purpose of this volume is to preserve some of the most interesting of these many cases of murder, mystery, and mayhem in chapters written by some of the best authors of the Rio Abajo community. Chapters range from heinous murders to bold train robberies, from religious miracles to unsolved mysteries, and from accounts of earthquakes to reports of terrible disease. All took place in the Rio Abajo, defined as Valencia and Socorro counties in north-central New Mexico.

So, put on your deerslayer cap and join us as we explore some of the most famous and least-well-known history of New Mexico's most colorful region, the Rio Abajo.

Section I—Crime, Lawmen, and Punishment

Death at the Depot:
Adelita Jaramillo, 1891

by Richard Melzer

Painting of Los Lunas Train Depot by K. Bruggemann (Los Lunas Museum of Heritage and Arts)

Several tragic deaths marred the history of the Rio Abajo in the late nineteenth and early twentieth centuries. The deaths of José Placido Romero in 1893, J. Francisco Chaves in 1904, and Solomon Luna in 1912 remain some of New Mexico's most famous unsolved mysteries. But perhaps the most tragic mystery of all involved the cold-blooded murder of an innocent young woman, 17-year-old Adelita Jaramillo, on November 8, 1891.

Adelita Jaramillo was born in 1875 at Fort Sumner, New Mexico. She was the daughter of Telefor Jaramillo of the wealthy Jaramillo family of Los Lunas, and Sophia Maxwell Jaramillo, the second youngest daughter of Lucien Maxwell, once the largest landowner in the entire United States. The Maxwell land grant encompassed no less than 97,000 acres in northeastern New Mexico.

As the daughter of such affluent parents, Adelita was raised in luxury. Her family's home near Tomé Hill was described as a two-story structure with a large front porch and as many as six fireplaces, three of which were made of marble.

By 1891, Adelita was quite beautiful and a favorite in local society. She had received her early education at the Loretto Academy in Santa Fe. Although their father, Telefor, had died of pneumonia earlier in 1891, it was decided that 17-year-old Adelita and her 15-year-old sister, Trinidad, should continue their education in Denver, Colorado.

The date was November 8, 1891. Accompanied by their grandmother, Trinidad Romero y Jaramillo, and a younger brother, Adelita and Trinidad had gone to the Los Lunas train depot to await the arrival of the evening train that would take the girls to school far to the north. The four family members sat peacefully on a bench in the small train station.

Suddenly, a bullet crashed through the station's window, hitting Adelita in the arm and passing through her small body. Adelita died in her grandmother's arms within minutes.

Adelita's lifeless body was taken to her grandmother's house where the local coroner held an immediate inquest. He determined that the young woman had been killed by a rifle shot. Her murderer had apparently fled in the dark of night.

News of Adelita's death spread through Valencia County and all of New Mexico, casting gloom over all who heard the sad news. Newspapers like the *Albuquerque Morning Democrat* were outraged, calling this "the most dastardly crime in the annals of New Mexico." Unfortunately, violence was still a frequent occurrence in the territory, but it seldom involved a young woman, no less the daughter of such a well-respected, powerful family.

All vowed that the killer must be found and punished immediately.

This did not seem like a difficult task, since all evidence pointed to one suspect: 22-year-old J. Francisco "Frank" Romero of Peralta. Romero was the number one suspect in Adelita's murder because he was the victim's rejected suitor. It was said that he had been turned away by Adelita's family because he was not considered good enough for their daughter. In fact, the family may well have decided to send Adelita away to Denver to distance her from Romero, especially after Telefor Jaramillo's recent death.

Based on this information, Valencia County Sheriff Tranquilino Luna summoned a posse and rode to Romero's Peralta home on the morning after Adelita's murder. The posse soon found Romero and placed him under arrest. Sheriff Luna also collected evidence, including a Winchester rifle (said to be the murder weapon), a knife, and some incriminating papers.

Luna was praised for personally taking charge of the arrest, especially when about thirty local men followed the sheriff to Romero's house with violent plans that had nothing to do with the accused's legal rights. Only Luna's presence had prevented an illegal rush to judgment. Unfortunately, Los Lunas had a reputation for lynchings in the 1880s and 1890s. Three men would hang in the village on a single night in March 1882. Another three would be killed on a single night in May 1893.

But fear of vigilante activity continued even after Romero was placed behind bars in Los Lunas. According to one Albuquerque newspaper, the residents of Los Lunas were "at a white heat with indignation" over the murder of such a young, innocent woman. Only the timely arrival of a special train of reinforcements from Albuquerque helped lawmen to secure the jail and prevent a lynching at Los Lunas's hanging tree on Main Street. Romero was transferred to the Bernalillo County jail for his own safety.

The case against Frank Romero seemed convincing enough. It was even rumored that Romero had admitted his guilt to a priest in confession, although the priest refused to share this evidence outside the confessional in a court of law.

But Frank Romero was never found guilty, no less punished for the murder of Adelita Jaramillo. His trial was moved to Santa Fe (in a change of venue), proceedings were delayed until 1892, and his legal counsel, Thomas B. Catron, had the reputation of being one of the best lawyers in the territory.

And Romero had an alibi. Yes, he admitted being at the scene of the crime on the night in question. In fact, he admitted being with a group of his friends outside the depot, when he claimed he saw a number of "tramps" who appeared to be looking for valuables to steal. To prevent such a theft, someone reportedly shot at or over the tramps' heads. But instead of hitting or scaring off the intended target, the bullet shot through the station window, accidentally hitting and killing Adelita. Adding credibility to this story, some baggage on the depot platform was, indeed, found to be missing. Without witnesses and with Romero's alibi, the jury at Frank's trial acquitted him in 1892. Once freed, he wisely left Valencia County to become a merchant in Magdalena where he remained for many years.

But Adelita's murder was avenged, at least according to newspaper reports of the day. In May 1893, a year-and-a-half after Adelita's death, Frank's father, J. Placido Romero, mysteriously disappeared, only to be found several days later when his body was discovered along the Rio Grande. Not able to punish the alleged murderer himself, a person (or persons) had punished his father instead.

And what of Adelita? Her funeral Mass was held at the old Catholic Church in Los Lunas at 10:00 a.m. on November 11, 1891. She was buried in the *camposanto* (cemetery) beside the church. There is no stone to mark her grave today because all of the weathered, deteriorated gravestones have long been removed.

But Adelita's name, along with dozens of others, appears on a plaque in the center of the cemetery. Otherwise, there is nothing left to remind us of the tragic events that ended her young life. It is perhaps fitting, because her life had ended far too soon for her to have left a lasting mark on the community that mourned her sudden death in the fall of 1891.

King Solomon's Mysterious Demise: Solomon Luna, 1912

by Richard Melzer

Solomon Luna (Valencia County Historical Society)

Mystery surrounds the death of one of Valencia County's most famous and power residents, Solomon Luna.

Luna's Power and Wealth

Born into the wealthy Luna family in 1858, Solomon was the great-great-grandson of Don Domingo de Luna, an early Spanish settler of New Mexico and the recipient of a 110,000-acre land grant from the King of Spain. Raised in affluence, Solomon was educated by tutors in this family's large home. When he was old enough, he was sent off to St. Louis to finish his education at St. Louis University. Returning to New Mexico as a young man, he was described as "about 5-foot-9-inches in height, not so handsome, yet distinctive in appearance with a resolute, self-confident bearing, and a determined, earnest face."

Solomon entered and vastly expanded his family's agriculture business, especially sheep ranching. By 1890, Luna owned 35,000 sheep,

7

yielding 40,000 pounds of wool a year. Fourteen years later, he owned 80,000 sheep with a yield of 80,000 pounds of wool per year. He was said to own the largest number of sheep in all of New Mexico. But Luna's business interests reached far beyond ranching. His diverse ventures included real estate, insurance, and banking. His assets totaled close to a million dollars.

Solomon Luna became as heavily involved in politics as he was in business. In Valencia County, voters elected him to the offices of probate clerk (in 1885), sheriff (in 1893), and county treasurer (in 1894). He reportedly held so much power as the Republican *patrón* (political chief) of Valencia County that he alone decided who ran for each office and who won each election. His enemies called him "King Solomon" and accused him of fixing elections in favor of his political allies, starting with his own relatives. His smoke-filled home office in the Luna Mansion was where most of the major political decisions regarding Valencia County were made in the late nineteenth and early twentieth centuries. The Luna family's influence led to the transfer of the Valencia County seat from Belen to Los Lunas in 1875.

Although he never held territorial or statewide office, Luna was nominated for the offices of congressional delegate, U.S. Senator, and state governor, but declined the nomination in each case. Luna did, however, serve as a member of the Republican National Committee from 1896 to 1912, making him a top leader of his party in the nation as well as in New Mexico. Luna was held in such high regard that when a new county was carved out in southern New Mexico in March 1901, it was named in his honor. Closer to home, Los Lunas's first high school was named for him as well. His name, high above the door of what would later become the Los Lunas Middle School, has greeted many generations of Valencia County students and teachers.

Not surprisingly, Luna was the most powerful Republican leader at the New Mexico State Constitutional Convention in 1910. It was said that all he had to do was nod and all of his fellow Republicans would vote as he wished, especially on questions involving the ironclad protection of Hispanic rights in New Mexico's first and only state constitution. With the creation of a state constitution, New Mexico was finally admitted as a state to the Union on January 6, 1912.

At the Sheep Ranch

But all of Luna's power and worldly success could not alter or prevent the early morning events of August 30, 1912. Luna and a crew of about fifty workers, including his favorite nephew, Eduardo Otero, had spent the previous two weeks cleaning thousands of Luna's sheep at Montague Stevens's ranch on the Plains of San Augustín in western Socorro County. Luna had leased Stevens's place for this annual event because water was more abundant there than at Luna's own nearby ranch.

As part of the cleaning process, sheep were led to a 3-foot wide, 75- to 100-foot long concrete vat. They were forced down a chute into hot water mixed with a strong solution of cresylic acid and soap called Cooper's Fluid Dip. Each sheep remained submerged long enough to kill all parasites on the wooly animal. Two dippings were required before a sheep could be sold outside New Mexico.

Sheep dipping trench (Los Lunas Museum of Heritage and Arts)

The work had gone well, although heavy rains had slowed it down and caused the ground to become slippery with mud. Eager to finish the job and return to his other business interests, Luna told his men to be ready to begin work as early as possible on August 30.

The men gathered to socialize the night before, but Luna turned in early, complaining of stomach trouble caused by eating too much fresh green chile. He had experienced similar trouble for several days, getting up to go the outhouse two or three times each night. Shortly after he retired to his room at about 10:00 p.m., Will Fullerton, a local rancher who was helping with the cleaning, came by to see if Luna had any matches to spare. "Yes," Luna replied, "Come in and help yourself." Neither man could have known that these helpful words would be Solomon Luna's last.

A Gruesome Discovery

Before sunrise the following morning, Inspector Edwin E. Spindler from the State Bureau of Animal Industry and several workers gathered to prepare the vat for the work that lay ahead. Spindler measured the water level in the vat and proceeded to fill it to the right level before the Cooper's Fluid Dip could be added and the work could begin. About three hundred gallons of steaming hot water, heated to nearly boiling, poured into the waiting trough.

But as the water level rose, one of the workers noticed something floating up in the mixture before them. At first, someone thought it was a lamb that had accidentally been caught in the vat the day before. It was only after closer inspection that the men realized that it was not an animal floating in the boiling water. It was the body of a dead person. One worker quickly assumed that the body belonged to Dave Farr, a crew foreman. But Farr quickly spoke up, proving that he was quite alive and well.

Then a terrible realization came to the men as the examined the remains by the light of a kerosene lantern. Although the sheep dip solution had damaged the body's physical characteristics beyond recognition, the crew quickly concluded that the undamaged religious medals, fine shoes, and silk underwear could only belong to one person in camp. "¡Es Don Solomón!" As Spindler later described that dreadful moment, "It was the most terrible shock that I and probably the others had ever experienced."

Word of Luna's death quickly spread through the camp. No one could believe that this tragedy had happened, especially with so many men camped outside, albeit at a distance from the fatal scene.

Muddy roads made it impossible for the undertaker to travel from Magdalena to care for Luna's body until that evening. Meanwhile, the corpse was placed on the only long flat surface they could find, a wooden door. In order to keep the body as cool as possible in the summer heat, Eduardo Otero had the men take shifts fanning his uncle's remains with palm leaf fans.

Funeral and Burial

Once prepared, Luna's body was transported to Magdalena and then on to the Strong Brothers Mortuary in Albuquerque where final arrangements were made. The funeral Mass was celebrated in Immaculate Conception Church in Albuquerque because the parish church in Los Lunas was far too small to accommodate the large crowds that attended. Father Anton Docher, pastor of the Isleta parish, presided.

Mourners came by train from all corners of the state to pay their last respects to the great man they had suddenly lost. A special train from Belen and Los Lunas brought dignitaries, friends, and relatives from Valencia County. Even President William Howard Taft sent a letter of condolence to Luna's widow.

The Knights of Columbus and the Benevolent and Protective Order of Elks led the procession that carried Luna's coffin to the Santa Bárbara cemetery (today's Mount Calvary Cemetery). Honorary and active pallbearers included John Becker, Thomas Catron, Albert B. Fall, H.O. Bursum, a U.S. Army general, and the Chief Justice of the New Mexico Supreme Court. Solomon's grave was soon marked with a tall, impressive obelisk that towered over all nearby stones, much as Luna had towered over most other men of his generation.

Theories of Conspiracy and Intrigue

So, where is the mystery in Solomon Luna's tragic death at the relatively young age of 54? The case seemed simple enough. He had apparently accidentally fallen into the vat while going to the outhouse.

One ranch hand testified that yes, he had heard what sounded like splashing from the direction of the vat in the early morning hours of August 30. But he was so tired from the previous day's labor that he had not gotten up to investigate. He and his fellow workers concluded that Luna had simply slipped in the mud while trying to get to the outhouse by going over the vat rather than taking a longer route around the crowded sheep corrals.

A small abrasion on the dead man's head showed where Luna had probably hit his head as he fell. Prints of his muddy palm and fingers on the vat's inner wall showed where his right hand had probably struck before slipping below the murky surface. Unconscious and unable to save himself, Luna drowned in the murky liquid.

The coroner's report agreed that this was an accidental death, leaving no room for the possibility of foul play as the cause of the fall, no less the drowning. But it was not long after Luna's elaborate funeral that at least three more sinister theories surfaced to explain how he had died on that fateful morning.

According to one theory that gained considerable currency, Luna was murdered. Those who believed this explanation suspected that someone either knocked Luna out in his room and dumped his body in the vat or pushed him into the vat as he stood by it. Likely suspects included anyone who felt cheated by Luna politically, financially, or personally. Even Eduardo Otero was accused, but never seriously enough to be officially charged.

Doubters responded to this theory by saying that Luna had no enemies who would want to see him dead, especially among the loyal workers present in his camp on August 30. Even his political rivals were counted among his personal friends. As his December 1906 will verified, no relative seemed cheated by this man who was as generous in death as he had been in life.

A second theory contended that Solomon Luna had committed suicide by drowning. Those who favored this explanation pointed to Luna's marital problems after thirty-one years of marriage to the former Adelaida Otero. Friction between Solomon and Adelaida had reportedly increased over the years and their union had borne no children. Rather than continue in an unsatisfactory marriage or face the scandal of a public divorce, Luna had taken matters into his own hands by ending his own life.

As proof of this theory, advocates discovered that Luna had canceled his upcoming reservations at the Alvarado Harvey House Hotel in Albuquerque because he had anticipated his own death, having planned it himself. In addition, Luna had just resigned as the president of the Sheep Sanitary Board, a powerful position he had held since 1897.

But few New Mexicans believed this suicide story. Well known for paying all outstanding debts, Luna had created two new ones just prior to his death, including a debt for the purchase of a new car in Albuquerque. Those closest to Luna knew that he would not have killed himself prior to settling all obligations, assuring that his estate would not be burdened with debts following his demise. Believers in the suicide theory also ignored the fact that the laces on Luna's shoes had been neatly tucked into his shoes to prevent an accident, not to intentionally create one. And why would someone of Luna's stature choose to end his life in this gruesome, demeaning manner?

A third theory of Luna's death is by far the most sensational and, as a result, the most appealing to many. It was rumored that Luna staged what appeared to be his own end, but what was really the murder of an innocent sheep herder. The victim was supposedly killed, dressed in Luna's clothes (or at least his medals, shoes, and silk underwear), and drowned in a poisonous liquid that would make physical recognition (long before DNA testing) impossible. After carrying out this elaborate ruse, Luna supposedly ran off to Europe to live out his life in luxury, receiving a handsome monthly income from his business operations via a co-conspirator, such as his loyal nephew, Eduardo.

This last theory definitely has sensational appeal, but, like most tabloid newspaper tales of the day, this one was undoubtedly the work of Luna's worst enemies, eager to finally ruin his name and reputation in death as they had been unable to in life. The surrogate victim theory was also the least likely explanation because it simply had too many holes to be viable. It would have required an exacting schedule and meticulous execution—neither of which Luna could have managed in an isolated sheep camp, despite all of his worldly wealth and influence. How could Luna and his co-conspirator(s) have snuck another person (or corpse) into the isolated camp without notice, especially down the muddy road that delayed an undertaker for hours on the day of the alleged murder? And how could Luna have made an effective getaway by car down those same bad roads? An accomplished horseman, he could have ridden off, but why hadn't those in camp noticed any unusual horse tracks in the mud? Or, more to the point, why didn't they notice any missing horses from their small herd?

How could Luna and his helper(s) have killed someone, hidden the body, and carried it to the vat so inconspicuously with so many men camped in the vicinity? Wouldn't there have been more commotion, and wouldn't more than one man have heard it? Finally, how could Luna have received a regular princely income from the United States without leaving a large paper trail that someone would have noticed over however many years his charade continued? No one need exhume Luna's remains to discover if it is really Solomon who is buried at the Mount Calvary Cemetery. The conspiracy theory just doesn't make sense.

The Most Likely Solution

And so, the most obvious solution is also the most likely, as is often the case in history: Solomon Luna died in a fluke accident while taking a shortcut over a sheep dipping vat during a hurried trip to the outhouse. We can safely believe the words of a *corrido* (ballad) later written in Luna's honor:

I am Don Solomon Luna
Who tried to help everyone
But at the hour of my death
No one took pity on me.
Everyone was asleep
And dawn found me dead in a vat.

At four in the morning
The inspector arose
In order to inspect his vats and to see
That everything was in order.
When he saw the corpose floating in the water
"Good heavens, what is this!"

Hearing the voices
The whole camp was alarmed
They took the body from the water
When a man recognized it.
Very alarmed, he told them,
"Oh, my God, it is our master!"

How my poor employees gather around me
Today they are all spectators
Of my unfortunate death,
See how sad they all are
Recalling to mind all my favors.

Farewell, my dear Eduardo,
My nephew beloved.
Do you not see how your uncle
died
By drowning in a vat
Full of lime and sulfur,
A place designed for the sheep?

I to my Redeemer recommend you
And hope He will have compassion
on you
Step carefully and do not slide.
Lest the same thing happen to you
For it was a false step that
Caused me to lose my life.

Who Killed El Colonél?
J. Francisco Chaves, 1904

by Richard Melzer

José Francisco Chaves (Museum of New Mexico, #27132)

In sharp contrast to the questions about the death of Solomon Luna in August 1912, there can be no doubt about the fate of another leader of early Valencia County history. José Francisco Chaves was killed by an assassin's bullet on the evening of November 26, 1904.

Similarities

Despite differences in their deaths, Solomon Luna and J. Francisco Chaves had many similarities in life. Both came from affluent, powerful Spanish families that had been among the New Mexico elite for over a century.

Both Luna and Chaves were born in the Rio Abajo and were educated back East. Specifically, Chaves was born in Los Padillas (just north of Isleta Pueblo) on June 27, 1833. When old enough, he attended schools in St. Louis and New York City. In a famous statement reflecting Hispanic concerns on the eve of the American conquest of New Mexico, Chaves's father sent Francisco off to school saying, "The heretics are going to overrun all this country. Go and learn their language and come back prepared to defend your people."

When Francisco returned to the Southwest, he used his acquired English skills to defend Hispanic rights in many ways, but especially in politics and education. After studying law, he was admitted to the bar and began a long, successful political career. Like Luna, he was a Republican kingpin and a strong advocate for New Mexico statehood. He served as a leader at New Mexico's constitutional convention of 1889, just as Luna was a dominant figure at the New Mexico constitutional convention of 1910.

Both Luna and Chaves were also large sheep ranchers. Chaves drove thousands of sheep to California in the mid-1850s to exploit that state's great prosperity following the gold rush of 1849. In 1854, he blazed a new trail through what is now northern Arizona, but found the market for his sheep temporarily depressed. He stayed in California long enough for the market to improve and to marry Mary Bowie, a native of Montreal, Canada, in November 1857.

Finally, as highly respected territorial leaders both Chaves and Luna had new counties named after them. Chaves County, carved out of Lincoln County, was created in February 1889, one of the sixty-nine places named after one or another member of the Chaves (or Chávez) family in New Mexico. Luna County was named in Solomon Luna's honor on March 16, 1901.

Differences

But Luna and Chaves had almost as many differences as they had similarities. Unlike Luna, who shunned political office outside Valencia County, Chaves served as Valencia County's representative in the territorial legislature for more than twenty years (1875-1904). Presiding over the legislature for eight terms, it was said that Chaves was so powerful in Santa Fe that no business took place in the legislature until he arrived on his buckboard, even if he was delayed for several days.

At a higher political level, the citizens of New Mexico elected Chaves as their territorial delegate in Washington, D.C., for three terms (1865-1871). He also served as a district attorney and was appointed as the New Mexico Superintendent of Public Education in 1901 and as the Territorial Historian in 1903.

Luna and Chaves were also different because Chaves, having lived through long periods of war, had more military experience. Francisco served in the Civil War, rising to the rank of lieutenant colonel and earning much praise for his fighting skills. He had received recognition not only in New Mexico but also from President Abraham Lincoln himself in Washington, D.C. In addition, Chaves fought against the Navajos and was the commanding officer at Fort Wingate for several years. Based on his military exploits of the 1860s, Chaves was thereafter addressed as "*El Colonél.*"

But the characteristics that made Luna and Chaves most different were their loyalties to different political factions within the Republican party of Valencia County and the territory as a whole. Although related, Chaves and Luna (in alliance with the Otero family) constantly fought for party control with all the political and economic advantages that went with it. Fighting between the Luna and Chaves factions became so heated that Father Jean B. Ralliere of Tomé wrote in his diary, "I don't even care to listen to their confessions any more."

After years of squabbling, a compromise of sorts was negotiated. Like medieval lords dividing fiefdoms, the warring factions split Valencia County in two, creating a new county from parts of Valencia, Lincoln, San Miguel, Socorro, and Santa Fe counties. The Luna-Otero faction retained control over the old Valencia County west of the Manzano Mountains, while the Chaves faction gained control over the new county east of the Manzanos. The new county was named Torrance (after railroad developer Francis J. Torrance), since the Chaves name had already been used elsewhere. As if to affirm Chaves's domination over Torrance County from its inception, the county seat was placed in Progresso, the location of a Chaves sheep ranch. It appeared that political peace had been achieved by 1903.

Murder in Pinos Wells

But peace ended quickly on November 26, 1904. On that Saturday afternoon, Francisco had completed some business in the small village of Pinos Wells near his ranch in the far southwest corner of Torrance County. Asked to stay for dinner, Chaves retired to the home of Juan Dios de Salas. Salas and Chaves were joined at their dinner table by Donaciano Chaves, the local mail carrier. Francisco sat next to an exterior window.

Suddenly, a shot was fired through the window. Aimed at Francisco, the fateful bullet hit its mark, piercing Chaves's lungs just above the heart and exiting his body under the right arm. The bullet left only a small hole in the window pane and finally rested several inches into the interior adobe wall of the room. It was reportedly fired from a large caliber, smokeless gun.

Severely wounded, the 71-year-old Chaves rose from his chair, took two steps toward the window and fell dead within seconds. Shocked, the other men in the room paused before pursuing the assassin. By the time Salas and the mail carrier had gathered their composure, it was already too late. Only the killer's fresh tracks were found, leading to a nearby corral where he fled by horse.

Search for the Killer

News of Chaves's "black and cowardly" murder "flashed over the wires" in the words of the *Santa Fe New Mexican*. The awful deed was the topic of all conversations, as was the need "to bring the inhuman wretches who perpetrated the murder" to swift and "well deserved justice." A posse was formed and blood hounds from the territorial prison were sent out immediately. A reward of $2,500 was offered for the "dastardly" assassin's arrest. According to the *New Mexican*, it "would be a foul blot upon New Mexico" and its criminal justice system if the killer somehow escaped. But the assassin had made a clean get-away. The hounds picked up the killer's scent at the scene of the crime, but lost it after about a mile where it was destroyed by the passing of a herd of sheep or goats.

Only one man was taken in for questioning. Suspected for unstated reasons, Domingo Vállez was transported to the territorial penitentiary in Santa Fe where authorities attempted to force a confession by stringing him up by his thumbs. In terrible pain, Vállez soon confessed, although he recanted within moments after he was lowered to the floor. Later asked why he had changed his mind, he replied, "Let me string you up by your thumbs, and you will confess that you did it too!" Vállez was never tried, no less convicted, for the Chaves murder. He, in fact, lived to be 103 years old, with five children, sixteen grandchildren, thirty-three great-grandchildren, and two great-great-grandchildren. He died of natural causes in Belen, having recently built his own pine coffin and whittled its wooden key in the fall of 1956.

Who Killed *El Colonel?*

If Vállez was not the murderer, who was? Some believe that Colonel Chaves was killed by men he had alienated by gathering evidence against them for rustling and other crimes in his new county. But most historians agree that Chaves's murder was probably politically motivated. In the words of one historian, the colonel "was sent to the holy land at the behest of highly placed Republican party leaders because they considered him inimical to their intrigues." Only the details of who was behind the plot and how they carried it out remain a mystery.

Could the infamous Santa Fe Ring that dominated New Mexico for much of the late nineteenth century have arranged for Chaves's murder or were his local political foes responsible? Could Solomon Luna or his Otero allies have been involved, although Luna was among those who met Chaves's body when it was transported to Santa Fe by train? If Luna was somehow involved, it was ironic that Luna also died six years later in what some considered a politically motivated "accident."

According to one popular theory, whoever arranged for Chaves's death had so much power and influence that he (or they) made a deal with a hardened convict serving a life sentence in the territorial prison: the convict agreed to cold-bloodedly murder Chaves in exchange for his early release from the penitentiary. If we believe this theory, we can also speculate that the convict/killer was able to flee from the murder scene with the help of the same power person (or group). How else can we explain the convenient destruction of his get-away trail by a herd of animals? (A similar ploy had been used to hide the get-away tracks in the famous abduction of Albert Fountain and his young son, Henry, in southern New Mexico in 1896.)

Perhaps Domingo Vállez's torture-provoked confession was part of the larger scheme, with Vállez used as a red herring to divert attention from the real killer in this tragic saga.

As a well respected, long-serving political leader, Colonel Chaves lay in state in the territorial Capitol until 10 a.m. on Wednesday, November 30. His body was then escorted to St. Francis Cathedral for a funeral Mass. Chaves was laid to rest at the National Cemetery in a ceremony attended by members of his family and all "prominent citizens of the city and the territory," according to the press.

But the mystery of Chaves's death remains unsolved. Unless foolproof new evidence or a convincing written confession is someday discovered, the true identity of Chaves's assassin will never be known, making the study of history as frustrating in this case as it is rewarding in others.

The Case of
The Dead Highway Commissioner:
Eugene Kempenich, 1921

by John Taylor

Eugene Kempenich's headstone in Albuquerque's Fairview Cemetery (John Taylor)

Two men gingerly pushed opened the front door of the house and called out, "Gene, Gene, are you here?" No one answered. They looked in the living room and kitchen and called again. Still, no answer. Noticing that the bedroom door was ajar, they went down the hall, and, as Demetrio Jaramillo looked into the room, he recoiled in horror. There beside the bed, wearing silk pajamas and lying in a pool of blood was his boss, Eugene Kempenich.

The Kempenich Family

The Kempenichs were active members of the Peralta community. They had immigrated to the New Mexico Territory from Austria in 1892, settling in Peralta. Although they were European and Jewish, they had fully assimilated into the Hispanic Catholic population of the Rio Abajo. In fact, the patriarch of the family, Abraham, and his wife, Jennie, were known locally as Abran and Juanita. In 1902, Father Rallière of Tomé had even hired Abran to design the steeples for the mission church of Sangre de Cristo in Valencia.

As the family put down roots and expanded their business interests, they kept their Peralta connection, operating a general store at the Peralta plaza, across from the Catholic Church of Our Lady of Guadalupe. They also ran the local post office, which was located in the plaza, and they bought and sold property in the area. Abraham died in 1905, and his wife and two of their three sons, Max and Eugene, took over management of the Peralta business. (A third son, Henry, lived in Portland, Oregon, and a daughter lived in Albuquerque.) Max died in the 1918 Spanish Flu epidemic, so by the early 1920s Eugene and his mother were running the Peralta operation alone. Eugene was also serving his second term on the State Highway Commission, and had been active in Sandoval County politics. In addition, he had owned a trading post in eastern Arizona for a time. He was a bachelor, and lived with his mother in the family home just north of the store.

The Crime Scene

On Friday morning, October 8, 1921, Demetrio Jaramillo had arrived at the store and noticed that, contrary to normal practice, his boss was not already there. Jaramillo thought that a few other things also seemed out of the ordinary—Kempenich's car, normally parked in the garage, had apparently been driven into a corral behind the house at a high rate of speed and had skidded to a stop, bumping the corral gate. The back seat of the car was askew and covered with tools.

Worried, Jaramillo called Henry Wortman, Kempenich's store manager, and together they entered the house. When they reached the bedroom, they found Kempenich, dressed in silk pajamas, lying on his back beside the bed with a .45 caliber revolver under his hand, dead from a single gunshot wound. The two men immediately called Valencia County Sheriff Joe Tondre who rushed to the scene.

As the investigation proceeded, the sheriff discovered that on Wednesday Kempenich had attended a special meeting of the State Highway Commission at which a proposal to change the routing of State Route 26 from Hillsboro to Elephant Butte was vetoed. He had driven to Moriarty on Thursday morning for a luncheon meeting with G. V. Johnson, a tire salesman for the Gates Tire and Rubber Company.

Kempenich had also set up an early afternoon appointment with Frank Gwinn, an engineer for the Highway Commission, to inspect a stretch of road. Finally, he had arranged to pick up his mother at the Santa Fe depot in Albuquerque at 4:00 p.m. on Thursday.

Kempenich kept his luncheon appointment with Johnson at a Moriarty hotel and left around noontime, apparently in good spirits. However, he failed to meet Gwinn and also failed to meet his mother's train.

Sheriff Tondre had a bit of a situation on his hands! Fingerprints wouldn't be very useful for another decade, luminol to detect bloodstains wouldn't be available until the late 1930s, and he would have to wait almost sixty years for DNA. But Tondre did know a few details that were pertinent: the victim was a single, middle-aged, well-to-do, Jewish male who had been active in business and state and local politics for some time. He was found wearing silk pajamas, lying on his back beside his bed with his right hand bent behind his head and his .45 caliber revolver under his hand. By examining the barrel and smelling for gunpowder Sheriff Tondre concluded that the revolver had not been fired recently. In addition, a bullet had been found under the bed. Kempenich's gun was a .45, and the badly deformed bullet under the bed was either a .41 or .44, so it did not appear to be a suicide.

The medical examiner's report said that Kempenich was shot in the back with the bullet entering slightly above his waist and to the right of his spine and exiting through his chest near the heart, suggesting that he was probably in bed, lying on his stomach when the assassination took place. In addition, no gunshot residue was found on his pajamas, indicating that the shooter was several feet away when the shot was made.

As for other clues, Wortman and Jaramillo noticed that their boss's car was in the corral where it had apparently been driven in haste. However, no one had seen Eugene come home, and he didn't contact anyone when he arrived. None of the neighbors had heard gunshots, although an occasional gunshot was not all that unusual in late-night Peralta in the 1920s.

In questioning Jaramillo and Wortman, Tondre had also learned that about three weeks before the incident, the victim had moved the revolver that he normally kept in the store to a shelf in his bedroom. This suggests that something or someone had been on his mind for a while. Whatever was bothering him didn't just pop up on Thursday afternoon!

It was apparent that something or someone he saw or someone he talked to either in person or on the phone early in the afternoon while he was still in Moriarty caused this normally punctual and businesslike individual to miss his appointments without notifying others and without arranging for someone to meet his mother at the train station in Albuquerque. No note had been found, so the message that initiated his bizarre behavior was probably delivered either in person or on the phone, and may have involved a threat to him, to his business, or to a family member or friend.

It also seemed unlikely that Kempenich was being chased, because his long desolate drive home from Moriarty would have afforded ample opportunity for the assailant to attack him under much more anonymous circumstances. The drive from Moriarty to Peralta only took between three and four hours, even if he had taken the cutoff through Escobosa and Hell Canyon, so there seems to have been several hours of "lost time." In that time, Kempenich could have gone almost anywhere from Santa Fe to Socorro, met with unknown folks, or perhaps even received more threats.

The authorities attempted to reconstruct Kempenich's behavior in the last few hours of his life. Despite an obvious concern for his own safety, he apparently didn't seek help from any friends or employees. This suggested that he arrived late at night, or at least after dark, or that he couldn't be sure that friends or employees would have been willing or able to help him. In appeared obvious that the urgency of the perceived threat caused the victim to drive into the corral and skid to a stop. Someone rummaged around the back seat of the car looking for something. If it was Kempenich himself, he may have believed that he was about to encounter someone in the house and may have been looking for a weapon to use. If it was the assailant, perhaps Kempenich had something that the assailant wanted. Whatever the threat had been, it did not immediately materialize once Kempenich got inside the house, so at some point he decided to put on his pajamas and go to bed, probably with his revolver close at hand.

Sometime during the night, the assailant who had either hidden in the house waiting for his victim to go to bed, had been invited in by the victim, or had sneaked in later, came into the bedroom and shot the victim from the foot of the bed as he lay sleeping. This would account for the bullet's trajectory. Kempenich rolled out of bed and died on the floor. The assailant then fled the scene.

Possible Motives

Based on the evidence, several common reasons for murder were eliminated. Except for the disarray in the back seat of the car, there was no evidence that robbery was involved. Although the silk pajamas on a middle-aged bachelor in his own house may have raised some eyebrows, there did not seem to be any evidence of a jilted lover, male or female. On the other hand, the fact that Kempenich moved his revolver from the store to the house and the apparent threat after lunch in Moriarty would seem to rule out a random act. The Kempenich family's full integration into the community would seem to eliminate the possibility that this was an anti-Semitic hate crime, although such feelings were widespread at the time.

The question of who might benefit from Kempenich's untimely departure focused some attention on Henry Wortman. After all, he eventually came to own the property and became the postmaster in Peralta. If he really was a close associate and Kempenich felt mortally threatened, why didn't Eugene solicit Wortman's help before he entered the house? However, everyone spoke very highly of Wortman and his loyalty, and Tondre thought that it was very unlikely that he was involved in this murder. In addition, since the threats had been going on for a few weeks and Kempenich did not seem to suspect Wortman, it seemed improbable that Henry would be a prime suspect.

This process of elimination seems to have eliminated everything except Kempenich's position on the Highway Commission. Even in the 1920s, before the advent of Route 66 and the Interstate Highway system, roads were big business—paving, grading, gravel, roadside concessions, etc.—all depended on routing and contract decisions made by the Commissioners. If Kempenich had voted the "wrong way" on some issue, was being pressured to vote one way or another, or if he was perceived as an impediment to an upcoming decision with significant financial ramifications for a powerful individual or group, perhaps "getting him out of the way" was the preferred alternative.

The murder of Eugene Kempenich was never officially solved. In early November 1921, the police arrested a Los Lunas man named J. Lucy Harrington as an "accessory after the fact," implying that someone else had actually committed the murder. But Harrington was released soon afterwards, and the Valencia County Grand Jury returned a "No Bill" on the charges against him the following March. The bottom line probably lies with the old-timers who remembered the tragedy and who were overheard decades later saying that whoever murdered Kempenich committed the crime because of "that highway business."

Joe Tondre and the Onion Skin Murder Mystery, 1926

by Richard Melzer

Joe Tondre (Anne T. Williams)

Forty-year-old Niichi "Nick" Yamate had just finished his evening shift as a railroad car inspector in the Santa Fe Railway yards of Belen. Tired, he had returned home at about midnight on Thursday, January 7, 1926. Yamate sat down at his kitchen table to relax and read a newspaper by the light of a kerosene lamp. A can of smoking tobacco lay open on the table, suggesting that he also planned to smoke his pipe before retiring to bed. Two houseguests were asleep elsewhere in the house. Yamate knew that both men were sound sleepers. Few, if any, sounds could awaken them.

A gunshot blast and the sound of breaking glass suddenly disrupted the quiet winter night. Hit in the head, Yamate slumped forward. He died almost instantly. Yamate's assassin turned from the shattered kitchen window and retreated across the yard. He vaulted the backyard fence and headed for a nearby truck. Throwing his rifle under the truck's seat, Yamate's killer slid off the sneakers he had worn to disguise his tracks. He put on his regular shoes and got into his truck. He had clearly planned his crime well. After a short drive, the killer arrived at a second house. He quickly undressed and went to bed, prepared to testify that he had slept through the night. Even his alibi had been carefully planned.

Yamate's body was discovered the following morning when his two houseguests awoke. They immediately reported the heinous crime to the local police. Neither man had heard Yamate arrive home, no less the single gunshot that had ended his life. They were, indeed, sound sleepers.

Newspapers in Belen and Albuquerque soon reported news of Yamate's murder. Front-page articles told how the police were initially baffled by the crime. They had little evidence, no witnesses, no immediate suspects, and no motive. An autopsy only added to the mystery. Four physicians, including Dr. Samuel Wilkinson of Belen and Dr. William Randolph Lovelace of Albuquerque, discovered that the fatal bullet had entered Yamate's head from above, exiting the head just above his left ear. How could this be when Yamate's head was supposedly turned so that his left ear was facing the window as the killer took his deadly aim?

The Investigation

Local police were soon joined by both private detectives and county lawmen. The Santa Fe dispatched railroad agents in case Yamate's murder was somehow tied to his job as a railway car inspector. Yamate's relatives in California hired a Burns Detective Agency investigator, perhaps fearing that a Japanese-American's case might not receive the same attention as a native in New Mexico. The family offered a $200 reward for information leading to the murderer's apprehension and arrest.

Valencia County Sheriff Antonio J. Archibeque and his deputy Joe Tondre completed the investigative team gathered to find Yamate's killer and bring him to justice. Investigators first searched for a motive for

Yamate's murder. They learned that Yamate had been born in Japan but had moved to California and then to New Mexico. For several years, he had owned and operated a grocery store at Fourth Street and Copper Avenue in Albuquerque. He had moved to Belen when he went to work for the Santa Fe Railway. He lived in a house on a five-acre plot not far from the roundhouse and railroad yards where he worked.

Once settled in Valencia County, Yamate had met and married a daughter from the Chávez family of Peralta. The couple had one child, a daughter, born in 1922. Unfortunately, Yamate's wife had grown ill and had died of natural causes in September 1925. Yamate's wife was not dead more than a few months when he asked his late wife's 18-year-old sister, Elisa, to marry him. Elisa accepted. They were to be married on January 18, 1926.

Marrying a deceased spouse's sibling was not unusual in New Mexico in the 1920s. Only Yamate's age, compared to Elisa's, and the short time between his first wife's death and his planned new marriage raised eyebrows in the community. So perhaps the killer was among those who disapproved of the marriage ceremony planned for early 1926. Or could the killer be a disgruntled former suitor? If so, it certainly would not be the first time that a disappointed suitor was accused of murder in Valencia County. Recall the tragic death of Adelita Jaramillo recounted earlier in this volume.

Mindful of this possible motive, investigators in 1926 learned that as many as three men had an interest in asking for Elisa's hand in marriage. All three were questioned. All three were now happily married to other women. The police and private investigator were stymied. According to the press, investigators did not even know if the killer had escaped from the murder scene by horse, by car, by truck, or even on foot.

Did the murder victim have any personal enemies? By all accounts Yamate was a well-liked neighbor, employee, and co-worker. Neighbors said that he was always willing to share anything he had with those in need. Reporters described him as a "perfect" citizen without a known enemy in the world.

But then Deputy Joe Tondre discovered a key piece of crime scene evidence. As the former county sheriff, Tondre was hardly a novice in police investigations. He had investigated and successfully solved many crimes in his career. Retracing the killer's route from Yamate's window to his get-away vehicle, Tondre discovered a tiny bit of evidence that only he and a few others could have recognized as significant. The Los Lunas lawman found onionskins where the killer had exchanged the footwear he had worn to disguise his footprints.

Why were onionskins significant in this case? Because, as Tondre recalled, Elisa's brothers, Emilio and Juan, had delivered a truckload of onions from Peralta to Belen just days before the murder. Could onionskins have dropped from one of the brothers' shoes as he removed the tennis shoes and replaced them with his regular footwear?

Based on this evidence, the police detained both Emilio and Juan for the murder of Niichi Yamate. By the next day, 26-year old Emilio confessed to the murder, taking sole responsibility for the deed so that his older brother could be exonerated and cleared as a suspect. Convinced that they had the right man, police officers released Juan and formally charged Emilio with the crime.

Confession

Emilio Chávez made a complete, signed confession. He freely admitted that he had purchased a .44 caliber Winchester rifle in late December 1925. He also told the police that he was staying at an in-law's house in Belen on the night of January 7. He had pretended to go to bed, but instead of dressing for bed, Emilio had kept his clothes and shoes on under the covers until all was quiet and he could leave the house undetected. He had left his in-law's house at about 11:30 p.m.

Driving to Yamate's, Chávez had put on his tennis shoes, climbed over the fence, approached the kitchen window, and found his human target quietly sitting at a table. After shooting a single shot, Chávez fled back across the fence, hurriedly changed his shoes, climbed into his truck, and made his escape. He returned to bed in his in-law's house so that no one would suspect his involvement in the crime. All those who had seen him go to bed earlier in the evening could unwittingly be used to corroborate his alibi.

But why would Emilio Chávez want to kill the husband of his deceased sister and the future husband of his younger sister, Elisa? Emilio was described as a bright young man who had studied at a Methodist school in Albuquerque before graduating from Belen High School in

1923. Since then, he had preached in Belen, and, most recently, grown crops, including onions, to sell in the valley.

Single, he was said be very close to his family, especially his youngest sister, Elisa. He worked hard to support his family and protect them in any way he could. Chávez was said to be a "quiet boy" and "friendly towards all." At 5 feet, 7 inches and 136 pounds, he was a slim youth who had never been in trouble with the law. What could possibly be his motive for such a cold-blooded murder? As it turns out, Chávez had two main motives for his actions.

First, he could not understand why Elisa would want to marry Nick Yamate. Chávez concluded that nothing short of magic could have convinced Elisa to marry her older brother-in-law. Yamate had, in fact, boasted to Chávez that he knew of a magical way to make any woman fall in love with him. Chávez was convinced that Yamate must have used this "improper spell" on Elisa. After all, Elisa had once told Chávez that she would never marry Yamate, not even if he were a king. But within weeks of uttering these words, Elisa had changed her mind and promised to marry Yamate. Only magic could have caused this sudden change of heart. Emilio claimed that he had killed Yamate to save Elisa.

As so often happens in criminal cases, Chávez's second motive had to do with money. When Chávez had learned that Yamate planned to marry Elisa, Chávez had asked Yamate for a "donation" to Elisa for "her protection" in case a disaster occurred sometime in her life. Yamate had refused, begging poverty. To prove his lack of financial resources, Yamate had gone so far as to let Chávez see his bank account at the First National Bank of Belen. Yamate's $56 account was not large, but Chávez and others suspected that the railway worker had additional savings stashed in a bank in San Francisco. He also had a "considerable" life insurance policy and had property interests, although, as a Japanese-American, he could not legally own land or property directly.

Upset that Chávez had pried into his business affairs, Yamate reportedly said that if it were not for Elisa, he would "get even" with his past and future brother-in-law. Chávez considered Yamate an enemy who might yet fulfill his threat to seek revenge.

Trial

With two clear motives, revealing evidence, and a signed written confession, Valencia County District Attorney Fred Nicolas felt confident of conviction. Chávez's trial was heard before Judge Henry Owen only two weeks following Yamate's murder and two days before Yamate and Elisa were to have been married. Well aware of the futility of pleading innocent to first-degree murder, Chávez pled guilty to the lesser charge of second-degree murder. He waived his right to a trial by jury and refused legal counsel. In essence, Chávez threw himself on the mercy of the court.

Judge Owen willingly showed mercy because Chávez had confessed, had pled guilty, and had saved the time and expense of a trial and prosecution. The judge may or may not have been further influenced by a letter that arrived in his chambers two days before Chávez's sentencing. The letter was written by A. L. Campo on behalf of himself and several other former students of the Harwood Methodist School that Chávez had attended for three years in Albuquerque. Campo stated that Chávez had been a good schoolmate and friend, although he had at times "acted queerly."

Campo believed that Chávez's unusual behavior was inherited from his now-deceased father. Campo concluded that anyone with such a background "cannot bear crisis and when it comes they are likely to do just exactly what this fellow did." The letter writer asked the court to show clemency to Chávez "for all the family depends on Emilio to run things for them since he is the best educated of them all." For his part, Chávez made a brief statement when asked if he had anything to say before sentencing. He asserted to the court, "What I did, I thought I did with good intentions" to save Elisa.

"But if I am guilty, I am willing to [face my penalty] and do the best I can. I believe that God will [intervene] and someday I will be a free man again. And I hope that what I did will help me later in life to be a better man and to lead a better life, because after you [have had such] an experience, you can do better. That is all I have to say."

Punishment

Judge Owen responded by sentencing Emilio Chávez to no less than ninety and no more than ninety-nine years at hard labor in the New

Mexico State Penitentiary. The judge minced few words in sentencing Chávez on January 20, 1926. According to Owen, Chávez had

...maliciously and willfully destroyed a God-given human life without legal justification or any moral excuse and without mitigating circumstances. Based on an imaginary grievance, you used a deadly gun, the weapon of a coward, and, at an hour when all was dark to cloak your cowardly action, you sent the bullet on its deadly mission.

Judge Owen declared that Chávez would have the rest of his life to suffer for his crime. As a high school graduate, Chávez "commanded an intelligence more keen than ordinary with which to comprehend the extent of your disgrace and the sorrow you have laid on your family and your friends." Chávez was led from the courtroom and transported to the state penitentiary in Santa Fe. He began serving his sentence on January 22, 1926.

Community residents were relieved that Yamate's murder mystery had been solved and that the streets and homes of Belen were safe again. And all were impressed by Joe Tondre's sharp detective work. The veteran lawman had found the key bit of evidence that others had ignored when it literally lay at their feet. For this and his other good work, Tondre was appointed as New Mexico's new U. S. Marshal later that same year.

The public was also impressed by how swiftly justice was served once the murder suspect had admitted his guilt. Chávez had escaped execution on the gallows by pleading guilty to second-degree murder but his stiff penalty seemed onerous enough to fit his terrible crime. While most seemed satisfied with the outcome of this case in 1926, we have no way of measuring public reaction to the news of Emilio Chávez's fate in early 1932. After serving only six years of his ninety to ninety-nine year sentence, Chávez realized his sentencing-day hope that "someday I will be a free man again." He was released on parole and allowed to return to Peralta to work and care for his family. A year later, Governor Arthur Seligman granted him a full pardon and a return of full citizenship.

Prison records do not reveal why Governor Seligman decided to parole Chávez at such an early date. Documents attest that Chávez had been a model prisoner, having "passed the entire period of his imprisonment without any violations of the rules and regulations of the penitentiary." We can only speculate that the governor might have hoped to cut prison expenses by paroling certain less troublesome prisoners during the depression year of 1932.

John W. Pope also reminds us that long sentences were not unusual in the early twentieth century. Based on a different system of sentencing and parole than we use today, parole boards enjoyed far more discretion in determining the actual punishment for crimes, including crimes as serious as murder.

There is at least one other explanation for Emilio Chávez's early release from prison. As Yamate's California relatives had feared from the moment they had learned of his death, perhaps state officials did not take the railway worker's murder as seriously as other killings because of his Japanese ancestry. Race may well have played a part in the early release and pardon of Yamate's murderer.

But Nick Yamate's relatives were at least grateful to Joe Tondre, the man who had ignored Yamate's race in solving the mystery of his murder and in apprehending his killer within a week of his death. Yamate's relatives also appreciated the compassion Tondre showed to Yamate's orphaned daughter, often looking out for her welfare in the succeeding years. Anne T. Williams, Joe Tondre's daughter, recalls that the Yamates expressed their appreciation to this dedicated police officer by taking him and his wife, Ruth, to dinner in San Francisco years later.

Joe Tondre never forgot that act of kindness in the wake of his most memorable murder case. And he never forgot what he firmly believed and expressed so well in a letter to a friend in 1930. "Racism," Tondre wrote, "gets us no place. After all, we are all equal. It is the individual that counts, and not the race he is from."

We can learn few greater lessons in our study of history.

Two Killings in Budville, 1967

by Richard Melzer

Historian Don Bullis holding the alleged Budville murder weapon (Richard Melzer)

By all accounts, Howard Neal "Bud" Rice was a big fish in a small pond in western Valencia County during the 1950s and 1960s. Born and raised in Cubero, New Mexico, Rice owned and operated a trading post, a gas station, a garage, and a towing business along old Route 66, about twenty miles east of Grants and forty-six miles west of Albuquerque. Completing his small empire, Rice had built his house adjacent to his trading post, with a door between for easy access in both directions.

Friends

Because Rice was the dominant personality along his stretch of Route 66, it was fitting that the small community surrounding Bud's house and businesses became known as Budville. Fifty-four years old in 1967, Bud Rice was well liked by many of the men and women who knew him. He counted Anglos, Indians, and Hispanics among his friends and neighbors in western New Mexico. Families recall his helping poor children in need of shoes to go to school. Neighbors recall his willingness to bail them out of jail when they occasionally ran afoul of the law.

Rice intentionally cultivated close ties to members of the New Mexico State Police. Rice gave each member of the force a bottle of good liquor and a carton of cigarettes each Christmas. The businessman threw a large barbeque for his state police friends each Fourth of July. Grateful, state policemen visited Rice often; their cars—and their presence—were highly visible in Bud's parking lot at all hours of the day and night. Rice also had friends in high political office. In 1939, he had been convicted of assault, but, thanks to well-placed connections, he received a suspended sentence and was eventually pardoned by the governor in 1942.

By the 1950s, Rice served as the local justice of the peace in Budville. And, while not a trained lawyer, Bud was known to effectively represent friends who appeared before the magistrate judge in Grants.

When the construction of I-40 threatened to destroy Bud's businesses along Route 66, he actively opposed construction of the modern highway. Rice lost the struggle (I-40 was completed through New Mexico in the mid-1960s), but made sure that the new highway's plans included an exit to tiny Budville.

Enemies

While a good many people liked and admired Bud Rice, there were just as many—or more—who had cause to dislike and distrust him over the years. As the only wrecker on Route 66 between the Rio Puerco and Grants, Rice enjoyed a monopoly he seldom hesitated to exploit. He was notorious for not only charging high towing prices, but also charging ridiculously high prices for repairs. According to an often-repeated story, Rice once towed a stranger's car into Budville and replaced the vehicle's fan belt. When the car owner heard the high price of the newly installed fan belt, he objected vehemently. Rice responded by taking out his pocketknife, cutting the new belt, and ordering the aghast traveler to get his vehicle off Bud's property.

Rice was also known to charge drivers inordinately high prices for tire chains during even the worst winter snowstorms. He routinely told out-of-state winter drivers that they would need chains west of Gallup where the weather was "bound to be rough." Falling for this con, worried drivers readily bought chains from Rice at higher than normal prices.

Other out-of-state drivers met Rice in his equally exploitative role as justice of the peace. Justice Rice was particularly hard on out-of-town speeders, seldom fining them less than $60 a ticket, an outrageously high amount in the 1950s and 1960s. (Sixty dollars in 1967 equals about $380 in today's money.) Enjoying extraordinary local power, Rice liked to be called "Juez de Boss," or "Judge Boss." Reminding many of Judge Roy Bean, who had been known as the "law west of the Pecos River," Rice became known as the "law west of the Rio Puerco."

Towing companies in Albuquerque also resented Rice because he arbitrarily decided that all car wreaks on Route 66 east of the Rio Puerco were theirs, while all wreaks west of the river were his to tow. This unfair arrangement gave the Albuquerque companies only eight miles of road to divide among themselves, leaving thirty-eight miles of highway for Rice to profit from alone.

Having angered so many people, some wondered if Bud Rice might someday go too far and suffer violent consequences, despite all his friends on the police force and in high places. These fears were realized at last on the evening of November 18, 1967.

Tragedy

About 8:00 p.m. that Saturday, a customer reportedly drove up to Rice's trading post and gasoline station just before closing. Bud went out to pump the man's gas, while the stranger went inside to pay for his two-gallon purchase and to buy cigarettes from Blanche Brown, an 82-year-old retired schoolteacher and long-time trading post employee.

When Rice finished pumping his customer's gas, he entered the store to find the stranger arguing with Blanche, perhaps over the price of his bill or his proper change. Seeing Bud, the man pulled out a pistol and pointed it at the trading post owner.

The two men struggled. Blanche yelled for Bud's wife, Flossie, and tried to stop the fight. Flossie ran out from her adjoining house, but it was too late. Six to eight shots rang out. Two shots hit Blanche. Three hit Bud. While Bud and Blanche lay dying, the man forced Flossie to hand over as much as $450 from the cash drawer, a cigar box, and her purse.

The robber put out the store's lights to discourage anyone from stopping by. No one did, as it was now past closing time and everyone—including the police—expected the outside lights to be off after 8:00 p.m.

The shooter tied Flossie up and placed tape over her mouth before dragging his two victims' bodies to the rear of the store and, in Blanche's case, into the kitchen of the Rices' home. Ordering Flossie not to move for at least fifteen minutes, the killer warned, "If anything goes wrong, I'll come back and kill you." The young man fled into the night.

The killer could not have known that another person was in the store that evening. Nettie Buckley, the Rices' housekeeper, had rushed into the store's bathroom, unnoticed when the violence had begun. Nettie now left her hiding place and untied Flossie. Finding both Bud and Blanche dead, Flossie called the police.

Search

Astonished by the news of Bud Rice's murder, state and local policemen raced to Budville at speeds of over 100 miles-per-hour, arriving moments after Flossie's call. Much of whatever evidence existed at the crime scene was undoubtedly compromised by the activity of so many police officers, all eager to find clues that could help them identify their friend's killer.

The police also launched a massive manhunt throughout Valencia County and beyond. Within half an hour roadblocks were set up along Route 66 and I-40 as far west as Gallup and as far east as Albuquerque. Other blockades were placed on roads as far north as Farmington and as far south as Belen. In the words of one press report, these roadblocks fairly "bristled with rifles and automatic weapons." In two instances, the police fired their weapons to halt confused drivers. One car overturned. A gun was discovered in a vehicle near Gallup, but nothing about the driver connected him to the crime in Budville.

Members of the Mount Taylor Search and Rescue Unit, four small planes, and students from the local Job Corps program joined eighty state, county, and local police officers in an extensive search through Saturday night and all day Sunday.

Searchers looked for a man described by Flossie Rice and depicted in a composite sketch made by an Albuquerque police artist. Flossie described the assailant as a clean-shaven young man, about five-feet, ten-inches tall, wearing black clothing and black pointed shoes. Somehow, Flossie had also seen a tattoo on the man's stomach. Police believed that the suspect drove a light brown or tan compact car and might still be carrying the 9-mm pistol used to commit his horrible crimes.

The First Suspect

Finally, at about midnight on Sunday night, police grew suspicious when they stopped a 1961 pale green Comet at a roadblock about a mile east of Grants. The driver wore black clothing and supposedly resembled the image in the composite sketch based on Flossie's description. Larry E. Bunten, a 23-year-old Navy chief petty officer, was arrested as he, his wife, their infant, and Bunten's brother-in-law were heading west on the new interstate, I-40. After booking him in Grants, the police brought their suspect to Budville about 2:00 a.m.

Although Flossie had been given a sedative and was already asleep in bed, the police awakened her and asked her to look through her front window to see Bunten, sitting in a police car with a flashlight shining on his face. Yes, Flossie said, the young man in the car resembled the cold-blooded murderer who had killed her husband and Blanche Brown.

Certain they had the right man, the police brought the sailor to Los Lunas where he was held without bond in the Valencia County jail. The authorities were so sure that they had the culprit in custody that all roadblocks were removed and all attention was focused on Larry Bunten. Home on leave and low on funds, Bunten requested legal assistance for his defense. Mayo T. "Terry" Boucher of Belen and James Toulouse of Albuquerque were assigned to the case. Working diligently, the attorneys gathered evidence to prove that their client had been wrongly accused.

Boucher and Toulouse produced witnesses to prove that Bunten was in Albuquerque at the time of the robbery and murders on Saturday night, November 18. These witnesses testified that Bunten had been visiting his brother-in-law's family in an Albuquerque apartment at the time the crime had been committed over forty miles away. Bunten had, in fact, been taking home movies of his kids as they played in front of a TV set showing "Mannix," a popular detective series of the 1960s. Ironically, a fictional crime story on "Mannix" was telecast just as a real-life drama unfolded in Budville. The court-appointed lawyers also showed that Bunten had passed both truth serum (sodium pentothal) and lie detector tests administered after his arrest. Only Flossie's identification of the sailor remained.

But Flossie's identification was highly suspect. How reliable could her testimony be when she had been awakened from a drug-induced sleep to look at the accused from a window in the middle of the night with only a flashlight to illuminate Bunten while he sat in a police car? Concluding that the latter evidence was hardly sufficient to hold Bunten, Judge Paul Tackett ordered the petty officer released eighteen days after his arrest. Tackett praised Boucher and Toulouse for their work, declaring that he'd sooner let ten guilty men walk free than have one innocent man be unfairly charged and punished. Tears ran down Bunten's face as he was released from jail and was reunited with his family. Dreading a stressful trial, a wrongful verdict, and a possible death sentence, the sailor declared that his time in jail represented "the longest weeks of my life."

But now the police were back to where they had started, if not further behind. While the authorities had focused their attention on Larry Bunten, the real killer had had plenty of time to destroy all evidence and flee the area undetected. His trail grew colder by the day.

Meanwhile, funeral services were held for Bud Rice and Blanche Brown at the Strong Thorne Mortuary in Albuquerque. A crowd of family members and friends filled the mortuary's chapel to overflowing. More than two dozen New Mexico State Police officers attended the services. Several officers formed an honor guard. Bud Rice's remains were cremated, with his ashes scattered over Route 66, the famous highway along which he had lived, had made a good living, had enjoyed inordinate power, and had met a terribly violent death. It would take another eight months before detectives finally arrested another suspect in the double murder and robbery.

The Police Get Lucky

Then the police got lucky. Three felons accused of other crimes, offered to share what they knew about the Budville murders in exchange for reduced charges. All three men identified 26-year-old Billy Ray White as the gunman who had eluded detection and arrest for the last three months. Born in Jasper, Alabama, White had been orphaned at an early age and had spent most of his adult life drifting from place to place. With as many as eight aliases (from Rudy Hill to Eric Lee Kendrick), White was a professional criminal with a string of convictions in states across the country. He once told an attorney that prison time was "just the cost of doing business" in his chosen "profession."

As of March 1968, Billy Ray White had become the number one suspect in the brutal slaying of 54-year-old Bud Rice and 82-year-old Blanche Brown. Unable to find, no less arrest White, the FBI went so far as to place the suspect on its Ten Most Wanted list in the summer of 1968. The gambit paid off. Within weeks, White was spotted in Springfield, Illinois. He was apprehended on August 17, 1968, surrendering to police without incident. Waiving extradition, White was brought back to New Mexico and arraigned on two counts of first-degree murder. A slim youth with a small goatee, White appeared for his September 28 arraignment at the Valencia County courthouse wearing an old sweatshirt, untied sneakers, and no socks. Made to shave so that he might look more like he would have appeared on the night of the murders, White stood in a line-up to face Bud Rice's widow. Flossie identified him as the killer without hesitation.

White was kept under heavy guard at the Albuquerque city jail and, later, at the state penitentiary in Santa Fe until his trial was scheduled to begin in Los Lunas. In an era before public defenders, the court assigned two Valencia County attorneys to defend White at his upcoming trial: H. Vern Payne of Los Lunas and "Terry" Boucher (who had earlier defended Larry Bunten) were given the unenviable legal task.

Vern Payne remembers the first time he met his new client. Considered an escape risk, White was being held in solitary confinement at the Albuquerque city jail. Payne could only talk to White through a small window in White's cell door and with a guard present at all times. Looking through the cell's window, Payne saw a young man dressed in a jail uniform and wearing sneakers without shoelaces, for security reasons. White was courteous and respectful, always calling his attorney "Mr. Payne." According to Payne, White reminded him of a "Sunday School boy" rather than a hardened criminal.

Having had bad experiences with lawyers in his past, White did not trust Payne initially, especially with a jail guard present to hear his every

42

word. But White eventually opened up to Payne as he saw his court-appointed lawyer consistently work in his behalf in the coming weeks.

In one of several motions, Payne arranged for a psychological evaluation of White, including a truth serum test. The truth serum test revealed that White had been abused as a child. More to the point, the test suggested that White may not have been responsible for the robbery and murders at Budville in November 1967.

Billy Ray White's Trial Begins

Billy Ray White's trial began at the old Valencia County courthouse in Los Lunas on Monday, March 3, 1969. Fifty-five county residents were called for jury selection. Eight women, four men, and one alternate were chosen in less than two hours on the trial's first morning. When asked, each of the thirteen jury members had responded that yes, he or she would be able to serve on a jury in a case that might end with the death penalty. Prosecutors sought nothing less than two first-degree murder convictions.

The young man who appeared in court that Monday morning did not resemble the scruffy-looking youth that had been arraigned the previous September. Gone were his dirty clothes, replaced by a white shirt, a tie, and a plaid sports jacket. White's improved image would have a positive impact on the perception of the press, the jury, and many in attendance.

The courtroom was packed on March 3, as it would be on each day of this sensational trial. In addition to the press, Flossie Rice, her new husband, 33-year-old Max Atkinson, Bud's two daughters from a previous marriage, the daughters' husbands, and students from a Los Lunas High School Civics class attended daily. Each of these individuals and groups would play an important role in the ensuing drama.

District Court Judge Frank Zinn opened proceedings on Monday in an uncomfortably cold courtroom because the courthouse's heating system had broken over the weekend. Zinn ordered his bailiff to install enough portable heaters to assure that the temperature in his courtroom was more comfortable by the afternoon. Zinn expected some heated moments in Billy Ray White's trial, but the judge could not rely on sparks of controversy to sufficiently heat the cold March days ahead.

The Prosecution

After opening statements, the prosecution, led by Assistant D.A.s Don Wilson and Frederick "Ted" Howden, called its first witness. Not surprisingly, they called Flossie Rice to the stand. Asked by the prosecution to identify her husband's killer, Flossie answered with a shaky voice. "That's him, right there," she asserted, pointing at the accused. Asked if she had any doubt about her identification, Flossie's voice became firmer, replying, "No doubt, whatsoever."

Knowing that Flossie's identification of their client was the most damaging evidence against him, White's defense team cross-examined the widow carefully. The attorneys made much of the fact that Flossie had, in fact, identified two men as the killer: Larry Bunten, the falsely accused sailor, as well as Billy Ray White, the newly accused defendant. How could Flossie have been so positive in her identification of both men? If she had been wrong about Bunten, couldn't she be just as wrong in her identification of White? White's attorneys also questioned the veracity of Flossie's identification of White because the police had had Flossie hypnotized several times in order to learn more details about the murders. Had Flossie's identification of White been compromised by a post-hypnotic condition? Should White be found guilty, and perhaps be executed in the gas chamber, based on such a questionable identification?

Next, the prosecution called three witnesses who gave increasingly damaging testimony against young Billy Ray White. Joseph V. Dean, a 33-year-old ex-convict, testified that he had sold White information about three possible targets for a robbery in the Albuquerque area: a bank, a loan company, and Bud Rice's Trading Post. The latter business seemed like a particularly easy mark because it was so isolated on old Route 66, after the recent construction of I-40. It was also rumored that Rice kept a lot of cash on hand from his towing business, from his store, and from the high fines he imposed on speeders in his role as the local justice of the peace. Dean testified that he had also helped White by "test driving" (stealing) a 1966 or 1967 blue Chevrolet at the Lloyd McKee car dealership in Albuquerque. Dean told the court that he had left the stolen vehicle for White to use in his anticipated crime.

Thirty-year-old David L. Patterson was called to the witness stand next. Patterson testified that he saw bloodstained clothes in White's bathroom when he went to Billy Ray White's apartment on the morning after the murder-robbery. Most damagingly, the heavily tattooed felon recalled White saying that things had gone badly with the robbery and that he had had to "wipe a couple of people out."

A third felon, Joe Cruz, testified for the prosecution that he had provided the gun White had used in Budville on November 18, 1967. David Patterson added that he and White had disposed of the weapon after the crime by throwing it in an irrigation ditch off Rio Bravo Boulevard in Albuquerque's South Valley. The police had recovered the gun, which was entered as the main piece of evidence against White.

White's attorneys cross-examined Dean, Patterson, and Cruz, focusing on their credibility as felons eager to make deals with the district attorney to have charges against them dismissed, even at the price of framing their friend and putting his life at risk in a capital crime. Prosecutor Howden knew that this would be a problem for the prosecution's case. Years later, he still insisted, "You can't always call a bank president or a church leader as witnesses. You simply have to go with what you've got, for better or for worse."

The Defense

The defense's first witness was hardly more credible. When the prosecution rested on Wednesday, March 5, attorneys Payne and Boucher called Richard Wehmeir to prove White's alibi that he was hundreds of miles away in East St. Louis on the night that Bud Rice and Blanche Brown were killed. Wehmeir was Billy Ray White's former cellmate in a federal prison in Terre Haute, Indiana. Wehmeir's criminal record was as long, if not longer than his jailhouse friend's. Wehmeir nevertheless testified that he and White had spent Saturday, November 18, 1967, in an East St. Louis motel room, drinking and carousing with two women.

But who could believe Wehmeir's story, especially when he could not remember the name or address of the East St. Louis motel he and White supposedly stayed in? And who could believe Wehmeir when he had been heard in the hall outside the courtroom claiming that his sole interest in coming to New Mexico was to "spring Billy Ray"?

Despite these glaring problems with Richard Wehmeir's testimony and behavior, defense attorney Payne had great faith in his next witness,

35-year-old Lyle Craig Boren. Payne says that Boren "clinched it for us" when he testified that he had seen Billy Ray White in Missouri where White had sold him a bottle of good whiskey for just $4 a week before Thanksgiving in 1967. Boren seemed believable because he was a disabled Korean War veteran whose only conviction had been for disturbing the peace. Boren seemed far too innocent to lie for a friend or for anyone else.

Relying on Boren's testimony, questioning the prosecution's witnesses, and doubting Flossie's ability to identify the killer, Vern Payne told the jury, "It is beyond my comprehension how the state can ask the death penalty on such flimsy evidence, full of inconsistencies, the evidence of scoundrels and a woman who, however well-intentioned, put another man [wrongly accused sailor Larry Bunten] in jail for three weeks."

The defense never called White to the stand to testify in his own behalf. His attorneys knew that if White appeared on the stand the prosecution could ask him anything they wanted about his past, including several previous crimes that sounded very much like the modus operandi used in the Budville robbery and murder. As White later told a reporter, he agreed not to testify because he knew "the state would make me look like the lowest thing that ever crawled." Such testimony would surely compromise White's "Sunday School" image and seal his fate.

In a real sense, the defense had let White testify for himself by simply having him sit in court looking as clean-cut and innocent as possible. Even assistant D.A. Ted Howden recalls how White's appearance helped his defense, noting that "to look at him you couldn't help but like him." The presence of the Los Lunas High School class only reinforced White's image as an innocent looking, wrongly accused youth. Although at least eight years their senior, White looked young enough to be their high school classmate, rather than a hardened criminal who could have robbed a business and cold-bloodedly killed two people, including Blanche Brown, an 82-year-old retired school teacher.

The Verdict

The defense rested on Thursday, March 6. Following a rebuttal and closing arguments, the case was handed to the jury at 4:12 that afternoon. The jury deliberated for less than two hours before announcing that they had reached a decision at 6:06 p.m. The crowded courtroom fell silent as the jury foreman stood to read the verdict. To the surprise of many, the jury declared Billy Ray White innocent of all charges against him. Many in the courtroom cheered, especially the students from the Los Lunas High School Civics class. A jubilant White shook hands and accepted congratulations. A woman in the crowd reportedly rushed forward to tell White, "God bless you, Billy Ray."

But the drama was not over. Flossie sobbed uncontrollably when she heard the verdict. Expressing his outrage in a different way, Flossie's new husband, Max Atkinson, jumped over the railing that separated the defendant's table from the rest of the courtroom. Wielding a knife, Atkinson attacked White, seeking the justice he and Flossie believed the young man deserved. Vern Payne remembers Atkinson's attack like it was yesterday. Standing next to White, Payne recalls seeing Bud Rice's son-in-law rush forward to stop the assault. A policeman from Arizona, the son-in-law probably saved White's life, not to mention attorney Payne's.

Assistant D.A. Wilson was shaken by Atkinson's attack, but was even more shaken by the jury's verdict. Wilson called the verdict "a serious blow against law and order." He declared that he had "never prosecuted a case in which I had more evidence against a defendant." But the jury clearly disagreed. Four members of the panel later told a reporter that "no member [of the jury] felt the state had presented concrete proof" of White's guilt. Circumstantial evidence just wasn't enough, they added, "when you have a man's life in your hands."

White in Louisiana

Thus ended one of the most dramatic trials in Valencia County history. But Billy Ray White's moment of victory was short-lived. Extradited to Louisiana, he faced trial for similar crimes committed just two months prior to the tragedy in Budville. In sharp contrast to the outcome of his trial in New Mexico, Billy Ray White was found guilty of all charges brought against him in Louisiana. The court sentenced him to a long prison term in the Louisiana state penitentiary at Angola.

Despite his conviction in Louisiana, White was always grateful to his defense attorneys in Valencia County. Vern Payne recalls receiving Christmas cards from White with vague promises of "putting bread on your table someday." Payne always worried that White would keep this promise, showing up at the attorney's office bearing a TV or some other stolen goods as illicit tokens of his appreciation for saving him from the gas chamber in New Mexico. To Payne's relief, White never appeared with a gift in hand. On the contrary, Billy Ray White died in the Louisiana state penitentiary on June 8, 1974. An apparent suicide, White had reportedly confessed to a fellow inmate that he was, in fact, guilty of the Budville robbery and murders.

Attorney Payne never believed the story of White's prison confession and suicide, especially because White was due to be paroled in just five months. According to Payne, who got to know White rather well before and during his trial, White simply wanted to do his time in prison so he could be released and continue his life of crime. When Payne had asked White what he intended to do if he was found innocent in 1969, White had told his lawyer that he had every intention of going back to his previous life as a pimp and a thief.

Who Killed Bud Rice

Vern Payne has defended hundreds of men and women in his long legal career. In the vast majority of cases, he's been able to conclude whether his clients have been innocent or guilty. But to this day he is not sure about Billy Ray White.

But if White didn't commit the Budville crimes, who did? When interviewed, some jury members say they suspected that Flossie and Max Atkinson were somehow involved. How else to explain the fact that Flossie was spared by the robber, while Bud and Blanche were not? Did Flossie commit the murders herself or perhaps have someone like Max do them for her?

Vern Payne remembers a rather mysterious visit by Nettie Buckley's sister to his office before White's 1969 trial had begun. Nettie Buckley, the Rice family employee who had hidden in the trading post's bathroom while the robbery and murders were taking place, had recently died of an apparent heart attack. Nettie's sister told Vern Payne that she was sure that Flossie and Max had kept Nettie in isolation since the murders and had denied her medical assistance when she most needed it because they feared that she would implicate Flossie and Max in court. Payne mentioned this accusation to the district attorney's office, but to no avail before or during Billy Ray White's trial.

Like Nettie Buckley's sister, some jury members were especially suspicious of Max Atkinson, a dark character who had married Flossie shortly after the murders took place. The jury could not have known that Atkinson could not have committed the murders because he had an airtight alibi of his own. A convicted felon, Atkinson had spent all of 1967 (including the night of the killings) in an Arizona state prison cell. (Max Atkinson, who took over Bud's businesses and succeeded in alienating most of the Budville community, was killed during an argument on June 7, 1973. After marrying yet again, Flossie died of natural causes on April 10, 1994.)

Who else could have killed Bud Rice and Blanche Brown? Was it someone Bud had angered in his political life or business dealings in western Valencia County? Was it someone connected to a Texas drug trial in which Bud had testified just days before he was killed? Or could it have been Joseph Dean, David Patterson, or Joe Cruz, the felons who had fingered White and provided such damning testimony during his trial in Los Lunas?

After so many years and with the deaths of so many key players, the crime will probably never be solved. Perhaps the best we can say is that the decline of Route 66, the famous old route that had been Bud Rice's main source of income and power for so long, had as much to do with Rice's death as any living mortal. When the new super highway, I-40, had bypassed Route 66 the traffic that normally flowed by Bud's trading post dried up, leaving the store and its owner vulnerable to intrusion and murder on a dark Saturday night in November 1967. Bud Rice had fought against the construction of I-40 to save his economic and political life in the mid-1960s. Little did he know at the time that he was also fighting against the increased isolation that would ultimately take his mortal life as well.

The Mystery of Eddie Martínez's Death in Vietnam, 1969

by Richard Melzer

Private Eddie Martínez in Vietnam (Martínez family)

Historians often spend time in cemeteries. This may sound like a morbid activity, but students of the past can learn a lot in cemeteries. Grave sites help us answer many questions about individuals, families, and whole communities. But grave sites can sometimes create as many questions as they answer. This is especially true with the grave site of a former Belen resident named Eddie A. Martínez, Jr. His mysterious death and subsequent burial pose questions that may never be answered, despite years of inquiry by the family, friends, political leaders, and the press.

Eddie Martínez was born on April 1, 1948, in Springer, New Mexico. His parents, Edward and Elizabeth Martínez, moved to Belen to raise their large family of six children—Eddie, Gary, Tommy, Bobby, Mary Ann, and Mary Jane. Eddie led a normal life in Belen with his share of good times and bad. As a teenager, he was involved in at least one fight—over a girl—that left an H-shaped scar under his left arm, a fact that would be significant later in his story. Dr. J. A. Rivas treated the knife wound and sent Eddie home. Another time, Eddie was arrested when riding with some friends who were found with stolen liquor. Questioned by the police, Eddie had an alibi and was released, but not before he was measured and fingerprinted at the police station. This information would also prove to be important years later.

On better days, Eddie enjoyed playing in local bands with such unusual names as the Teen Beats, the Minute Men, The Creatures, and Scott and the Tissues. Always popular, these bands played at local dances, graduations, and weddings. Scott and the Tissues won a Battle of the Bands competition for the entire state of New Mexico. As lead guitarist and soloist, Eddie enjoyed playing popular songs of the 1960s, while composing several of his own. Classmates remember him as a nice, quiet boy who, with his natural good looks and proven musical talent, was a favorite with the girls.

Eddie never finished high school, opting to go to California to look for work, preferably in the music business. He left with some friends, but returned after three months. "They only believe in smoking pot out there," he told family members. "They called me a square."

Enlistment and Vietnam

But there was little for Eddie to do in Belen. After several months, he decided to join the Army. Although the war in Vietnam had escalated (with 2,000 more combat deaths in the first three months of 1967, compared to the entire previous six years), Eddie enlisted on August 16, 1967. His goal was to earn enough money to pursue his real interest in music.

Once enlisted, Eddie received his basic training at Fort Bliss, Texas. He also received training as a mechanic. It was only a matter of time before he was scheduled to be shipped out to Vietnam. Upset by Eddie's impending departure, his mother offered to try to prevent it. But little could be done, and Eddie insisted, "I'm no coward, Mom, I want to fight for my country." He left for Vietnam in April 1968.

First stationed at Camp Eneiea and later at Camp Radcliff in Vietnam, Eddie wrote home regularly to reassure his family that he was safe. A month after his arrival in Vietnam, he told his mother, "Don't worry about me here. It's not as bad as people say." By June 1968, he assured his mother, "I'll make it home." He ended each of his letters optimistically with the words, "Keep the candle burning cuz this kid is coming home."

The young private also wrote about his future. He planned to take night classes in order to finish his high school education while still in the service. He looked forward to college and a well-paying job. He wrote that he was determined to "make life more pleasant."

Eddie sometimes used his letters home to describe the conditions in Vietnam. He wrote about the country's long monsoon season when it rained almost constantly for six months "and I mean hard." He told his mother about the local Vietnamese and their hardships. "They live in huts made of straw and plastered with mud. Houses that they put animals in. Little children crying in the nude for food. Vietnam is a sorry place. These people don't have any future."

Conditions were increasingly rough for Eddie, too. Although he received medals for good conduct, as a sharpshooter, and for participating in two battles, he wrote about the hardship of working seven days a week with only half a day off each Sunday. The rain was so bad that when "we sleep in holes...the rain seeps in and you're sleeping in mud." By the fall of 1968, Eddie was still determined to do his duty. "I have a job to do here in Vietnam," but he was growing war-weary and wrote of "pushing time here in ol' Vietnam."

His attitude about the people of Vietnam had also changed from pity to disgust. On November 10, he wrote, "Oh, how I hate these stupid, ugly, little people. Mother, I have seen things here that would make you sick just to hear them." Eddie also lost respect for several of his fellow soldiers. In at least one fight with another American, he hurt his left ear. Ten stitches were required to treat this new wound.

To cope with his surroundings, Eddie turned to the only thing that had consistently given him pleasure in life: music. He asked his family to send him his electric guitar so he could audition for Armed Forces Radio and Television. He planned to sing "If I were a Carpenter" and was sure "I'll go over good. I just need a break."

But not even music could distract Eddie by early 1969. With seventy-five days left to serve in Vietnam, he was almost desperate for leave time.

"I just have to go on R&R [rest and recreation]. I'm getting fed up with this lousy country." Eddie asked his mother to return $150 he had recently sent her. "I need a break. Help me out. OK?"

Eddie Martínez's last letter home was dated February 1, 1969. In it he confessed to his mother that "things aren't going so good here, and I have a very important decision to make. ... I have a chance of getting out of the Army on an unsuitability discharge. That means unsuitable or can't adjust to the military. ... What do you think I should do? Stay with the Army or come home? ... Oh, how I hate to work for these sorry people in the Army. You meet all types. Also, you have to put up with a lot of nonsense. .... Mom, if I could get out, where would I go to work? You know all I'm good for is playing music. I'm in a tight situation. ..."

Nine days later, on his mother's birthday, the Army claimed that despondent Eddie Martínez shot himself in the chest with a bullet fired from his M-16 rifle. He died instantly.

Three soldiers were reportedly present when the tragedy occurred in their Company B, 29th Artillery barracks. SP4 Gerald Gordier reported that he heard a gunshot and, looking in the direction of its sound, saw Eddie fall back on his bunk, his M-16 dropping from his hands. Gordier testified that there was no one near Eddie at the time and no one was seen running from the area of Eddie's bunk. SP4 Phillip Tarzia and PFC Ronald Carter also heard the fatal shot and confirmed that it was Eddie who had been killed.

Statements by an officer, Captain Antonio Gonzales, and a fellow soldier, SP4 Bruce Peters, indicated that Eddie had had emotional problems in the preceding weeks. He seemed to lack confidence in coping with "personal problems concerning both his family and Army life." A suicide note was found at the scene. Eddie's death appeared to be a simple suicide. Notified by Army personnel, the Martínez family grieved terribly for their lost son and sibling. Having recently found his music book on a closet shelf in their home, they discovered the lyrics of two songs written by Eddie, ironically titled "Don't Look Back" and "Your Last Day."

Mystery

And that would seem to be the end of a sad story about another American tragedy in Vietnam. But that's where the mystery began.

Eddie's mother noticed several inconsistencies from the start. She noticed, for example, that three of her son's last four letters were sent from a different address than he normally used. There were no postal markings and the handwriting on the envelopes was not Eddie's. Even more strangely, Betty Martínez later obtained a copy of an Army document that showed that Eddie was issued his regular $203 pay on March 4, 1969, about a month after he reportedly died. The document was clearly signed with Eddie Martínez's signature. But this is only the beginning of this complex mystery. The rest began when Eddie's body was shipped home to Belen for final burial.

The day after Eddie's remains arrived in Belen, family members were told that they could view the body. Although the casket had a glass cover and was never completely opened, Eddie's mother quickly noticed some strange, inexplicable things. She noted, for example, that the body before her "looked large in size" when Eddie only weighed 145 pounds, according to a government driver's license issued to him just three days before his death. Other marks and body characteristics were similarly puzzling to family members and friends. Betty recalls that at Eddie's funeral "everyone that knew my son said it didn't look like him."

Other strange events occurred within days after Eddie's burial. His family received his personal belongings, but they did not include his dog tags (ID), his clothes, or several pictures of his family that he had taken with him to Vietnam. Instead, the returned belongings included a small wedding ring, although Eddie was never married and, as a guitarist, never wore hand jewelry.

Upset by these many inconsistencies, Betty could not rest until she learned more about her son's fate. She eventually saved enough money for Eddie's body to be exhumed so an autopsy could take place. Dr. Richard E. Brubaker examined the exhumed body, but did not perform a complete autopsy. Instead, in a graveside procedure, the doctor simply confirmed that a chest wound was the cause of death, as originally reported by the Army.

Hardly satisfied, Betty insisted on a second examination of the body buried in the Catholic cemetery in Belen. But this 1980 examination only added more doubts. While Eddie's eyes were hazel, his hair was light brown, and his skin color was "fair," the autopsy revealed that the exhumed body's eyes were brown, its hair was black or brown, and its skin was rather dark. Moreover, Eddie was five-feet, nine inches tall and weighed 145 pounds. The exhumed body was that of a man who was five-feet, six-inches tall and weighed 175 pounds. Eddie had large hands; the body's were small.

Also, the body had no H-shaped scar under its left arm, as Eddie's had had following his teenage scuffle over a girl. And, while Eddie's left ear had been injured during his fight with a fellow soldier in Vietnam, the exhumed body's ears shows no sign of damage. The body had a four-inch scar on its right forearm and a second scar on its left knee. Eddie's Army medical records showed that he was never treated for such injuries overseas.

Given these many inconsistencies, the Martínez family sought the help of several high-ranking government officials, including senators Pete Domenici and Jeff Bingaman. While at first willing to accept the Army's conclusions about Eddie's death, Domenici re-examined the physical evidence and reconsidered his conclusions. By mid-1981, he agreed that "numerous inconsistencies and irregularities" indicated that the body buried in Belen might not be Eddie's. Domenici called on Secretary of the Army John O. March, Jr., to continue the investigation because "there are sufficient discrepancies to make further questioning valid by all involved." Bingaman agreed, especially after a laboratory DNA test confirmed that the corpse in Belen did not belong to Eddie Martínez.

But little more was ever done and Eddie's case is still open in almost everyone's mind but the Army's.

What Happened to Eddie Martínez?

So what could have happened to Eddie Martínez? Did he die of a self-inflicted gunshot wound and was he buried in Belen as the military has long contended? Or was he killed in his barracks in a fight with a fellow soldier? Embarrassed for some reason by Eddie's death, did the Army substitute another man's body as part of a larger cover-up of the mysterious crime. Or was this simply a case of body shuffling in a war zone where so many bodies were sent home to the States that mistakes were bound to happen and hearts were bound to be broken in the aftermath?

Or was Eddie never shot, no less killed, in his barracks in early 1969? If so, why would the government stage his death and send a bogus body back to his family for burial in New Mexico? And what has happened to Eddie over all these years? The Martínez family would clearly prefer the latter conspiracy theory because the evidence simply doesn't add up. As Betty put it, "I feel like the government is trying to play a joke on me."

One incident seems to help prove the family's case. According to Eddie's younger brother, the late Gary Martínez, a stranger once approached him in a bar in Belen. The stranger said that he had known Eddie in the Army and had attended his funeral but "that wasn't your brother in the casket. Your brother is on an island and he's got some sort of disease." The bar music was too loud for Gary to hear everything the man said, and Gary never got his name and address. But Gary did remember the man urging him to "tell your mother she should be happy. Eddie is still alive."

Was this a true story or one fabricated to help console Eddie's family in their prolonged grief? Betty Martínez would like to believe it. As she asserts, "Eddie was born on April Fools Day. Someday he's going to fool us all and walk in that door alive." She never conceded that her son would kill himself, no less shoot himself on her birthday. "Eddie loved me too much to want to hurt me like that."

Meanwhile, Betty Martínez sat, waiting for news, and willingly talking to curious reporters and at least one historian. "If the story is printed in the newspaper, maybe somebody somewhere in the world will read it and will tell me what really happened to my son, Eddie." Betty died at the age of 79 in 2005. According to her obituary, "She dedicated her life to uncover the truth about her son's death in Vietnam."

Ten residents of Valencia County were killed in Vietnam by 1969. We mourn and honor them all, but should never stop until all ten rest peacefully, starting with the still unsettled memory of Eddie Martínez.

Collecting Cacti and Chasing
Butterflies in Mexico:
Denis Cowper, 1974

by Richard Melzer

Denis Cowper (Daphne Cowper)

Many able attorneys have practiced law in the Rio Abajo. Any list of notable lawyers must include an attorney from Belen who practiced law with great skill and good humor for nearly twenty-five years: the incomparable, six-feet, three-inches tall Denis Cowper. Those who remember Cowper inevitably mention his four main characteristics.

First, they recall Cowper's great intelligence. Born in 1922 and raised in England, he and his older sister, Daphne, were the only children of a highly successful English doctor and his brilliant wife. When interviewed, Daphne said that Cowper received a good private school education in England, with additional study in Switzerland.

Always a curious—and often mischievous—child, Cowper seemed to learn as much outside the classroom as in. He and Daphne met many fascinating people who knew their parents and often visited their large country home. Cowper may have acquired his spirit of adventure after meeting men like Lawrence of Arabia and other English heroes of his parents' generation. Coming to the United States when he was 17 in 1939, Cowper attended Harvard University, UCLA, and the University of California, Berkeley, before studying law at Tulane University in New Orleans. Only severe headaches prevented him from graduating from Tulane.

Cowper moved to the drier, healthier climate of New Mexico to finish his law degree at the University of New Mexico. He was among the law school's first graduates in 1950. Cowper held an assortment of odd jobs during his years in school, including parking lot attendant, timekeeper, waiter, cook, carpet layer, candy maker, hardware salesman, bill collector, and ghost writer. Cowper said he benefited from each job, learning much about human nature in general and American ways in particular.

An Able Attorney

Once admitted to the bar, Cowper became an exceptional lawyer. An associate or partner in Tibo J. Chávez, Sr.'s Belen law firm for twenty-four years, Cowper complimented Tibo's skills in many ways. According to Filomena Baca, the firm's legal secretary, Tibo was always well-organized and punctual, while Cowper was far more spontaneous and was known to procrastinate. Filomena says she enjoyed typing Cowper's legal briefs because they were often original and never dull. Sylvia Storey, another secretary in the firm, said that Cowper was so sharp that he could be interrupted while giving dictation and later return to dictating at the exact place where he had left off.

Cowper never carried law books or legal pads filled with notes to court, relying on his remarkable, almost photographic memory to cite appropriate laws and precedents. His lack of books and notes and somewhat disheveled appearance often disarmed opposing counsel not familiar with his formidable legal skills.

Attorney Norm McDonald recalls a typically clever defense used by Cowper in a workmen's compensation case. Cowper's female client had been receiving workmen's compensation for a back injury suffered on the job. But a witness had seen Cowper's client carrying two large grocery bags from a local food store to her parked car. The woman was charged with fraudulently receiving workmen's compensation checks. Despite this seemingly damaging evidence, Cowper calmly asked the witness who had testified against his client, "Do you know if the bags my client was carrying were full of potatoes or potato chips?" When the witness was unable to reply, the case was dismissed.

Tibo Chávez's wife, Betty, said that her husband was always glad to have Cowper as a partner. But there were some trying moments. Filomena once asked Tibo if he needed any help on one of his many political campaigns, to which Tibo answered, "I'll take care of the campaign if you take care of Denis and the firm." Cowper entered the political arena twice. As a young attorney, he ran successfully for the New Mexico state House of Representatives, serving one term, from 1955 to 1957. He also ran for a district court judgeship in 1970. After someone told him he looked like John Wayne, Cowper ran his own picture in a newspaper ad that asked, "Will the real John Wayne please stand up?" Apparently the ad did not make a difference. In a close contest, Cowper lost by less than two hundred votes.

Other Interests

The second thing that people inevitably remember about Denis Cowper was his amazing skills as a linguist. Cowper learned languages easily. As a boy, he had had several German nannies from whom he learned German. In Switzerland, he reportedly mastered several languages when he was not busy skiing on mountain ski slopes. He learned to speak Italian in a neighborhood bar while vacationing in Italy. In all, Cowper was fluent in eight languages: English, German, Italian, French, Czech, Russian, Navajo, and Spanish. What impressed people most was Cowper's ability to speak various dialects of each language he knew. Filomena Baca and Sylvia Storey recall that Cowper could speak whatever Spanish dialect a person spoke when visiting their law office. This skill helped Cowper relate to and befriend everyone who sought his legal services.

Next, people remember Cowper as an avid collector of both butterflies and cacti. His sister, Daphne, recalls that Cowper collected butterflies from an early age and, at 16, became the youngest member of the Royal Academy of Entomology. Over the years, Cowper became an expert on butterflies and accumulated one of the most impressive collections in the Southwest. He even discovered new genii, including one he named after his stepdaughter, Francine Moore.

Cowper also began collecting cacti when he moved to the United States. His interest in succulent plants soon equaled his interest in butterflies. Acknowledged as an authority in his new field of study, Cowper published several articles on the subject and was invited to lecture to audiences across the United States and Europe. According to an article in the *Valencia County News-Bulletin* of May 25, 1954, his collection of plants included as many as five hundred kinds of cacti. Cowper was known to go anyplace at any time in search of butterflies and cacti. He never went anywhere without a net to catch butterflies and a pick and shovel to dig up cacti.

Horst Kuenzler, who was Cowper's partner in a cacti-growing business, remembered flying to Europe with Cowper. When their plane made a stop in an East Coast city, Cowper could not resist leaving his seat, exiting the plane, and searching for butterflies between airstrips. He hurried back just in time for the plane to take off.

Finally, those who remember Cowper always mention his love of Mexico, its people, its cultures, its terrain, and its potential as a rich source of butterflies and cacti. "My happiest hours," Cowper once wrote, "are crawling through the mountains of Mexico looking for new species." Cowper traveled to Mexico as often as he could, staying anywhere from a long weekend to several months at a time. Lee Auge, a close friend and local car dealer, recalled selling Cowper a low-mileage car shortly before Cowper left on one of his many sojourns to Mexico. When Cowper reappeared in Belen months later, Auge asked him what had delayed his return. Cowper replied that the car Auge had sold him had broken down and parts were hard to find in Mexico. Curious why the car would need new parts so soon, Lee checked the odometer and discovered that Cowper and the car had traveled more than 80,000 miles!

Cowper had many adventures—and misadventures—in Mexico. On one occasion, Cowper was traveling at night on a remote Mexican road that he had driven several times before. Anticipating a bridge that he had previously traversed, Cowper was surprised—and undoubtedly shocked—to discover the bridge gone. Cowper stopped just in time to prevent a disaster and save his own life.

In addition to remembering Cowper for his intelligence, language skills, collections, and love of Mexico, friends and relatives recall many details about his life and habits. They remember his love of reading and his interest in knowledge of any kind. They remember his favorite, beat-up old sheepherder's hat, sadly stolen from a peg where he had left it in a café. They remember his preference for strong coffee, rather than English tea, and they remember the aroma of the apple-scented tobacco he smoked in his favorite pipe. Everyone remembers Cowper as a kind, generous gentleman. His wife, Josephine, says that "no one was too big or too small to get his full attention."

Mexico, 1974

Many of Denis Cowper's characteristics and interests may well have contributed to circumstances and events in the final chapter of his interesting life. It was November 1974. Fifty-two-year-old Cowper had driven to Puerto Vallarta, Mexico, in a new four-wheel-drive Chevy Blazer. Josephine, his wife of eleven years, had flown down to meet him. They planned to search for butterflies and cacti while enjoying a two-week vacation at the Tropicana Hotel.

On Friday morning, November 29, the couple went butterfly hunting, driving two vehicles in case either of them decided to return to the hotel before the other. Finding a likely area to explore, they chose to search in different directions: Cowper to the south and Josephine to the north. As they parted, Cowper's last words to his wife were, "Put on your best bib and tucker, old girl, and we'll go out to dinner tonight."

After several hours searching for butterflies, Josephine returned to their hotel to get ready for dinner at 7:00 p.m., their usual dining hour. But 7:00 p.m. came and went without any word from Cowper. Josephine grew more anxious by the minute. She notified the local police that Cowper was missing, but was dismissed as simply an excitable woman.

Over the next several days Josephine tried everything she could think of to get help, including calling New Mexico's two U.S. Senators and hiring a search helicopter for hundreds of dollars a day. Hearing of their friend's disappearance, Tibo Chávez, District Judge Filo M. Sedillo, and Lucy Keys Brubaker in Belen appealed to U.S. government officials in Washington and at the U.S. embassy in Mexico City. Nothing produced results.

Josephine went so far as to visit a Mexican army base in search of help. Initially greeted with several rifles pointed in her direction, Josephine eventually recruited fifteen Mexican soldiers to help search for Cowper. Their efforts were to no avail. Increasingly desperate, Josephine contacted a Mexican television station and offered a $5,000 reward to anyone with information that might lead to the discovery of Cowper's whereabouts. An anonymous viewer called and told Josephine where to look. The caller never asked for the cash reward. Based on this new information, the police found Cowper's truck parked along an isolated road. But there was no sign of Cowper inside or anywhere near his vehicle.

Bloodhounds picked up Cowper's scent from a pair of boots left in his truck. The dogs went to work, finally discovering Cowper's remains in the jungle, quite a distance from where his vehicle had been parked. After eight days in the wild, Cowper's body was badly decomposed. It was, however, undisturbed. His wallet (with about a hundred dollars in cash), his gold watch, and his turquoise belt buckle were not taken.

Return Home

Josephine now faced the daunting task of bringing Cowper's body home to Belen with the help of her daughter Francine and Francine's friend, Eloy Padilla, Jr., who had arrived by Tuesday, December 2. Leaving Mexico required paying fees and dealing with seemingly endless rules and regulations. Mexican officials even interfered when Josephine, Francine, and Eloy attempted to transport Cowper's body from the small village where his remains had been taken and were kept in an ambulance. While Josephine and Francine bantered with officials, Eloy says he simply got in the ambulance and drove off. A procession of vehicles chased him until he arrived at the American consulate and, finally, at a local funeral home.

Carrying cash to pay for final transport of Cowper's body to the United States, John C. Johnson, president of the First National Bank of Belen, flew a commercial flight to Mexico for fear that the money might be lost, confiscated, or delayed in the mail. John Pope, then a young attorney and one of Cowper's law partners, also traveled to Mexico with his wife, Linda, to assist with arrangements to transport the body home. Joe Martínez from Albuquerque and Tom Newboldt, a private investigator from Socorro, arrived as well.

Finally back home in Belen, Denis Cowper was buried at the Terrace Grove Cemetery. Many friends and relatives attended his funeral. Appropriately, Cowper's headstone included cacti designs engraved on either side of his name and the dates of his birth and death. Tibo Chávez said he was "stunned" by the loss of his law partner and friend. An editorial in the *Valencia County News-Bulletin* spoke for the entire community in offering Cowper's family its "deepest sympathy."

What Happened to Denis Cowper?

Denis Cowper was laid to rest in 1974, but the circumstances of his death remain a mystery. There are two main theories regarding his demise. The first theory is that Cowper simply died of natural causes. Cowper had suffered from heart disease, for which he took regular medication. Just prior to his final trip to Mexico, he had confided in Horst Kuenzler that his health had grown worse. On the morning of his disappearance, he had felt badly and had debated whether or not to even leave the hotel. According to this theory, Cowper, without medication or immediate medical care, simply succumbed to a heart attack and died in the wilderness.

The second explanation for Cowper's death is far more sinister. Some believe that Cowper may have walked into the middle of a drug deal. Rather than leave a witness who might later turn them in, the drug dealers might have killed Cowper and made a hurried escape, not stopping to steal his cash or belongings. One of the drug dealers may have been the anonymous caller who had told Josephine where Cowper's body could be found. Perhaps he did not ask for the $5,000 reward because he did not want to be identified and implicated in drug trafficking or the far more serious crime of murder. An autopsy was never performed to prove or disprove the theory that Denis Cowper was simply at the wrong place at the wrong time.

Unfortunately, we will probably never know what happened to Denis Cowper on the day of his tragic death. It is nevertheless comforting to know that he died doing what he enjoyed the most in the place he most wanted to be. We should all be so fortunate in our last moments of life on this earth.

Los Ladrones:
Thieves Mountain in New Mexico

by Richard Melzer

Ladrón Peak (Paul Harden)

Located twenty-five miles southwest of Belen and 9,143 feet above sea level, the Sierra Ladrones rise from a mesa base like a rugged island surrounded by an enormous sea. Like an island, the mountain is isolated, distant, majestic, and mysterious.

Like an island frequented by sea pirates, the Sierra Ladrones was once a favorite haunt of land pirates who hid their stolen treasures in caves and hideouts, fully expecting to someday return to claim their ill-gotten wealth before others discovered their prizes and, ironically, robbed the robbers.

Historian Francisco Sisneros has discovered that the earliest Spanish reference to "Los Ladrones" appeared on a map drawn by cartographer

Bernardo Miera y Pacheco in 1758. Meaning "thieves" in Spanish, the mountain's name suggests its main role in history. There have been other treasure mountains in New Mexico, including Starvation Peak, Victorio Peak, and the Manzanos, but few live more vividly in local legend as the Sierra Ladrones in the Rio Abajo.

Apache Indians apparently used the Sierra Ladrones for their treasure caves as early as the seventeenth century. The mountain served as an ideal place from which to raid travelers on the old Camino Real, or main royal highway into New Mexico. Apaches also raided valley settlements along the Rio Grande, often hiding stolen livestock in the Sierra Ladrones' steep canyons.

Discovering Spanish Treasure

A cowhand discovered evidence of these Indian raids in the spring of 1917. The cowhand spotted the entrance to a well-concealed cave while herding cattle on the east side of the mountain. Curious, he left his horse and cautiously explored the cave's dark interior. To his amazement, the cowhand found an old Spanish trunk, made of thick buffalo hide, with heavy wrought-iron hinges. We can only imagine this accidental explorer's anticipation as he opened the trunk, no doubt hoping to find a chest brimming with treasure. The cowhand discovered a treasure, but hardly the type he had anticipated. Instead of gold or silver, he found six books. One volume was the Bible, in both Hebrew and Greek. The five other books included a book of poetry and a tome of sermons.

Such books were rare in colonial New Mexico for three main reasons. First, few settlers on the frontier could afford such luxuries. Second, few settlers could read; tutors were seldom available; and schools as we know them did not exist. Perhaps most importantly, reading could be a dangerous activity in the seventeenth century. Books not written in Spanish were assumed to contain treasonous plots against the Spanish king or sacrilegious beliefs against the Catholic Church. Some colonists, including Governor Bernardo López de Mendizábal's wife, had been arrested and imprisoned by the dreaded Spanish Inquisition because she had engaged in such suspicious behavior. Doña Teresa became the only woman arrested by the Inquisition in New Mexico when she was discovered reading an Italian novel, among other supposedly irregular conduct.

But the Apaches who abandoned Spanish books in a mountain cave had none of these reasons for leaving the volumes behind. They simply had no use for books in their culture. Instead, the Indians probably salvaged their more valuable loot and left the books behind, much to the chagrin of the cowhand who discovered the small collection centuries later.

Historian Marc Simmons has suggested that the chest of books and whatever treasure was hauled to the Ladrones might have been captured by the Apaches when they allied with the Pueblo Indians to attack Spanish settlements in the Revolt of 1680. With all six of the discovered books predating 1680, this conclusion seems quite probable, although impossible to prove.

"Bronco Bill" and His Loot

Other raiders, including outlaws, also used the Sierra Ladrones as a convenient hideout to stash their stolen goods in the years that followed the Pueblo Revolt. Perhaps the most famous of these was "Bronco Bill" Walters and his gang who robbed Train No. 21 in Belen on May 24, 1898. Bill and his cronies probably buried much of their take (as much as $50,000) in the Ladrones before making their escape to Arizona. There, on July 28, Walters was captured and later found guilty of murder, receiving a life sentence.

Bronco Bill was released from prison in 1917 after serving more than seventeen years behind bars. Despite long hours of searching, he could not find the stash of coins he had buried, either because it had already been found and removed or because the landmarks he had remembered had changed over time.

Later employed on the Diamond A Ranch near Hachita, Bronco Bill died on June 16, 1921, four hours after he accidentally fell off a windmill he was fixing. On his deathbed he asked to see Jethro S. Vaught, Jr., a boy he had befriended. The boy arrived too late to speak to the old outlaw. We can only wonder if Bronco Bill was eager to tell his young friend something about the treasure he had supposedly buried at or near the Ladrones twenty-three years earlier.

Bronco Bill's gravestone in Hachita, New Mexico (Richard Melzer)

Hearing of this legend of possible buried treasure in the Sierra Ladrones, many have searched the mountain and its hideouts. Two men from Albuquerque spent many weekends intensely exploring the area in the 1980s. They had heard that Bronco Bill's gang had buried silver coins from the train robbery between two trees on a small hill. Using Geiger counters, the treasure hunters were finally successful when they uncovered 332 silver coins buried between two trees on a small hill east of the Sierra Ladrones. Imprinted with dates between 1878 and 1898, these coins fit the description of the long-lost loot from Bronco Bill's train robbery.

According to legend, local residents had also discovered large sums of money after years of deliberate searching or, more often, by pure accident. A poor sheepherder named José M. Jaramillo suddenly became wealthy enough to build a stone ranch house and purchase a large flock of sheep about 1908. Some say that José had uncovered money from the 1898 train robbery and had wisely hid it until enough time had passed that it was safe to spend it freely.

Other local residents may have also discovered parts of the loot from the train robbery. Two women who lived in the Sierra Ladrones region in the 1890s claimed that Indians from the nearby Alamo Navajo Reservation had found much of the money. One woman even claimed that the Navajos who discovered the cash spent some of it in her father's general store. "The money smelled like smoke, like it had been in a safe that had been blown up with dynamite," which is exactly how Bronco Bill and his cohorts had forced the train's safe open in 1898. Some local residents also recall seeing silver coins from the robbery in Navajo homes on the Alamo reservation. Navajo families reportedly vowed to never spend the coins outside their small community. With little other use for the coins, families were known to use them as poker chips.

Other Legends

Other legends about hidden wealth in the Sierra Ladrones abound. Kirk Gilcrease, who grew up near the Ladrones in the 1930s, knew a certain sheepherder who Kirk occasionally visited on trips to the mountain. While serving his young guest coffee at his campsite, the sheepherder proudly displayed a jar half filled with gold he claimed he had collected in his travels around the Sierra Ladrones. The sheepherder trusted young Kirk with knowledge of the gold's existence but never revealed the main source of his small fortune.

Kirk also remembers Miguel Sarracino of Polvadera who often traveled to the Sierra Ladrones and, after some time away, returned with gold coins and other artifacts, including a Spanish helmet and sword. Sarracino, who owned a store, a bar, and a service station, sold some of these collector items to those who could afford them during the Great Depression.

People attempted to follow Sarricino on his trips to the mountain in order to find his treasures and, undoubtedly, exploit the source of his wealth for themselves. But Miguel always left home before sunrise and took no one but his nephew Ramon with him. No one ever tracked the man's route, much less discovered his secret treasure trove.

Alvino Contreras was a young sheepherder in the Sierra Ladrones in the 1930s and the 1940s and, while he never discovered cash or coins, he knew a hermit who apparently had. The hermit, known as Mayamas, had a long white beard that he would wash in one of Alvino's water buckets whenever he stopped by the boy's camp. To wash his beard, Mayamas would remove his coat, often revealing a vest full of cash.

Years later, after he had grown up and had left to join the Army during the Korean conflict, Alvino read a newspaper account that reported that the hermit's dead body had been found along the Rio Puerco. According to the newspaper article, Mayamas had died of natural causes. Remarkably, a large sum of cash was found on his body, undisturbed.

Members of the Gabaldón family tell the story of Frank Gabaldón's experience in the Ladrones. Long-time railroad workers based in Belen,

Frank and a friend were exploring the mountain when they came across a large cave. Curious to know what treasure the cave held, the two men vowed to return someday to find out.

Frank's friend left for California before the pair could return to the cave they had discovered, but Frank eventually went back on his own. Looking down into the cave, Frank found that it was infested with rattlesnakes. Needless to say, Frank went no further. But some Gabaldón descendents still wonder if his friend may have entered the cave on his own, found something valuable, and suddenly left for California to live in luxury rather than share his treasure with Frank.

Not willing to leave nature well enough alone, humans have used the Sierra Ladrones for other legal and illegal pursuits. Civil War soldiers in the retreating Confederate army of 1862 were said to have buried a cannon in the area when the weapon's axle broke. The rebels were in such a rush to return to Texas that they probably didn't stop to notice what many people have observed ever since: that the mountain resembles the profile of the Confederates' arch enemy, President Abraham Lincoln. The buried cannon was later recovered, either by a local ranch hand in the 1930s or by a Socorro businessman in the 1950s, depending on which story you prefer to believe.

Outlaws on the lam used the Sierra Ladrones not just to hide their loot, but also to hide themselves in the mountain's high, rugged terrain; pursuers could be spotted from long distances from this ideal vantage-point. When, for example, two masked men held up the First National Bank of Belen in 1904, the fifty-man posse headed for the Ladrones first. But the bank robbers were never apprehended and the $600 they had stolen was never recovered in what was the only successful heist in the bank's long history.

Old-timers remember that moonshiners also used the mountain as an ideal location to operate their stills and hide their illegal liquor during Prohibition in the 1920s and early 1930s.

In the 1950s, at the height of the uranium boom near Grants, mining companies drilled near the Ladrones in hopes of finding deposits of lucrative uranium-bearing ore during the Cold War era. For better or worse, this exploration failed to reveal uranium in large enough quantities to warrant further development and the massive intrusion of modern change.

While some profited from treasures found in the Sierra Ladrones, most families that lived and worked nearby did not. In fact, a great many suffered from their proximity to the robbers' roost. Quite a few residents became the victims of crime, especially when outlaws in need of fresh mounts did not hesitate to steal good horses from local ranches in the late nineteenth century. To discourage such behavior, ranchers were known to hide their best horses and tie old nags to their front gateposts. They hoped that fleeing outlaws would take the more readily available nags while leaving the better animals behind.

Still Treasures?

Is there still buried treasure to be found in the Sierra Ladrones? Perhaps, although most of the area is not easily accessible by four-wheel-drive vehicle, much less by foot. Exploring the mountain can be dangerous, especially for those who are ill prepared. Ralph Castillo learned this lesson the hard way when he brought his fiancée (and future wife) Roseann to explore a large cave in the mountain during their courtship in the 1970s. Ralph brought three flashlights along, but two burned out and the young couple was lost below ground for about two hours. They can laugh about the experience now, but it was quite unnerving at the time.

About the same year a Socorro High School teacher had his own brush with danger when he fell and broke his leg while climbing in the Sierra Ladrones. The hiker was rescued and a new search and rescue team, consisting of mostly student volunteers from New Mexico Tech, was created to deal with future mishaps in the Ladrones and elsewhere.

If Ralph Castillo's story and the high school teacher's accident were not enough to discourage explorers, a 1972 story in the *Valencia County News-Bulletin* told of a bottle of nitroglycerin that reportedly sat on a ledge in one of the mountain's caves. The article's author advised, "Anyone poking around a cave in Ladron [sic] and seeing a bottle of liquid should have the sense to leave it alone and get out of the cave."

While some will persist to ignore the dangers and search for adventure and wealth in the Sierra Ladrones, most observers are content to admire the mountain from afar and simply ponder its majestic image and mysterious past. As low clouds encircle this pirate island in the desert, the view and the memories are treasure enough.

The Great Belen Train Robbery, 1898

by Richard Melzer

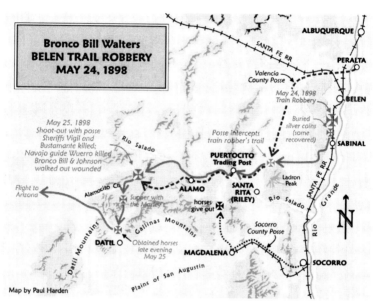

A map of the Great Belen Train Robbery Events (Paul Harden)

The scene was the railroad depot in Belen. The date was May 23, 1898. It was a day like many others in Belen since the Santa Fe Railway had built its tracks into town eighteen years before. Trains came and went with their regular cargo and weary passengers en route to destinations near and far. But May 23, 1898, was about to become a day unlike any other in history. The small town was about to experience its first and only train robbery.

The train robbers were two Texans: William "Bronco Bill" Walters and William "Kid" Johnson. As criminal activity went, the pair had chosen a hazardous, if lucrative, "trade" when they engaged in robbing trains. In fact, train robbery was considered the elite crime in the Old West. To rob a train, an outlaw gang had to somehow stop a mammoth, speeding machine, enter its usually well-guarded express car, extract its valuable cargo (stored in a thick metal safe), and hopefully make a clean getaway. Few outlaws had the nerve, much less the skills, to attempt such a high-risk operation. Few of those who attempted it were successful, and those who were, like the Black Jack Gang and the High Fives, were notorious.

"Bronco Bill" Walters and "Kid" Johnson knew the odds were stacked against them as they planned their robbery of Train No. 21. Their plan was clever, if not unique. As evidence later showed, the pair had ridden their horses about three miles south of Belen and tied them up by the tracks near the small settlement of Pueblitos. They then walked back to Belen in plenty of time to board their targeted train just as it was about to pull out of the town on schedule at 1:45 a.m. Walters and Johnson wore cowboy clothes and long canvas coats.

Train No. 21's newest passengers were hardly new to the life of crime. Standing five feet, nine inches tall and weighing no more than 138 pounds, the blue-eyed, brown-haired Walters had begun his criminal career in New Mexico as early as 1889 when he was only 19-years-old. From 1889 to 1898, he was implicated in any number of crimes, from horse theft and larceny to shootings and train robbery. Walters had served eight months in the New Mexico territorial prison in Santa Fe, from August 1891 to April 1892, but on at least two other occasions he had outsmarted his captors and escaped from local jails. By 1896, the *Albuquerque Daily Citizen* characterized Walters as "a tough of the toughest sort" and a "bad man generally."

Bronco Bill Walters prison photo (New Mexico State Records Center and Archives)

Much less is known about Walters's partner, "Kid" Johnson. Some believed that he had used several aliases, including Joe Evans and Ben Masterson. He was released from the territorial prison in 1897 after serving two years for the crime of bigamy. No one seems to know how or when the Kid's path crossed Walters's, but their fate was sealed in May 1898.

Robbing Train No. 21

Climbing into the engineer's cab, the two outlaws brandished their six-shooters and ordered the engineer to pull out of the train station in Belen. About two miles south, the engineer was told to stop his train so that one of the robbers could uncouple the locomotive and express car from the remaining passenger cars. After completing his task, the robber got back on board and instructed the engineer to drive further down the track.

When the locomotive and its single car stopped again, the outlaws broke into the valuable express car. To their surprise, the car was left unguarded. Its express manager, Edward Hicock, had escaped into the night when the locomotive and express car had been separated from the rest of the train. Hicock had hurried back to Belen to sound the alarm about the robbery.

Meanwhile, Walters and Johnson dragged the Wells Fargo safe out of the express car and employed dynamite to tear one side of the safe completely off. As Bronco Bill later described the scene, "Paper money came floating down like snow."

The outlaws stuffed as much cash as they could into large pouches, hesitating only long enough to toss over $500 in coins into the locomotive cab in a traditional gesture practiced by train robbers to share at least a portion of their loot with the victimized train crew. Estimates on the amount of cash they carried off ranged from $250 (a regulation estimate always given after Wells Fargo robberies) to $50,000 (or over $800,000 in today's money).

The Getaway

The cash-laden robbers rode southwest to the Sierra Ladrones. From there, Walters and Johnson headed west to Alamosa Creek in northern

Socorro County. Arriving in the tiny village of Puertecito, they entered Anastasio Baca's general store to purchase food for themselves and feed for their horses.

Years later, Baca's daughter recalled seeing big money belts around each stranger's waist. Juanita Baca also saw a thick pouch across the saddle of each horse the men rode. "I was sure their money belts and saddle pouches were filled with money," Juanita said in a 1956 interview.

Back in Belen, news of the train robbery spread like wildfire. Valencia County Sheriff Jesús Sánchez turned to his chief deputy, Francisco X. Vigil, to raise a posse and track down the perpetrators of this bold crime. At 37, Francisco Vigil was a veteran lawman from a large family in Los Chávez. Married with an adopted daughter, he was known for two characteristics in particular: his generosity to the poor and his bravery in the face of danger. Mounting his favorite *alazan* (sorrel), the highly respected lawman acted quickly to raise a posse and begin his pursuit before the outlaws' tracks grew cold.

But Vigil was frustrated in his efforts. Serving on posses required not only bravery, but also a willingness to ride long hours over difficult terrain for little pay. Many refused to serve, claiming they were busy with spring planting and with other pressing concerns. Although they hardly admitted it, many men probably refused to volunteer because they had no vested interest in recovering money stolen from a train simply passing through their community. Their attitude would have changed radically if their own money had been taken, as would happen in 1904 with the first robbery of the First National Bank of Belen. Finally, some residents of Valencia County, including former sheriff Maximiliano Luna, could not join Vigil's posse because they had volunteered to serve with the famous Rough Riders and were off in San Antonio, Texas, training for their eventual invasion of Cuba during the Spanish-American War.

Only one man volunteered, Los Chávez blacksmith Daniel Bustamante. He had served on posses before and was known as a crack shot with his favorite "*la cuarenta y uno*" (probably a .41 Long Colt revolver, introduced in 1877). In May 1898, he was 30-years-old, married, and the father of two children. He felt a particular loyalty to Vigil, his *primo* (cousin) and the best man at his wedding several years before. The small posse of Francisco Vigil and Daniel Bustamante began their pursuit, correctly tracking Walters and Johnson in the direction of Sierra Ladrones (Thieves Mountain).

Further south, Socorro County Sheriff Holm O. Bursum had enjoyed only slightly greater success in raising a posse of his own. Bursum was joined by two local men and Deputy U.S. Marshal Cipriano Baca, who had once arrested Bill Walters after tracking him all the way to Mexico in 1891. Sheriff Bursum was especially eager to find Walters because the notorious outlaw had been one of ten prisoners who had embarrassed the lawman by breaking out of the Socorro County jail in February 1896, using a makeshift key and an ax.

Francisco Vigil   Daniel Bustamante
(Vigil photo courtesy Tibo Chávez, Jr.; Bustamante photo courtesy Paul Harden)

Shootout on Alamosa Creek

Vigil and Bustamante discovered Bronco Bill and Kid Johnson first. Arriving in the small Navajo community of Alamo early on the morning of May 25, they were told that two strangers had been seen camping on Alamosa Creek. Two Navajos accompanied the deputy sheriff and his *primo* to the outlaws' isolated camp.

From a distance, the newly enlarged posse saw Walters and Johnson breaking camp. As the outlaws worked, their horses were still picketed on the edge of camp and their weapons were laid aside, seemingly out of reach. Vigil's posse surrounded the camp and silently led the outlaws' horses off. One Navajo urged Vigil to take the robbers' guns before moving in, but the deputy sheriff ignored this wise advice. Instead, Francisco Vigil stood up, waved some papers over his head, and loudly announced that he had warrants for Walters's and Johnson's arrest. He ordered them to surrender by throwing their hands up.

Although surprised, the robbers remained calm and, in fact, smiled at their apparent captors. Suddenly, the two dove for their rifles and threw themselves behind some cottonwood trees for cover. They opened fire, killing Vigil, Bustamante, and a Navajo, Vicente Wuerro (also spelled Guerro), within minutes.

Scene of the Alamosa Shootout (Paul Harden)

The outlaws were wounded, but only superficially and not enough to prevent them from escaping on foot. They reportedly buried most of the cash they had stolen from Train No. 21, but carried several thousand dollars away with them. Obtaining fresh horses near Datil, they continued their escape westward. Unbeknownst to them, $4,000 in reward money had been offered for their arrest.

Captured

Traveling into eastern Arizona, Walters and Johnson found refuge in the rugged Black River country. There they were aided by local cowhands and at least one previous partner in crime. After recovering from their wounds, they foolishly began to draw attention to themselves by displaying their stolen money and shooting up a Fourth of July dance near Geronimo, Arizona.

Hearing of the outlaws' brash behavior, a team of Wells Fargo detectives headed for Arizona and tracked the fugitives to a horse camp on the Black River. In a shootout on July 29, 1898, the detectives killed Kid Johnson and severely wounded Bill Walters. Brought back to stand trial in Socorro, Walters eventually pleaded guilty to second-degree murder. He began to serve a life sentence on December 14, 1899.

Designated as inmate number 1282, Bronco Bill became known as a model prisoner during this, his second term in the territorial prison. Prison guards grew less vigilant, despite Walters's earlier escapes from several county jails. Walters and a fellow inmate exploited the guards' laxness, climbing over the prison's walls and escaping from Santa Fe on April 16, 1911. Walters walked south to Albuquerque, enjoyed a good meal at the Mint Restaurant and continued to Isleta. After a $100 reward was offered for Walters's arrest, a Santa Fe Railway officer recognized the fugitive and informed authorities. Bronco Bill was arrested without resistance in Isleta on April 19. In his ever-confident words, "I could have fought my way out of New Mexico, but I've quit the bad game for good."

Walters served six more years in the territorial penitentiary. Released in April 1917 due to failing health, he is said to have traveled south again in search of the loot he and Kid Johnson had buried between three trees on a hill southwest of Belen. He never recovered the money that had cost so much pain and agony for so many.

Walters was soon hired as a cowhand on the Diamond A ranch in the extreme southwest corner of New Mexico. Working on a windmill near Hachita, he was thrown to the ground when a fierce gust of wind caused the windmill to spin out of control. He died of a broken neck later that same day in June 1921. Bronco Bill was 51.

Walters was one of the last train robbers in New Mexico history. "Black Jack" Ketchum attempted a foolish one-man theft near Folsom, New Mexico, in August 1899, and paid for his misdeed with his life in April 1901. His bungled execution by an inexperienced hangman left him not only dead, but decapitated, to the horror of 150 witnesses at the scene in Clayton.

It is ironic that the last recorded train robbery in not only New Mexico but the entire West took place within a short distance from where Bill Walters died in southern New Mexico. The attempted theft by two tenderfeet from the Mid-West was botched from the outset. The nearly comical episode on the Southern Pacific Railroad in November 1937, ended with the would-be robbers badly roughed up by angered fellow passengers. According to one witness, "If it hadn't been that we had women passengers on the coach, those robbers would have been beaten to death."

Amalia Tafoya of Belen composed a *corrido* to honor the memory of Valencia County's fallen heroes. Originally translated from Spanish by Tibo J. Chávez, Sr., and Gilberto Espinosa, it reads:

We are saddened
With great pain
To learn how he died
In such a major tragedy.

God give me courage
To relate this sad event,
To note a sad story
That touches my heart.

The year was '98.
Ah! What a sad tragedy occurred
On the 25th of May.

And Don Daniel Bustamante also expired,
But almost at the moment of his death
He fired seven times
And until the last he defended his rights.

Let us pray a prayer for the redemption of the two
And ask each of you
For a final remembrance
For the sake of God.

The story has been told,
My name I shall expose
I am Amalia Tafoya
Who today has finished this sad tale
To extend my sympathy to
All the members of
The dead heroes' families.

Daniel Bustamante was found
Soaked in his own blood.
It was Don Francisco Vigil
Who had left Belen
In the company of Daniel Bustamante
Along with some Indians
To arrest the Texan thieves.

Where are the Texan outlaws?
Soon Vigil and Bustamante arrived
The deputy sheriff
Commanded in a positive voice
For them to give up
And to follow him

The outlaws never obeyed,
But took to their guns,
First killing the deputy sheriff.
Later they killed an Indian
Of the Indians who had come along.

But what of the dead heroes of the tragic robbery of Train No. 21 in 1898? Daniel Bustamante was buried in the Catholic Church cemetery in the village of Santa Rita (now called Riley) where his mother lived. Francisco Vigil was buried in the same cemetery near his primo, but his remains were later moved to the cemetery at the Sangre de Cristo Catholic Church near today's Valencia Y on State Road 47. A humble gravestone marks the location of his body near the church door. Vicente Wuerro's remains were returned to his family in Alamo.

Francisco Vigil and Daniel Bustamante had bravely done their duty when few others dared. And it was Francisco's sense of fairness to the accused that cost both lawmen and Vicente Wuerro their lives. Courage, duty, and fairness—no one could ask more of their fellow citizens in 1898 or a century later.

The Abo Pass Gang, 1911

by John Taylor

A typical 1911 locomotive (Museum of Albuquerque # 1990.013.138)

The Belen Cutoff was long awaited by the managers and shareholders of the Santa Fe Railway. This new trackage from Dalies, just west of Belen, through Belen, to Mountainair and across the eastern plains of New Mexico was completed in 1908, saving freight operators thousands of dollars on every train. No longer did these trains have to traverse the steep and dangerous tracks through Raton Pass—they saved almost 2,000 feet of elevation gain by going through Abo Canyon instead.

However, every silver lining has a cloud! Slow-moving freight trains crawling up the west approach to Abo Canyon from Belen to Mountainair proved to be an irresistible target for train robbers. The miscreants would jump onto the slow-moving trains, break into the freight cars, and simply toss cargo off to be picked up by their colleagues who followed behind in a wagon. The Santa Fe Railway was fed up with these affronts, and on Wednesday, January 22, 1911, two of their railroad police officers boarded one of the eastbound freights at Belen to investigate and put a stop to these robberies.

One of the officers got off at Scholle, a coal and water stop east of Belen, to send a telegram, but failed to reboard the train before it departed.

The remaining agent, J. A. McClure, rode on alone but would not be seen alive again. McClure apparently left the train as it reached Abo Canyon in pursuit of the thieves.

When no report was received from McClure by Friday, January 24, the head of the Railway Police, Bill Williams, took over the investigation, and a posse, led by Bill Olds of the Railway Police and Lieutenant John Collier of the New Mexico Mounted Police (the predecessor to today's New Mexico State Police), was organized to look for the missing agent.

The *Albuquerque Morning Journal* reported that the officers believed,

McClure is a dead man; we are satisfied of that. With unusual cunning, the slayers have concealed the body and successfully covered their trail. We expect to have them in custody or dead by sundown today!"

The reporter further noted,

The Santa Fe depot this morning, prior to departure of the cut-off train, looked like an arsenal. The officers carried Winchesters and six-shooters, and wore heavy belts filled with cartridges.

Following a trail of kernels that had dropped from a torn bag of stolen corn from the tracks in Abo Canyon, the posse came to the ranch of Fred Howe and his sons, Robert and Guy. The Howe family was suspected to be a part of a loosely organized group of outlaws known as the Abo Pass Gang.

Reaching the ranch on the afternoon of Saturday, January 28, the posse found the body of McClure, shot and thrown head-first into a deep well. After retrieving the body, they concluded that he had probably been shot from ambush as he tracked the thieves from the railroad to their ranch. McClure had been shot four times: in the wrist, the arm, the stomach, and the head, and the fall down the well had fractured his skull. By the time the posse reached the ranch, the Howes were long gone, but a large quantity of stolen material was found on the premises and in a nearby cave.

The Santa Fe offered a $500 reward for the arrest and conviction of the Howes, and several posses were now in pursuit. The Howes had apparently ridden east through Abo Canyon to Gallinas where they boarded a southbound El Paso and Southwestern freight train heading for the Mexican border somewhere east of El Paso, Texas. The three men were put off the train around noon on Monday, January 30, near the Rio Grande, and they started walking east. They were noticed by a U.S. Mounted Custom Inspector named Thomas O'Conner who enlisted the help of a local Justice of the Peace named Myron Hemley (also spelled Hemly). The two mounted lawmen caught up with the Howes near Fort Hancock and asked where they were going, to which the Howes replied that they were just looking for work.

Suspicious, O'Conner and Hemley drew their weapons and started to search the men. While Hemley was searching Fred and O'Conner was searching Guy, Robert Howe pulled a rifle that was concealed in some bedding and shot O'Conner four times in the mouth and chest. The firefight continued, ending with O'Conner fatally wounded, 17-year-old Robert Howe wounded in the shoulder, and Hemley wounded in the wrist. The Justice of the Peace fled with the dying O'Conner to round up a posse. When they returned, they found the Howes gone.

Now guilty of killing two law enforcement officers, the Howes slipped across the river into Mexico. Meanwhile, four Texas Rangers joined in the hunt. The Howes crossed back into Texas near Sierra Blanca, about one hundred miles east of El Paso. Fred and Guy abandoned Robert, but they were overtaken by the Rangers at about 9:00 a.m. on Tuesday, January 31. During another gunfight, Fred and Guy ran into a thicket of brush which was quickly surrounded by the Rangers. After about an hour, the two men rushed from the thicket, guns blazing. Both were shot and killed. Robert was captured and jailed in El Paso where he confessed that his brother had killed agent McClure and that he had killed Thomas O'Conner. He was indicted by a Grand Jury and held on $25,000 bond. Unfortunately, no record exists of his trial and sentencing.

Years later old-timers said that the Abo Pass Gang was substantially assisted by a compatriot in the Belen depot who let them know about which trains had attractive loads. However, no one in Belen was ever called on the carpet, and the memory of the Abo Pass Gang faded away.

Gangsters, Los Lunas, and Route 66, 1928

by Richard Melzer

It's hard to imagine that Los Lunas was once a small, quiet village dwarfed in size by both Belen to the south and Albuquerque to the north. Boleslo Romero is one of the few old-timers who still remembers Los Lunas long before it became today's growing community, filled with traffic and bursting with new housing and big box stores.

Boleslo M. Romero was born in Los Lunas on December 8, 1917, the oldest of four children born to Andrés Adrián and Emilia Isidora Romero. His memories of childhood in the 1920s and 1930s are as vivid as if they had happened yesterday.

Boleslo remembers when Los Lunas was so small that its post office was just a room attached to the south side of the Huning Mercantile Store (now Leftovers Etc., west of McDonald's). Running the office was a small operation, handled ably by postmaster Joe Baca.

Boleslo says that once a day Don Juan Gurulé would pick up the mail pouch at the post office and bring it to the railroad station. After delivering the mail at the depot, Don Juan would pick up whatever mail had arrived by train and carry it back to Postmaster Baca's office. Remarkably, Don Juan carried the entire community's load of outgoing and incoming mail in a single wheelbarrow.

Boleslo made his own deliveries on the streets of Los Lunas when he delivered the *Albuquerque Journal* to subscribers' homes, using a bike in good weather and a horse when weather conditions turned inclement. Boleslo remembers one customer in particular: Ed Otero, the rich and powerful owner of what is now the Luna Mansion. Boleslo says that Otero often waited for his newspaper by the mansion's front gate. Otero was so rich that he paid his newspaper subscription an entire year at a time, rather than monthly, like most customers. The price of a month's subscription? Sixty-five cents!

On a few occasions, Ed Otero even invited Boleslo into his kitchen for coffee and a roll. The newsboy was impressed by Otero's generosity, but he was even more impressed by a beautiful silver-trimmed saddle displayed on a workbench in the mansion's kitchen. Otero probably kept his valuable saddle indoors where it was less likely to be stolen than if it were stored in a far less secure stable or barn.

Boleslo has many other memories of life in Los Lunas, but he recalls one exciting moment in particular. Boleslo's uncle owned a gas station and garage on the corner of Main St. (old Route 66) and Los Lentes (old Route 85), where the Home Furniture and Carpet Store now stands. With its ideal location at the intersection of two important highways, the business was called the "66-85."

Boleslo's Uncle Albert and his friend Nash Sánchez managed the 66-85. Boleslo often worked at the station, pumping gas and sweeping out the garage early each morning. One day about 1928, Albert had gone to Albuquerque to buy parts, leaving Nash and young Boleslo behind in Los Lunas. Nothing unusual occurred until the station's telephone rang. The Albuquerque police alerted Nash that a gang of thieves was headed for Los Lunas in a large black car.

The 66-85 Gas Station (Los Lunas Museum of Heritage and Arts)

Unwisely, Nash and his young companion rushed out to the roadside, just in time to see a black sedan and its occupants speed down Main Street from the east. To Boleslo's surprise, Nash pulled out a gun and began shooting at the gangsters as they drove by. Luckily, the car did not stop, although there is reason to believe that Nash hit his mark. The black car disappeared in a cloud of dust, heading westward towards Arizona. About ten minutes later an Albuquerque police car arrived at the intersection. Two lawmen rode on the car's running boards, while several others rode inside, armed with machine guns. Boleslo says it reminded him of a scene out of an old Keystone Kops silent movie.

Twelve years later, as a young adult, Boleslo became the first man from Los Lunas to enlist in the Army on the eve of World War II. He served with distinction in Europe from 1940 to 1945, flying thirty missions as the flight engineer on a B-24 bomber nicknamed Stardust.

Soon after the war ended, Boleslo met a pretty young woman named Dora C de Baca, the daughter of Manuel and Maria C de Baca. Raised mostly in New Mexico, Dora had spent several years of her youth in Arizona where her father had managed a large farm near Tempe. During World War II Dora had proudly served in the Women's Army Auxiliary Corps (WAACs) before returning home to New Mexico in 1943.

Boleslo and Dora soon fell in love and became engaged to be married. While courting Dora, Boleslo told his fiancée many stories about life in Los Lunas: about Don Juan and his wheelbarrow mail truck and about Ed Otero and his silver saddle. Then Boleslo told Dora about the exciting day when gangsters raced down Route 66 and Nash Sánchez fired gunshots into their large black car as they sped off towards Arizona. Dora's mouth must have dropped open when she heard Boleslo's story. Dora remembered a day in about 1928 when she had noticed a similar black car parked on the road when she returned home from school near Tempe. Leery, Dora started walking home, but soon came across a small campsite and a bloody coat. Continuing on, she found more bloody clothes along the way. Dora rushed home to tell her parents of her gruesome discoveries.

Dora's father searched the area and reported the incident to the local police. But whoever had driven the abandoned car, built the campsite, and discarded the bloody clothes had either succumbed to their injuries or had already fled the scene. Could the black car that Dora had seen near Tempe have been the same vehicle that Boleslo had seen as it sped through Los Lunas? Could the bloodstained clothes that Dora had discovered in Arizona have belonged to gangsters wounded by Nash Sánchez in New Mexico?

We'll probably never know the answers to these questions about the fleeing outlaws and their fate. But if mystery helps kindle romance, the mystery of a carload of bad men helped bring Dora and Boleslo much closer together. Dora and Boleslo were married on December 18, 1945. With two sons and three grandsons, they have been happily married ever since.

Boleslo and Dora Romero now live in retirement in a beautiful home in a new section of Los Lunas. After years of travel around the world, they now stay closer to home and their many interests in New Mexico. But Boleslo is always willing to share his memories of the much slower, usually more peaceful days of his youth. And a certain grateful historian is always willing to listen and learn more about the Rio Abajo and its most colorful past.

A. S. Torres and
the Shootout in Adelino, 1949

by Richard Melzer

Long before "big box" or convenience chain stores arrived in Valencia County, there were "mom and pop" grocery stores in almost every community of the Rio Abajo. These small, friendly establishments are remembered fondly for their social as well as their commercial functions. Local residents often met and shared news of the day as they purchased needed food and supplies. Unfortunately, small grocery stores were also vulnerable targets for thefts and, in some cases, more violent crimes.

Alvarado "A.S." Torres (Valencia County News-Bulletin)

Alvarado "A.S." Torres and his wife, Helen, ran one such store on Highway 47 in Adelino. The Torres's store was actually two operations: a grocery store on the south end of the building and a bar, known as the Diamond T, on the north end. The bar was called the Diamond T (for Torres) because A.S. was such a dapper dresser, much like the legendary

Diamond Jim Brady. A single gas pump stood out front of the store and bar. The business also served as the local Greyhound bus depot. The Torres family, including young daughters Bessie, Carmen, Frances, and Lorraine, lived in a house attached to the premises to the east.

A.S. Torres had always been an industrious, enterprising man. Born in Tomé in 1911, he had used his bilingual skills to translate court proceedings from a very young age. Marrying Helen Jaramillo in 1937, Torres had run his Adelino store until 1942, when he moved his family to San Diego, California, to work in the war industry. Torres worked at the Consolidated Aircraft Company, helping to build B-24 bombers for the duration of World War II. After the war, the Torres family returned to Adelino to operate their store and buy and sell local real estate. Torres was said to be among the largest landowners in Adelino by 1949. His ads for property sales often appeared in the *Belen News*.

Wednesday, April 6, 1949, was uneventful at the Torres store until about 8:00 that evening. It was then that a neighbor, 38-year-old Nicanor "Nick" Sánchez, came by to purchase some items. Although the store had already closed, Torres let his friend in, leaving the front door unlocked. Crime was rare in small communities like Adelino in the late 1940s, but A.S. Torres was usually cautious, especially because his family lived in quarters so close to his two business establishments. And the world was changing after World War II. You never knew who might be traveling through a small rural community like Adelino with mischief on their minds. So Torres kept a loaded .38 caliber Colt 6-shooter on a small table by his kitchen so that he could grab it quickly, if needed. Having served as a deputy sheriff, Torres was an excellent marksman.

Torres's daughter, Frances, remembers her father lecturing his children about the proper use of guns so that they'd never think of them as toys. A dutiful father, Torres would sometimes take his daughters out back to shoot at watermelon targets to demonstrate how terribly destructive guns could be.

An Attempted Robbery

The Torres family was eating dinner when A.S. went to serve their after-hours customer, Nick Sánchez. Sánchez's pickup truck was the only vehicle in the parking lot. Neither Torres nor Sánchez could have known that a dark sedan with Ohio license plates was headed their way, driving north on Highway 47. Three young men rode in the sedan. Army soldiers on furloughs, they had spent the afternoon at Carter's Bar on North 2nd St. in Belen. Fellow patrons recall that the soldiers drank quite a bit before leaving with the bar owner's teenage son, Frankie. They dropped Frankie off at Belen's Teen Town club.

Leaving Belen, the trio crossed the bridge over the Rio Grande and proceeded north through La Constancia and into Adelino. They stopped at the Torres store. Two men got out. The driver stayed behind. At 8:15 p.m. the two strangers entered the grocery's front door with white handkerchiefs over their faces and with newly purchased coveralls over their Army uniforms. Twenty-two-year-old Thomas Jewels pointed a .32 caliber automatic pistol at Nick Sánchez. Twenty-year-old Timothy Myers rushed around the north end of the counter and aimed a similar weapon at A.S. Torres.

Speaking at the same time, the robbers demanded that Torres and Sánchez, "Put your hands up," to which Torres replied, "What's going on? Are you trying to pull something funny?" Bravely, Torres and Sánchez began wrestling with the robbers. Shoving Myers aside, Torres rushed into his living quarters, grabbed his Colt 6-shooter, and told his family to hide. Myers recovered his balance and fled through the store's front door and into the parking lot.

Circling outside, Torres peered around the northwest corner of his building. Seeing Myers near the store's gas pump, Torres fired a quick shot and stepped back out of sight. Myers returned six rounds, foolishly using the gas pump for cover. He jumped into the getaway car and driver Bobby Clark sped away.

Meanwhile, Sánchez and Jewels continued their struggle inside. Jewels struck Sánchez on the head with his Army pistol and tried to escape through the Torres' kitchen. By now, Torres had reentered his house from a back door, just as Jewels entered the kitchen, posing a direct threat to the Torres family's safety. The storekeeper shot three times from a distance of from fifteen to twenty feet. One shot hit Jewels squarely in the heart, killing him instantly. Frances remembers seeing the dead man on the floor, his military uniform clearly showing under his coveralls.

Torres instructed his older daughter, Bessie, to run across the street to tell her uncle, 27-year-old Alfonso Torres, what had happened so that he could relay the news to the sheriff in Belen. On hearing the news, Alfonso jumped into his car and hurried off toward Belen on Highway 47. As he drove, Alfonso noticed a dark 1935 model car with out-of-state license plates. Thinking that the car and its passengers may somehow be involved in the failed robbery, Alfonso memorized the plate: K743-OHIO.

Alfonso Torres brought Sheriff Elfego Baca and Assistant District Attorney George P. Seery back to the scene of the crime. By then almost everyone in Adelino had gathered at the Torres store. As nearby residents recall, it was not everyday that their small community experienced such excitement. The local newspaper would call the event, "a spectacular gun battle" and an "action-packed drama."

A coroner's jury of six men soon gathered and determined that "the cause of death was the result of a gunshot wound fired by Alvarado Torres in defense of his home and family." In other words, the jury confirmed that Torres had shot Thomas Jewels in self-defense.

Hours later, an overturned dark car was found abandoned in a ditch about four miles north of Adelino. If their car had been traveling south when Alfonso Torres had seen it on his way to Belen, the suspects must have veered their get-away vehicle in the opposite direction when they realized they had been spotted. Footprints from the overturned car indicated that two men had fled the scene in the direction of the Rio Grande. But where had the two fugitives gone? State and local policemen set up roadblocks throughout the area, but no one was apprehended that night and into the next day. The police were baffled.

Capture

The lawmen's luck changed on late Thursday afternoon when Bernalillo County sheriffs arrested Timothy Myers and 17-year-old Bobby B. Clark as they walked along East Central Avenue in Albuquerque. The two offered no resistance, partly because Myers suffered a minor chest wound as a result of his shoot-out with A.S. Torres in Adelino.

Treated at the Veterans Hospital in Albuquerque, Myers was soon released and transported to the Bernalillo County jail, where Clark was already in custody. A.S. Torres identified Myers as one of his assailants when the storeowner came to Albuquerque the following day. The police quickly placed the pieces of the puzzle together. Based on orders found in Thomas Jewels's Army uniform, the police learned that Jewels had been ordered to report from his last base in occupied Japan to his new assignment at Camp Campbell, Kentucky, by April 21, 1949.

Somewhere en route to Camp Campbell, Jewels had met up with fellow parachute infantrymen Myers and Clark. Myers came from Fostoria, Ohio, and undoubtedly owned, or had stolen, the get-away car with Ohio state license plates. Bobby Clark had previously lived in Belen where police records revealed that he had been involved in petty juvenile offenses. He left Belen and had joined the Army, but had apparently returned to town with Jewels and Myers.

Familiar with Valencia County, Clark had likely identified the isolated Torres store as an easy mark for a quick robbery. Clark might have assumed that with income from its bar, grocery, gas pump, bus depot, and land sales the Torres business was likely to have more cash on hand than most small operations.

On April 12, Myers and Clark appeared before Justice of the Peace John Elliott in Los Lunas. Although only a preliminary hearing, the session drew a standing-room-only crowd. Myers pleaded guilty to attempted robbery. When offered a court-appointed attorney, he replied, "I don't know what for." Clark, on the other hand, pleaded not guilty and claimed that he was only 17, which meant he should be tried as a minor.

Held on bond, Myers and Clark awaited the next district court session. They didn't need to wait long. Within two weeks after the botched crime in Adelino, District Court Judge Edwin L. Swope accepted Myers's guilty plea and ordered him to serve three years in the state penitentiary in Santa Fe. Unshaven and disheveled, Myers appeared relieved that his sentence was so short. Judge Swope stressed the seriousness of the crime, but Myers did not seem to notice or, at this point, care.

Clark still insisted on his innocence, admitting that he had been with Jewels and Myers at Carter's Bar on April 6, but claiming that he had parted company with the pair before they left Belen that evening. With no witnesses at the crime scene, the state's case against Clark was weak. Clark's case records at the Valencia county courthouse are now missing so nothing is known of how his case was finally resolved.

Getting on with their Lives

Meanwhile, A.S. Torres and his family attempted to get on with their lives the best they could in Adelino. Not long after the foiled robbery, a fire broke out in a back storeroom. Only the quick help of neighbors contained the fire before it destroyed the entire building.

Concerned for their family's safety, A.S. and Helen sold their store in Adelino and moved to Belen in 1951. Another daughter, Mary Ellen, was born to the family, and Torres began a new 23-year career as a technical engineer at Sandia National Labs. A.S. drove a carpool of fellow lab employees for many years. In retirement A.S. and Helen traveled to places across the United States and around the world. Their journeys took them to countries in Europe, Africa, Asia, and South America.

In 1976, during the nation's Bicentennial Celebration, Torres played the role of Father Jean B. Ralliere in a grand historical drama performed on the Tomé plaza. As a direct descendent of Spanish settlers who arrived in New Mexico with Don Juan de Oñate in the conquest of 1598 and with Don Diego de Vargas in the reconquest of the 1690s, it was fitting that he played this important role, spoken in both Spanish and English.

Those who knew A.S. Torres respectfully referred to him as "Mr. Torres." Ironically, he entered a third career in his later years: the locksmith trade to help others secure their property against potential theft. The author spent many interesting hours with this slim, unassuming man. If he ever mentioned the most frightful, dramatic moment of his life, it was only in passing. He much preferred to talk about his life as an interpreter and his pride in New Mexico history and culture.

A.S. Torres died on August 2, 1999. According to his daughter, Frances, he had lived "an interesting, full life, with many adventures." No one could disagree. Today, hundreds of cars speed by the Torres' old place in Adelino. The business has changed hands several times and was once even owned by Nadine Brady, the granddaughter of legendary Lincoln County sheriff William Brady who was shot by Billy the Kid in 1878.

Fortunately Nadine's Fiesta Inn and its successors were never disturbed by any outlaws following the failed robbery of 1949. Only a few old-timers still remember it as the scene of one of the most famous, tragic shoot-outs in Rio Abajo history.

Kidnapping La Conquistadora, 1973

by Richard Melzer

La Conquistatora (Archdiocese of Santa Fe)

She stands only twenty-eight inches tall. She is made of willow wood from her native Spain. Having arrived in New Mexico in 1625, she is at least 388 years old, but she is well preserved, thanks to the excellent care she receives from La Confradía de Nuestra Señora del Rosario (The Confraternity of Our Lady of the Rosary).

Her wardrobe of over 200 elaborate dresses would be the envy of almost any woman in history. One dress, made by Cochití Pueblo artist Dorothy Trujillo, is of Native American design and includes small silver bracelets and a miniature squash blossom necklace. The statue's jeweled crown's replacement value equals $65,378, while her pectoral cross, donated in 1960 by an anonymous admirer, is currently valued at $97,529. The replacement value of all of her jewelry equaled $180,856 in 2000.

Whole books have been written about her, and thousands of visitors have come to admire her at her special chapel at St. Francis Cathedral in Santa Fe. She is the center of attention at the annual Santa Fe Fiesta, where she is carried through the capital city's streets at the head of a grand procession.

She is the image of the Virgin Mary, the most venerated saint in the Catholic Church. She is the oldest Madonna figure in the United States. She is the most famous religious, cultural, and historical artifact in all of New Mexico. She is listed as a New Mexico Registered Cultural Property. Originally known as Our Lady of the Rosary or Our Lady of the Conquest, she is currently called Our Lady of Peace. She is best known as La Conquistadora.

Kidnapped

But on Sunday, March 18, 1973, La Conquistadora was kidnapped from her sheltered place of honor at St. Francis Cathedral. How could this have happened? Who could have committed such a terrible crime? Why would anyone have stolen such a sacred symbol of love and peace? To begin to answer these questions, we must return to the day and scene of the crime.

As usual, the cathedral's sacristan, Della García, had locked and secured the cathedral's exterior doors by 9:15 p.m. on Sunday, March 18. The church remained closed until it was time for 6:00 a.m. Mass the following morning. Within moments parishioners noticed La Conquistadora's conspicuous absence. Church officials quickly notified the police. The press announced the shocking crime with front-page headlines. The public was horrified. Grown men and women wept at the news.

As if appealing for the safe return of a human victim, Santa Fe mayor Joseph E. Valdes vowed to "do anything in my power to be sure that La Conquistadora is found." At St. Francis Cathedral Father Miguel Baca publicly pled with the kidnappers to show mercy. Archbishop James Peter Davis expressed shock and dismay, telling reporters that he only hoped the thieves were not be so "deranged" that they would destroy the famous statue, although he admitted that "you don't know what to expect these days."

Outraged, Fray Angélico Chávez, a noted historian and the author of two books about La Conquistadora, declared that the crime was an act of sacrilege in an age when not even churches were respected by "the crooks" any more. According to Fray Angélico, the statue's disappearance in New Mexico was as traumatic to the people of this state as the disappearance of the Statue of Liberty would be for the nation as a whole.

State and local police used all available manpower as they launched their search and investigation. La Conquistadora's altar was meticulously checked for fingerprints, but none were found. Only a single set of footprints was discovered to help the police identify La Conquistadora's abductor. There was no sign of breaking and entering at any of the cathedral's exterior doors.

Santa Fe detectives, led by Paul Baca and state police investigator Mike Montoya, surmised that one or two perpetrators had probably hidden in the choir loft or elsewhere in the huge cathedral as the building was being locked for the night on March 18. When all was quiet, the intruders had apparently climbed to the high niche where La Conquistadora normally stood, grabbed the holy statue, and fled from the church in the dark of night. If true, theirs had been a direct and simple plan, as most successful criminal plans are in history.

With few physical clues to work with, detectives interviewed at least eight persons who might have had information about the theft. Several suspects agreed to take lie detector tests. Unfortunately, these interviews left the police with as many questions as answers in the puzzling mystery.

Theories

The police pondered why La Conquistadora had been kidnapped in the first place. Given her fame, she could not possibly be sold either in the legitimate art world or on the nefarious black market. Some wondered if the kidnappers had taken La Conquistadora in hopes of portraying themselves as innocent citizens who had somehow discovered the lost statue and had turned it over to the police to reap the reward that was bound to be offered. In fact, about $1,500 in reward money had been pledged by local businesses and groups within days after the crime was committed. Or would the kidnappers soon contact church leaders to make demands for a ransom of much higher value? Would they threaten to damage or even destroy the sacred image if their demands were not met?

Police also wondered if this crime was related to recent thefts of other religious art in the capital. On July 5, 1972, a valuable statue of San Miguel, as well as other statues and paintings, had been stolen from San Miguel Mission, the oldest church in the United States. (According to one facetious theory, La Conquistadora had gone off in search of the lost San Miguel because he'd been gone so long and clearly needed help in finding his way back home!)

Or could the crimes at St. Francis and San Miguel be related to a series of thefts from twenty-four churches and *moradas* (penitente chapels) in northern New Mexico over the previous two years? Close to a hundred religious artifacts, valued at over $100,000, were recovered from galleries, private collections, and art dealers by November 1972, but no arrests had been made and the perpetrators were still on the loose in the spring of the following year.

Finally, there was the possibility that La Conquistadora's kidnappers may have learned of these previous crimes and were attempting a copycat caper with far higher stakes and much greater risks. Rumors of La Conquistadora's possible whereabouts circulated widely, as rumors often do in the capital city. Some speculated that La Conquistadora was being kept in northern New Mexico, not far from Santa Fe. Others believed that she had been taken south to Albuquerque. Another group thought that La Conquistadora had been transported as far away as the East Coast where she was less well known and could fetch a handsome price on the national or international black markets. Legitimate art dealers, museums, and collectors across the nation were notified to be on the alert.

But nothing happened for several days, despite the relentless efforts of police officers and the countless prayers of Catholics across the state. Reflecting the anguish of many New Mexicans, a poet named Magdalena Vigil wrote:

How sad we are without you!
What are we to do now?
Return quickly to us,
O Virgin Conquistadora!

Catholics in the Rio Abajo had an especially strong devotion to La Conquistadora. Although the statue of Mary had been permanently displayed at St. Francis Cathedral, La Conquistadora had occasionally traveled to various parts of New Mexico on special religious occasions. In May 1954, for example, La Conquistadora had toured several central and southern New Mexico communities to the enthusiastic reception of thousands of devout church members. Accompanied by Fray Angélico Chávez, the statue visited churches in Isleta, Tomé, La Joya, and Socorro. On Thursday, May 20, it visited Belen for the first time in the town's history.

La Conquistadora arrived in Belen on schedule that Thursday afternoon. A large procession was planned, with the statue carried from the home of Placido Jaramillo, at 700 North Main St. (where the Circle K now stands at Aragon and Main), to Our Lady of Belen Church off South Main. Senior Girl Scouts of the parish carried La Conquistadora on a portable throne. Fourth-degree Knights of Columbus served as her honor guard. Once at the church, an estimated three thousand parishioners attended a solemn High Mass celebrated by Our Lady of Belen's Reverend Aloysius Boland. Fray Angélico delivered a stirring sermon.

Years had passed since that eventful day in 1954, but many residents of Valencia County remembered the procession and Mass quite vividly. Learning of La Conquistadora's disappearance, these local men and women prayed fervently for the statue's safe return. Little did the people of Valencia County know that their region of the state was about to play a key role in resolving the mystery of La Conquistadora's disappearance in 1973. No one in the county or the state could have anticipated the dramatic events that were about to unfold.

Meanwhile, an older woman in Santa Fe recalled a strange occurrence at the Santa Fe Fiesta the previous summer. As usual, the fiesta's procession had begun at Rosario Chapel northwest of town where La Conquistadora had been taken so she could be carried back to the cathedral at the head of the annual procession. The elderly woman remembered that when several men had attempted to lift La Conquistadora at Rosario Chapel, the statue had grown inexplicably heavy, as if it had wanted to remain at the chapel rather than return to the cathedral and eminent danger. Stories of suddenly heavy religious statues abound, but this one seemed particularly ominous, at least in retrospect.

Contact

Three weeks after La Conquistadora's kidnapping in 1973, the police and church officials had yet to receive word from her abductors, either by mail or by phone. Santa Fe and the entire state held its collective breath. The case suddenly broke on Saturday, April 7, 1973. On that date, Father Baca at St. Francis Cathedral received a letter from someone who claimed to know of La Conquistadora's whereabouts. To prove that the ransom note was authentic, its author went so far as to enclose a small cross from La Conquistadora's crown.

Written in poor Italian, the note stated that La Conquistadora would be returned unharmed in exchange for a ransom of $150,000 and a promise from Governor Bruce King that those involved in the crime would not face criminal prosecution. If church leaders agreed to these terms, Father Baca was instructed to ring the cathedral's bells exactly ten times at 4:45 p.m. on Wednesday, April 11. If the bells were rung at the designated time, the kidnappers would deliver additional instructions by phone the following day.

Encouraged, lead detectives Montoya and Baca told Father Baca to ring the cathedral's bells as instructed in the ransom note. The bells rang ten times at precisely the right moment. Meanwhile, the police installed electronic equipment to intercept calls received in offices at St. Francis Cathedral. Detectives hoped they'd be able to trace incoming calls when the kidnappers attempted to communicate, as promised in their note.

But the phone call never came on Thursday, April 12. Instead, church officials and city police had to wait until 8:20 on Friday evening. This first phone contact did not last long enough to trace the caller. But a second call, made moments later, produced the desired results, thanks to Father Baca's success in stalling the kidnapper. The call was traced to a residential address in Santa Fe. Events unfolded quickly. Armed with a search warrant, detectives Montoya and Baca rushed to the Santa Fe address and arrested their suspect, a slim 17-year-old Hispanic youth the police had had under surveillance for some time, thanks to the help of an informant whose identity was withheld for his (or her) protection.

After two hours of questioning in his parents' presence, the teenager confessed and, in the process, implicated an 18-year-old friend who had attended high school in Santa Fe, but who now lived in northeast

Albuquerque. The police arrested eighteen-year-old Arthur W. McComb within hours. The older boy was charged with larceny, desecration of a church, criminal damage of property, and contributing to the delinquency of a minor. With a previous juvenile record, McComb was held on $40,000 bond.

The Santa Fe minor was so cooperative that he soon agreed to lead the police to where La Conquistadora could be found. Eager to retrieve the statue as soon as possible, Montoya, Baca, Santa Fe police chief Felix Lujan, and police captain Alfred Lucero accompanied the 17-year-old to La Conquistadora's location in the cold early morning hours of Saturday, April 14.

Recovery

Despite previous rumors that La Conquistadora had been hidden somewhere north of Santa Fe or south in Albuquerque, her actual location was in Valencia County. The minor, whose name was withheld from the press because of his age, led police to the foothills of the Manzano Mountains, east of Los Lunas. The small group hiked about three miles, and, after crossing a stream, approached a remote, abandoned mine. Carrying only two flashlights, the four men followed the youth about two hundred yards into the mine. There the police finally found La Conquistadora, safely wrapped in foam padding and secured in a large plastic bag. Other works of art were also discovered, including the invaluable missing artifacts from San Miguel mission church.

The detectives carefully carried La Conquistadora and the San Miguel art to their police car and began the long journey home. La Conquistadora and her entourage arrived at Santa Fe police headquarters at 7:00 a.m. Bells from the nearby cathedral rang just as the police removed La Conquistadora from their vehicle. Tears streamed down the faces of policemen and reporters at the scene.

Newspapers across the Southwest announced La Conquistadora's recovery with banner headlines. Santa Fe's downtown merchants displayed pictures of the rescued statue in their storefront windows. Catholics uttered prayers of thanksgiving and planned both a grand procession and a solemn Mass to welcome La Conquistadora home. New Mexicans had much to celebrate.

But there were many unresolved loose ends in this mystery. Where, for example, was La Conquistadora's crown? The statue's original crown had not been stolen in March because it was normally stored in a heavily-insured First National Bank of Santa Fe vault. But La Conquistadora had been wearing an imitation gold crown when she'd been kidnapped and this second, still-valuable headpiece was missing when the statue was brought to police headquarters in Santa Fe.

Detective Baca worried that in his haste to move La Conquistadora from the mine to his police car on April 14 the crown may have accidentally fallen off, unnoticed in the dim pre-dawn light. And so detectives Baca and Montoya returned to Valencia County by helicopter to retrace their steps to and from the abandoned mine in the Manzano Mountains. They searched for three hours on Monday, April 16, but found no sign of the crown. Instead, they discovered a large quantity of explosives, making La Conquistadora's survival in the mine even more miraculous.

To everyone's relief, La Conquistadora's crown was soon discovered in an arroyo six miles south of Santa Fe where it had apparently been left by the teenage thieves. Hand-carved antique wooden frames from the San Miguel mission theft were also found in an arroyo near St. John's College. Although damaged, the frames were soon repaired and returned to the old mission church.

Homecoming

After two weeks in custody as evidence, La Conquistadora's homecoming to St. Francis Cathedral took place on Sunday, April 29, 1973. Reporters on the scene noted that few people lined the streets of Santa Fe because most people—an estimated 2,500—took part in the procession itself. Three city blocks in length, the procession was the largest held in Santa Fe in many years. Appropriately, detectives Montoya and Baca were among those chosen to carry (and guard) La Conquistadora on her throne. According to the press, cathedral bells rang joyously throughout the momentous event.

Once in St. Francis Cathedral, the capacity crowd watched as La Conquistadora was triumphantly placed back in her chapel to the north of the cathedral's main sanctuary. At 3:00 p.m., Archbishop James Peter Davis celebrated a solemn Mass of thanksgiving. Father Baca delivered the sermon. La Conquistadora was safely home at last.

To the relief of many, La Conquistadora was able to play her traditional role in the annual procession during the Santa Fe Fiesta less than four months later. As usual, her impressive entourage included Santa Fe policemen on motorcycles, a color guard (bearing papal and American flags), the fiesta queen (and her court), Catholic clergy, a choir, flower girls, the Confraternity of La Conquistadora, and the Caballeros de Vargas, who bore the esteemed statue.

And what became of the teenage thieves? Arthur McComb was said to have had a "smart mouth" when first arrested; after a two-month evaluation, a psychologist concluded that the youth had had an overriding "desire to become a master criminal." Only the prospect of a long prison term at the state penitentiary changed McComb's attitude and career goal. In June 1973, he and his accomplice agreed to plea bargains. Showing overt remorse for his actions, McComb announced to the court that he was "finished with crime" and had devoted his life to God.

Tried as an adult, McComb received the maximum sentence of one to five years in prison. Still a juvenile, McComb's younger friend was sentenced to the New Mexico State Boys Home in Springer until he reached his eighteenth birthday. Some observers thought that these punishments were too lax. Others believed it would be best for the boys to serve longer prison terms for their own protection from the bitter public at large.

But most New Mexicans were simply glad that La Conquistadora's ordeal was over and that she had somehow remained safe in a desolate mountain mineshaft. We can only speculate about how she escaped greater harm.

Rio Abajo Legend

Perhaps a legend of the Rio Abajo can help explain what transpired. According to this legend, a Spanish colonial soldier named Juan Soldado discovered a valuable mine in the Manzanos sometime in the eighteenth century. To this day, Juan's ghost reportedly guards his find from intruders who might try to steal its riches for themselves. Even when travelers have discovered his treasure and have left items (from bandanas to rifles) to identify the mine's location, their markers have disappeared when they eventually returned to the area. Thanks to Juan, the remote location remained a secret for centuries.

We can only speculate that Arthur McComb and his friend had found Juan's secluded mineshaft and had hidden La Conquistadora in it shortly after her abduction on March 18. It was Juan's devout ghost who had kept watch over the statue and had assured its safety for the three weeks it was detained in his mine. A good soldier, Juan had guarded the mine's entrance, keeping out trespassers and only permitting the police to enter so they could rescue the priceless icon at last.

Pedro Ribera-Ortega, a highly respected leader of La Confradía de Nuestra Señora del Rosario, had a much different explanation of how La Conquistadora had survived. According to Ribera-Ortega, La Conquistadora had "allowed herself to be stolen to show us that we weren't taking care of our saints" and that security needed to be vastly improved. If this was her intent, La Conquistadora succeeded. Security at St. Francis Cathedral has improved considerably, and church officials have gone so far as to have a replica of La Conquistadora made so the replica, known as La Conquistadora Peregrina (or the Traveling Conquistadora), can travel around the state while the original statue remains safely at home.

La Conquistadora (or at least La Peregrina) returned to Valencia County when she visited Our Lady of Belen Church on April 30, 1998, as part of that year's Cuarto Centenario celebration. Arriving at noon in a chauffeured, air-conditioned RV, La Conquistadora was received by a crowd of devoted local parishioners. Twenty-five years and a day had passed since the statue's triumphant return to St. Francis Cathedral in 1973. The residents of Belen were glad to help La Conquistadora, the church, and all New Mexicans celebrate the anniversary of a perplexing mystery of the Rio Arriba that was ultimately resolved in the Rio Abajo.

Danny Hawkes and the
Trembly Jewelry Store Heist, 1979

by Jim Boeck

Danny Hawkes and Ernesto Montaño (Hawkes and Montaño families)

September 22, 1979, started out as an ordinary day for 23-year-old Belen police officer Danny Hawkes. It was Saturday, the weather was still warm, and Hawkes was off duty. He had gone to the police station to finish some routine paperwork and take his police car to Caldwell Motors for some needed repairs. Assistant Police Chief Ernest Montaño accompanied Hawkes to Caldwell's on North Main Street so that Montaño could give his fellow police officer a ride back to the station once he dropped off his car.

Shortly after 1:00 p.m., Hawkes was talking to a mechanic at the garage when a call came over the police radio. A robbery was in progress at Trembly's Jewelry Store on South Main. Frank Cruz, his 27-year-old girlfriend Lorraine Martínez, and a 16-year-old juvenile had just stolen $100,000 worth of merchandise and $700 in cash from Trembly's. After taping the wrists of storeowners Marvin and Jeff Trembly, employee Stephanie Pino, and two customers, the robbers had fled through the business's back door. The three thieves ran south down the alley behind the Pizza Hut restaurant. Meanwhile, Marvin Trembly ran south on Main Street, parallel to the robbers' flight. He yelled for a passerby to stop Martínez, who struggled with the heavy bag of loot.

As soon as Montaño and Hawkes heard the dispatcher's message, they jumped into Montaño's patrol car and raced south towards Trembly's. As they sped away, Hawkes, in civilian clothes and without a gun, asked Montaño if he had an extra weapon. Montaño pointed to the glove compartment and a five-shot .38-caliber revolver stored there. Hawkes took out the small pistol, wishing that he had a larger weapon with which to face the dangerous situation that lay ahead.

Approaching the crime scene, Hawkes could hear people on the street yelling that the robbers were running behind Steve's Lounge toward the Santa Fe Railway's lodging quarters on South Main. Hawkes bolted out of the car, chasing the fleeing thieves behind Steve's Lounge. He called to the robbers to stop and fired a warning shot in the air. Driving ahead, Montaño attempted to cut the robbers off at a parking lot further south.

Confrontation

Hawkes quickly caught up to Lorraine Martínez who was still struggling with the heavy bag of stolen goods. Running hard, Hawkes did not see Frank Cruz as he hid behind a nearby car, armed with a gun. Tackling Martínez, Hawkes slammed her to the ground. But as Hawkes subdued the female suspect he heard a gruff voice that made the hair on the back of his neck rise. Behind him, Cruz declared, "I am going to blow your head off if you don't let her go!" Wheeling without hesitation, Hawkes shot his would-be assassin in the head. Cruz fell, dying instantly. Arriving at the scene, Montaño handcuffed Martínez.

Hawkes took off in pursuit of the juvenile who was also armed. Hawkes soon cornered the teenager. Remaining calm, Hawkes told the kid to put his gun down. Aware of what had just happened to Cruz, the juvenile knew that Hawkes meant business. The boy dropped his gun and surrendered, much to the police officer's relief. Hawkes had had no desire to kill Cruz, much less a youngster, even in the line of duty.

As the dust settled, Hawkes did his own crime scene investigation, questioning witnesses to the robbery and the pursuit. A background check showed that Frank Cruz was a felon from Albuquerque with a long arrest record. His attempted robbery was the second such crime at the jewelry store in two months. The Tremblys suspected that Cruz had heard about the first successful robbery and thought he'd try his luck at the same location. While the first robbers acted like pros, Cruz and his band seemed like amateurs.

Within a week of the robbery, District Attorney Tom Esquibel announced that Frank Cruz's death was a justifiable homicide. An editorial in the *Valencia County News-Bulletin* suggested that Hawkes should receive a commendation and "the congratulations of the entire community" for his brave, off-duty deed. Lorraine Martínez was found guilty for her part in the crime and served several years in prison. The juvenile was killed a few years later in what was thought to be a gang-related murder.

But the September 22 incident still troubled Danny Hawkes. Nightmares haunted him in much the same way as a soldier experiences when he still sees the eyes of the men he has killed in combat.

Life After 1979

Despite his personal troubles, Hawkes's professional career seemed to benefit from the violent incident of 1979. People in law enforcement took notice of the young police officer. Lawrence Romero, running as a Republican candidate for county sheriff, asked Hawkes to be his undersheriff, and Hawkes jumped at the chance to serve with Romero, who he admired.

In 1984, as Romero's term was coming to an end, he encouraged Hawkes to run for sheriff. Hawkes threw his hat into the political ring and ran as a Republican. He defeated his Democratic rival, although Democrats outnumbered Republicans two to one in the county. Eventually, Hawkes decided to resign as sheriff and join the Air National Guard. His decision was based primarily on his desire to serve his country.

This was the beginning of what Hawkes describes as "the hurting time" of his life. After returning from active duty in the Guard, Hawkes was at a loss as to what to do next. All he knew was that he wanted to serve the public. And so he put his gun belt back on and started over as a patrolman. Those were rough years for Hawkes, working for law enforcement agencies from Bosque Farms to Socorro. He also sold cars to make ends meet.

But things began to improve. Hawkes went back to work for Lawrence Romero when Romero served as Belen's police chief. Later, in the Socorro police department, he rose to the rank of captain. Moving back to Valencia County, Hawkes served the public in a new way. He ran for the Los Lunas Board of Education in a non-partisan election. His goal was to help youth by improving the quality of education in the Los Lunas community. He won with 56 percent of the vote.

It was in the spirit of public service that Hawkes later sought the job of magistrate judge in Belen. He felt that Judge Gillie Sánchez had always been fair and just, and he hoped to follow in the long-serving magistrate's tradition. Campaigning hard, Hawkes rang doorbells, shook hands, and spoke out on the issues. When the votes were tallied, Hawkes had won by 806 votes.

Magistrate Judge Danny Hawkes (Hawkes family)

Hawkes's life improved in other ways as well. The producer of "Top Cop," a nationally syndicated television series dedicated to the heroic exploits of lawmen nationwide, learned the story of Hawkes's fortitude in foiling the Trembly store robbers. The producer thought that the incident would make an excellent story for his series. He contacted Hawkes who agreed to appear on the show with an actor portraying him in a dramatic reenactment of the 1979 crime. In 1998, the Air National Guard sent Hawkes to Kuwait for a short period of active duty. Returning home safely, he was appointed to serve in the Magistrate Judges Association. Later, the New Mexico Supreme Court appointed him to serve on the state's Judicial Rules Committee.

When asked why he has worked as a public servant throughout his life, Hawkes reply is simple: "I find it very gratifying to serve the public and I want to continue to serve the people of Valencia County." A grateful public appreciates his unselfish, brave dedication, dating back to a warm but violent Saturday afternoon in September 1979.

Sheriffs of Valencia County, 1846-2012

by Matt Baca

The word sheriff evokes images of bravery, dedication, and chivalry. A sheriff's mission is to serve and protect his community, despite daunting challenges and often unfavorable odds.

The office of sheriff dates back to ninth century England. Sheriffs represented the English monarchy in local government, with a long list of powers and responsibilities. The badge or shield that Western sheriffs and their deputies later wore probably originated in Medieval Europe during the era of knighthood. It symbolized strength and authority for whoever wore it.

When English settlers arrived on the East Coast of North America and American pioneers began moving west, sheriffs became a vital part of local government, helping to bring law and order to newly formed communities.

Sheriffs in New Mexico have Spanish as well as English roots. In Spanish colonial times, an alcalde mayor governed each community with duties that included the enforcement of royal laws within his jurisdiction. Rather than wearing a badge to represent his authority, an *alcalde mayor* carried a *bastón de justicia* (black cane) with a silver tip. According to historian Marc Simmons, an *alcalde mayor* carried his cane "on all occasions when he acted in his official capacity as an arm of the law."

The first U.S. governor of New Mexico, Charles Bent, appointed the first sheriff of the newly created Valencia County in September 1846. James Lawrence Hubbell had arrived in the region in 1844 and had married into the prominent Gutiérrez family. Respectfully known as Don Santiago, Sheriff Hubbell served a single two-year term. Thomas Hubbell, one of Don Santiago's several sons, also served as a noted sheriff in Bernalillo County, from 1895 to 1905.

Don Santiago Hubbell, first Sheriff of Valencia County, in his Civil War uniform (New Mexico State Records Center and Archives, Hubbell collection, 12306)

Sheriffs performed many tasks during the U.S. territorial period. In maintaining law and order, they served warrants and subpoenas, had charge of jails and inmates, formed posses, and sometimes headed the local militia. Sheriff Matías Baca (the author's great-grandfather) led the militia against raiding Indians in 1870.

Jailbreaks were common in territorial New Mexico and Valencia County was no exception. For example, in June 1881, the famous Elfego Baca helped his incarcerated father, Francisco Baca, break out of the Los Lunas county jail where he was being held for murder.

County size and terrain helped make a territorial sheriff's job extremely difficult. For much of its history Valencia County stretched from the Colorado River to the west into much of today's Torrance County to the east. Filled with mountains, deserts, and valleys, Valencia County's rugged terrain was ideal for outlaws evading the law. The long arm of the law was considerably shorter and far less effective in these adverse conditions.

Sheriffs were also responsible for the execution of condemned prisoners within their jurisdiction. Valencia County Sheriff Lorenzo Labadie oversaw the first legal execution in New Mexico's territorial history when Felipe García was hanged in Tomé on May 25, 1852, for the murder of Thaddeus E. C. S. Canter. Only one month and two days separated the date of García's crime and the day of his execution. In the only other legal hanging in Valencia County, an unidentified prisoner was executed on July 28, 1855.

Territorial sheriffs enjoyed considerable power, but not much compensation. Most earned more money as tax collectors (a major part of their assigned duties) than as lawmen. It took truly dedicated men to carry out their often-dangerous assignments, pursuing thieves, murderers, and every other kind of outlaw that plagued Valencia County.

Sheriffs were assisted by deputy sheriffs, who often filled in for sheriffs when they were out of town or otherwise unavailable. Deputies' jobs were no less dangerous, as proven in the case of Francisco X. Vigil. Vigil was on duty when a Santa Fe railroad train was robbed south of Belen on May 23, 1898. Pursuing the thieves, Vigil and his two-man posse (his cousin, Daniel Bustamante, and a Navajo volunteer, Vicente Wuerro) were killed in a shootout the following morning.

Of the forty-two sheriffs who have served Valencia County since 1846, the vast majority have been Hispanic. In fact, so many political offices in Valencia County were held by leaders of Spanish descent in the 1800s and early 1900s that newspapers of that era often referred to the county as the "Kingdom of Valencia." The "kingdom" was "ruled" by one family in particular: the rich and powerful Lunas. The Lunas or their handpicked allies used the sheriff's office as the base of their political power in the Rio Abajo. Many Lunas who served as sheriff went on to serve in higher offices, including Congressional Delegate (Tranquilino

Luna), speaker of the territorial House of Representatives (Maximiliano Luna), and dominant leader of the 1910 State Constitutional Convention (Solomon Luna).

The office of sheriff in Valencia began to change after New Mexico achieved statehood in 1912, but the job was no less dangerous and hardly more lucrative. No sheriffs have been killed, but several have been wounded in the line of duty. On Saturday, March 1, 1930, Sheriff Ignacio Aragón y García and two other lawmen attempted to take 19-year-old Bonifacio Torres into custody at his grandmother's house in Jarales when his family complained about his drinking and abusive behavior. Torres and deputy sheriff Charles "Casey" Cunningham were killed during an all-day standoff in Jarales.

Several years later, Sheriff Elfego Baca (no relation to the famous Socorro lawman) was summoned to a bar on South Main Street in Belen. According to the *Belen News*, Sheriff Baca and city policeman Luciano Sánchez answered the report that a patron was armed and disorderly. As Baca later recalled,

> When we walked into the place a man was standing at the bar with his back to the door. I grabbed him from behind and Luciano disarmed him, removing a .32 caliber pistol from a shoulder holster. We got him on the ground and were trying to put handcuffs on him when he got my finger in his mouth and bit it to the bone, almost tearing it off. I pulled my pistol and struck him twice over the head. That quieted him down. Both of us received treatment at the hospital.

Luis A. Esquibel, the apprehended prisoner, had recently escaped from an Oklahoma state prison. Returned to his cell in Oklahoma, Esquibel wrote Baca a bitter letter in which he expressed his anger at being captured and his strong desire to see Baca burn in hell for eternity.

Sheriffs responded to calls of all kinds, some of which required tactful counseling, rather than ordinary law enforcement skills. Sheriff Baca received many calls—especially on weekends—from women who claimed that their husbands had been either physically or verbally abusive to them. When Baca arrived at the scene of a domestic quarrel, he often acted as a marriage counselor, helping couples work out their issues for the evening. Baca said that many couples later came to his home to thank him for helping to save their marriages.

Most sheriffs have enjoyed job satisfaction, especially when they solved a major case or caught a notorious criminal during their terms in office. But some crimes were never solved and have remained forever frustrating.

The sheriffs of Valencia County have varied widely in characteristics and personalities. Most have been middle aged, but some (like 28-year-old Danny Hawkes) have been quite young. Most have been Hispanic, but others, including one of our most famous, Joe Tondre, were Anglo.

Most sheriffs served only one term, but others (Emiliano Castillo and Lawrence Romero) have served as many as three. Sheriff Castillo holds the record for the most number of years served, a total of twelve. Most sheriffs were elected, although some (like our first) were appointed, usually to complete the term of a predecessor who had died before his term in office had expired.

Several sheriffs have gone on to serve in higher public offices. In addition to the Lunas, Joe Tondre became a U.S. Marshal and a warden at the New Mexico State Penitentiary in Santa Fe. Ignacio Aragón y García served on the Belen school board for over twenty years, including a term as the board's president. Most recently, Danny Hawkes serves as an able magistrate judge in Belen.

Despite their many differences and occasional flaws, the sheriffs of Valencia County share one overriding characteristic. They have all worked tirelessly for the safety and welfare of the citizens of Valencia County. Often under-staffed, under-financed, under-paid, and overworked, they have faced incredible danger with unflinching valor and pride in the Rio Abajo.

Valencia County Sheriffs Since 1846

1846-48	James L. Hubbell	1929-31	Ignacio Aragón y García
1849-53	Lorenzo Labadie		
1854-55	Anastacio García	1931-33	Pablo Gallegos
1856	Jesús Aragón y Chávez	1933-35	Abelicio Sánchez
		1935-39	Henry T. Jaramillo
1857-59	Francisco Chávez y Armijo	1939-41	Manuel García
		1941-45	Liberato Gabaldón
1860-61	Clemente Chávez	1945-51	Elfego G. Baca
1862-67	Dionicio Chávez	1951-53	Emiliano (Mily) Castillo
1868-69	Antonio Luna		
1870-71	Matías Baca	1953-59	Medardo Sánchez
1872-73	Jesús María Sena	1959-63	Emiliano (Mily) Castillo
1874-75	Jesús M. Luna		
1876-80	Patrocinio Luna	1963-67	Medardo Sánchez
1881-82	Henry Connelly	1967-71	Jack Elkins
1883-85	Patrocinio Luna	1971-75	Emiliano (Mily) Castillo
1886-88	Jesús M. Luna		
1889-92	Tranquilino Luna	1975-77	Nick Sánchez
1893-94	Solomon Luna	1977-79	Lawrence Romero
1895-96	Maximiliano Luna	1979-81	Billy Holiday
1897	Jesús Sánchez	1981-85	Lawrence Romero
1898-1908	Carlos Baca	1985-87	Danny Hawkes
1909-17	Ruperto Jaramillo	1987	Bill Roach
1917-21	Placido Jaramillo	1987-91	Lawrence Romero
1921-25	Joe Tondre	1991-95	Anthony Ortega
1925-27	Antonio J. Archibeque	1995-2003	Juan Julian
		2003-07	Richard Perea
1927-29	Jesús Gallegos	2007-10	Rene Rivera
		2010-	Louis Burkhard

"The Judge:" José María Baca

by Richard Melzer

José María Baca was born on February 19, 1889, the fifth of eleven children. He grew up on his family's farm in Bosque and learned to read and write in both Spanish and English from his father, Damion Baca. In January 1912, only days after New Mexico became a state, José married Teresa Sánchez. Well respected in his community, José was elected the Justice of the Peace in Bosque four years later when he was only 27-years-old.

In 1922, José and Teresa moved to Belen to open a café on South First Street, across from the Harvey House and the Santa Fe Railway depot. Known as the Depot Café, the restaurant was a popular eating establishment for railroad passengers, railroad workers, local residents, and people from more rural parts of the county who came to town to shop and do business. José, Teresa, and their three children (Reynaldo, Bernieres, and Ernestina) lived in adjacent rooms on the café's north side. The family operated the café until 1952 when José retired. Still popular, the much-expanded restaurant is now operated by the Torres family and is known as Pete's Café.

A staunch Republican, José ran for the office of Belen's Justice of the Peace in 1936 and won. He served as his community's Justice of the Peace for the next sixteen years, hearing cases and marrying couples in his café much as Gillie Sánchez did in his bakery on South Main Street years later. Until his death at age 101, José was respectfully known as "The Judge."

Judge Baca typed each legal case he heard on a manual typewriter whose ribbon faded quickly from frequent use. His volume of case records filled over 1,300 pages. The book was enclosed in a rough, durable homemade cover and bound with two 4" screws. It symbolized the very practical justice citizens came to expect when they entered Judge Baca's café courtroom.

Judge José María Baca and his wife, Teresa (José María Baca family)

Reading Judge Baca's records, one is first struck by some old laws that seem quaint and even humorous today. Using "vile language" in public, for example, could lead to arrest, a court appearance, and fine in the late 1930s. Long before there were seat belt laws, Belen had a local law against four passengers sitting in the front seat of a moving vehicle. The fine for such unsafe behavior was $4.50 (plus $2.50 in court costs) in 1942. Speed limits were much lower, of course. In 1937 a motorist was fined $5.00 for driving a reckless 35-miles-per hour on Main Street, the speed limit on the same road today.

Reading old court records, one is also impressed by the near absence of certain problems we face today. DWI's, for example, were rare. Public intoxication was nevertheless a problem, especially in the last years of the Great Depression, 1937-39. In 1937 alone there were 133 cases of public intoxication, representing 72 percent of all cases on the criminal docket that year. Unfortunately, many of these cases, as well as many cases of disorderly conduct, took place during major social events, including the Belen fiestas. As might be expected, vagrancy was a problem in the depression years when thousands of unemployed men and women crossed the country, hitchhiking on highways or jumping railroad freight cars at all hours of the day and night.

Two tragic deaths occurred on or near busy railroad tracks. In May 1938, a coroner's jury concluded that an unidentified male was accidentally killed "by the cylinder of south bound #31 freight train." Two months later another coroner's jury declared that a man "came to his death by foul play by being placed on the tracks…by an unknown person to be run over by a train." No arrests were reported, and, surprisingly, the press made no mention of the incident.

Thefts were apparently rare and, most often, petty. In 1939, the last year of the Depression and the worst year for petty thefts, stolen items included wine, coal, gasoline, and a coat from the Becker-Dalies Store on South Main Street. Only seven cases of grand theft were listed, all surprisingly in the post-depression era. Pilfered items included rings, an antique rifle, a car, a horse, and some ranch cattle.

Several local trends can be directly tied to larger historical events in the United States and, in fact, the world. This was true of the Great Depression. It was also true of World War II. In 1942, shortly after Pearl Harbor was attacked and our country entered the war, many couples married as young males faced the draft or volunteered for military service. While most couples were married in local churches, the number married by Justice of the Peace Baca more than tripled from 1941 to 1942. Judge Baca's daughters, Ernestina and Bernieres, often served as official witnesses at these rather informal events in their father's café. The number of weddings conducted by Justice Baca declined to pre-war levels for the balance of the conflict while many men served in uniform overseas. But the number rose dramatically as soon as the war ended in 1945 and young veterans returned home to marry their local sweethearts.

Nineteen forty-eight represented the record year for weddings conducted by Justice of the Peace Baca. In fact, over 56 percent of all marriages conducted by Justice Baca between 1937 and 1950 took place in 1948 alone. Nationally, the offspring of these post-war unions formed the "baby boom" generation, the largest generation of newborns in American history.

Many couples married by Justice Baca were Valencia County residents who later took the time to have more formal church weddings with their family and friends in attendance. But a large percentage of couples were from outside the county, coming from as near as Albuquerque and Socorro and from as far as Denver and Los Angeles to exchange their wedding vows. This large percentage of non-resident newlyweds can be explained in several ways. For one, Belen's location on a major north-south highway (old 85) and at the intersection of two Santa Fe Railroad routes meant that couples relocating from one section of the country to another often stopped in Belen to "tie the knot" before continuing on to their final destinations.

Couples from closer communities, like Albuquerque, Socorro, Grants, and Mountainair, might well have eloped to Belen if families and friends back home disapproved of their nuptial unions for one reason or another. In an era when marriages between Anglos and Hispanics or between Protestants and Catholics were still frowned on by many, "mixed" couples were known to elope in defiance of church rules, parental authority, and local traditions.

High divorce rates were an unfortunate trend of the future in Valencia County and the nation as a whole. Divorce still carried a social stigma and few women had the means to survive alone, much less with children, without a husband's financial support in these earlier times. However, an increasing number of women appealed to Justice Baca's court for protection against verbal and physical abuse by their spouses. Some women obtained relief in the form of "peace bonds," or bonds paid with the promise of restraint over a period of time. But court records show that most women who turned to the court for legal protection asked that their cases be dismissed by the time they were scheduled to be heard. Did women opt for dismissal because their husbands threatened additional abuse if their cases came to court? Or did wives use the court to simply teach their husbands a personal lesson through public embarrassment? We'll never know. Motivations for dismissal surely varied, but it is significant that more and more women thought of the legal system as a viable means of defense against abusive males, even in a still heavily traditional rural community.

Individuals and whole companies also turned to the Justice of the Peace to recover money owed in debts or damages. Large and small stores alike sought help in collecting unpaid bills from their most derelict customers.

This, then, is a partial view of Belen as seen through the historical window of Judge Baca's local court records. Belen was still generally a small, peaceful community in the era 1937 to 1950, although some signs of modern change had, for better or worse, begun to appear.

To Justice of the Peace Baca's great credit, it appears that he handled his cases and ran his courtroom fairly and justly, given the ideas and values of his day. This is all we can ask of any judge at whatever level he or she might serve and in whatever period of history he or she might live. The rule of law—as opposed to the rule of force and violence—depends on it.

Doug Hall: Santa Fe Railway Agent, 1951-1983

by Richard Melzer

A train whistle blows in the distance as Doug Hall settles back to share some of his favorite stories about working for the Atchison, Topeka and Santa Fe Railway. Hall worked for the Santa Fe for a total of thirty-two years, from 1951 to 1983. Hall and his wife, Bettie, even built their beautiful home near the Santa Fe tracks south of Belen in the mid-1960s. Hall spent most of his railroad career as a special agent, or chief investigator of incidents ranging from petty crimes and minor accidents to major train wrecks and business scandals. As Hall puts it, his job "covered a lot of territory."

Three Deaths in a Single Day

Special Agent Hall began the memories of his career with a story about the time he dealt with three deaths in a single day at the Belen railroad yard. Early on that fateful day, a Santa Fe Railway official who had arrived in Belen on company business suffered a massive heart attack at the local depot; the out-of-town visitor died instantly. Hall called Arno Romero, owner of Belen's Romero Funeral Home, and notified Trinidad Anaya, the local coroner and justice of the peace, who immediately arranged an inquest.

Hours later, a passenger train heading for Belen wired that a passenger onboard had become ill and had died before medical help was available. Once the train arrived in Belen, Hall had the deceased traveler transported to the Romero Funeral Home and, for the second time that day, called Trinidad Anaya. Stunned by the news, Anaya convened a second inquest.

Unbelievably, a third death occurred shortly thereafter. While making his rounds, Hall had encountered a hobo in the yard. Smelling liquor on the man's clothes and breath and concerned about the fellow's safety among rolling stock and heavy equipment, Hall had chased the stranger from the area. Foolishly, the hobo had returned to the yard and had attempted to board a slow-moving freight train heading out of town. Still intoxicated, the man had lost his grip on the car he was trying to

120

board and had slipped beneath the train. Rushing to the scene, Hall knew that the man could not have survived his massive injuries. With some difficulty, Hall and Arno Romero pulled the lifeless body out from under the train. Hall then phoned Trinidad Anaya to report the tragic accident and death.

Doug Hall (photo courtesy Betty Hall)

The coroner could not believe his ears. Three deaths in one day were highly unusual in Belen. Three deaths in one day at the Belen railroad yard was unheard of. A coroner's jury was organized, although it was getting hard to find six available men to serve that day. Even a retired railroad man on crutches was asked to serve on the jury when he came to visit friends on the work crew.

Questioning what his duties on the coroner's jury would include, the retiree learned that members of the jury would have to view the deceased. The squeamish man suddenly remembered an errand he had to run in town. Eventually six men were found. The group investigated the incident, viewed the body, and within moments, declared that the homeless man's death had resulted from an accident beyond the railroad's control.

Tragic Accidents

Doug Hall recalls other tragic accidents resulting from failed attempts to secure rides on moving trains. In one particularly sad incident, a handsome young Mexican immigrant tried to hitch a ride on a train traveling on tracks about a quarter of a mile west of the Rio Grande. Losing his grip, the man fell under a moving freight car. The youth's legs were crushed. Notified in Belen, Hall raced to the scene of the accident to find the young man sitting on the tracks, staring forlornly at his injured legs. Hall ordered train traffic halted in both directions until an ambulance arrived and the man was lifted into the emergency vehicle. The ambulance had taken longer than usual to arrive because it had gotten stuck in the mud en route. Although the fellow was rushed to the hospital on North Main Street in Belen (where the public school administration building now stands), a local physician gave little hope for his survival.

Transferring the young man to the Bernalillo County Medical Center (now the University of New Mexico Hospital), doctors succeeded in saving his life, but only by amputating both of his legs nearly to his hips. After three weeks of hospitalization, the man was deported back to Mexico. While not responsible for the tragedy, the Santa Fe Railway paid the injured man several thousand dollars in compensation. Hall still shakes his head at the memory, knowing that the railroad's generosity could never compensate for the life the young man might have enjoyed but for one terrible moment on the tracks west of Belen.

Hall has memories of other careless people who put themselves and even their children at risk near dangerous freight trains. One father regularly drove his five children to their assigned school bus stop, located on the other side of an isolated railroad crossing. Arriving one day when a freight train was stopped at the crossing, the irresponsible parent instructed his kids to go under the train to get to their waiting school bus.

In another instance, a mother was seen passing her infant over the coupling between two parked freight cars; a waiting friend or relative reached out to receive the child on the other side of the tracks. Fortunately, alert conductors witnessed these incidents and made sure that the trains did not resume travel before the children were out of harm's way. Hall severely reprimanded both parents for their reckless behavior.

Railroad Robberies

Special agent Hall was also kept busy investigating thefts on the railroad. The Santa Fe Railway had more than 12,000 miles of track, stretching from Chicago in the east to Los Angeles in the west. Valuable property moved in both directions, thanks to the hard work of thousands of honest men and women employed by the Santa Fe. But with so many miles, so many valuables, and so many people involved, devious schemes were concocted and sometimes carried out. This was when Doug Hall went to work.

In one case, large shipments of cigarettes en route to California were being stolen from Santa Fe trains on a regular basis. Like all freight cars, those carrying cigarettes were sealed after being loaded at their point of origin. The seals were only to be broken when the cars and their cargo reached their destination, as listed on a train's manifest, or list of transported goods. Passing through Belen, seals on cars carrying boxes of cigarettes were still intact. But the seals were broken and most of the cigarettes were gone by the time trains reached the West Coast. How could anyone have committed this blatant crime over and over in a crime spree that lasted several months?

Asked to investigate, Hall was originally stymied by this mystery. The Santa Fe Railway grew so concerned that it sent two company officials to visit Hall and check on the progress of his investigation in Belen. Questioning Hall, the officials even implied that Hall might be involved in the robberies. Frustrated, Hall used four vacation days to pursue the mystery far beyond his home base in Belen. Using his railroad pass, the special agent rode a passenger train to Gallup and borrowed a friend's car from which he could conduct surveillance near the Gallup rail yards. While Hall watched the yards, it began to snow, obstructing much of his visibility. Leaving the borrowed auto, Hall lay in a snow bank and continued to look for suspicious behavior. His determination paid off when a freight train pulled in with a carload of cigarettes. Hall saw a local switchman sneak up to the freight car, break its seal, and unload several cartons of the valuable goods.

Caught red-handed, the worker was arrested, tried, and convicted of taking no less than $75,000 worth of cigarettes over a nine-month period. Further investigation revealed that the thief had regularly sold his loot to a man named Pino. Pino had been selling the stolen cigarettes in cigarette machines to hundreds of unsuspecting customers in western New Mexico. Arranging a plea bargain before State District Court Judge David Chávez, each of the thieves served a nine-month prison term for his nefarious deeds.

On another occasion, special agent Hall was sent to check into a similar series of robberies at the Houston, Texas, rail yards. This time the stolen property was liquor. Arriving in the south Texas city, Hall went undercover, posing as a newly hired yard worker. Dressed in overalls to look the part, he patiently observed his fellow workers and their movements over several days. It did not take long before Hall spotted two switchmen unloading crates of whiskey from a freight car and hauling them to a private vehicle parked nearby. Approaching the thieves as they loaded their car trunk, Hall politely inquired if the men needed help in their labor. The pair declined Hall's offer, to which Hall suggested that they would need lots of help where they were going—to prison. Hall revealed his true identity and apprehended the thieves. With only one set of handcuffs, Hall cuffed the two men together and escorted them to the nearest police station. The culprits were tried, convicted, and sentenced to prison terms at the Texas State Penitentiary in Huntsville.

Only a small percentage of retirees can say that they had worked in careers that truly matched their personalities, interests, and skills. Doug Hall can make this claim, to the lasting benefit of the Santa Fe Railway, the town of Belen, and the citizens of the Rio Abajo.

Valentín Torres and the
Turnpike Phantom Slayer, 1953

by Richard Melzer

A blue sedan barreled down State Road 85 (now 314) at speeds of up to one hundred miles-per-hour on Sunday, October 12, 1953. Three young men were on board: the 24-year-old driver, John Wesley Wable, and passengers Marvin Henry Parson and J.D. Francis, both of whom had hitched a ride with Wable when their car had broken down in California's Mojave Desert.

Wable and his companions were speeding south through Valencia County because they had just robbed the Whiting Brothers Service Station on West Central Avenue in Albuquerque. The three strangers had pulled into the filling station and had asked the lone attendant, 13-year-old Andrew Gutiérrez, to check their oil.

While Gutiérrez checked their oil, Wable entered the station, took $81 from the cash register, and came back out. Telling young Gutiérrez to "forget about the oil," the robber had jumped into his car and sped away. Alerted of this crime about 5:00 p.m., police in Bernalillo, Valencia, and Socorro counties prepared to set up roadblocks to apprehend the fleeing outlaws. Late on a Sunday afternoon, there were few policemen on duty, especially outside the Albuquerque area.

In Los Lunas, state policemen T.J. Chávez and B.E. Lucas received instructions to set up roadblocks on both sides of the Rio Grande, on routes 85 and 47. In Belen, 29-year-old patrolman Valentín Torres was the only officer at the local police station. Receiving word from Albuquerque, he drove his patrol car to the railroad overpass on North Main Street and waited. A wise lawman once said that police work consists of 99 percent waiting and one percent excitement. Few truer words were ever spoken, as Valentín Torres was about to discover.

As Torres watched traffic coming south on 85, the fugitives' vehicle suddenly came into view at 5:45 p.m. Without hesitation, Torres turned on his warning light and swung his patrol car in the speeding car's path. Rather than stop or plow into Torres's car, Wable veered to his right, pulling into the parking lot at the old 85 Courts Motel, located about where the Mesa Motel is located today. With no place to escape, the sedan came to a screeching halt.

Torres pursued the out-of-state car and easily captured and handcuffed its two youngest occupants, 20-year-old Marvin Parson and 17-year-old J.D. Francis. Meanwhile, Wable had fled on foot, crossing North Main Street and heading east. Torres noticed that the fugitive was about six feet tall and wore a blue shirt and brown pants. Patrolman Torres shared Wable's description with state policemen T.J. Chávez and B.E. Lucas when they arrived on the scene moments later. Two additional state policemen, a deputy sheriff from Socorro County, and several Santa Fe Railway agents also converged on the scene.

Capturing the Turnpike Phantom Slayer

As darkness fell, the policemen searched Belen for any sign of Wable. After several hours, they finally met success with the aid of two observant young women, 23-year-old Carolyn Smith, a nurse, and 20-year-old Midge Harmon, a billing clerk for the Santa Fe Railway. Hearing of Wable's escape, Smith and Harmon had noticed a suspicious hitchhiker at the sharp turn on Jarales Road, not far from the Santa Fe Railway's tracks. Wisely contacting the police rather than confronting Wable alone, the two women watched as Torres and his fellow policemen finally apprehended Wable near Auge's Service Station on River Road. Dirty, tired, and unarmed, Wable was taken into custody without a struggle. In Torres's words, the fugitive "didn't have a chance."

Wable was kept in the Belen city jail overnight. Authorities arrived the following day to accompany the prisoner north to his final destination in Greensburg, Pennsylvania. Once in Greensburg's county jail, Wable was considered such a dangerous criminal that he was placed in solitary confinement with a guard in his cell 24-hours-a-day. In fact, the guard was required to report on the prisoner's status every fifteen minutes!

News of Wable's capture in Belen spread quickly in Valencia County and, in fact, the entire United States. What might have seemed like a simple local arrest was national news because, to Valentín Torres's and many Belenites' surprise, John Wable was identified as one of the most wanted criminals in the country.

Valentín Torres (on far right) (City of Belen)

Wable was, in fact, suspected of being the notorious Turnpike Phantom Slayer who had brutally shot and robbed three truckers as they rested in their vehicles along the Pennsylvania Turnpike. Two of the three victims had died of gunshot wounds to the back of their heads in July 1953. Wable had been on the run ever since. All travelers on the Pennsylvania Turnpike had lived in what was described as a "reign of terror" while the killer had remained on the loose. Newspapers across the country carried reports of the frustrated nationwide manhunt.

Several false alarms had brought policemen to various locations, but with no success. Eager to catch the man who had shot three of its members, the Teamsters Union had offered an $11,000 reward for information leading to his final arrest and conviction. Ironically, Wable had been in police custody in Uniontown, Pennsylvania, on an unrelated charge while authorities continued their search in all other directions. While in jail, Wable had even confessed to a guard and several fellow prisoners that he was, in fact, the Turnpike Slayer. But Uniontown police dismissed Wable as a "screwball" incapable of such terrible crimes.

Released from jail, Wable had fled west to California and, eventually, to New Mexico.

Once Wable was caught in Belen and securely behind bars in Pennsylvania, as many as thirty individuals came forward to claim all or part of the Teamsters' $11,000 reward money. In Belen, those who hoped to be compensated for their part in the capture included Carolyn Smith and Midge Harmon who had promptly alerted lawmen after spotting Wable on Jarales Road.

Officer Valentín Torres

Valentín Torres may well have added his name to the list of those eligible to collect the reward money. After all, it was his quick action that had forced Wable to turn off the road, abandon his car, and flee on foot on that fateful Sunday afternoon. But Torres refused to apply for the coveted reward money. He humbly accepted an official commendation from the Belen town council, but stated that he was simply doing his job when he helped capture the notorious Turnpike Slayer.

Valentín Torres had served on the Belen police force for five years prior to the events of October 1953. Born and raised in Belen, he was a proud descendent of Captain Diego de Torres, one of the founders of the original Belen land grant in 1740. Torres had attended public school in Belen, including high school where he played several sports, especially baseball. After school, he had joined in the Civilian Conservation Corps (CCC), had worked, ironically, as a trucker (like those whom John Wable had murdered), and had served in the U.S. Army during World War II.

Returning home after the war, Torres was applying for a job with the town of Belen when a local official suggested that he apply for a job on the police force. Torres was not very interested in a career in law enforcement, but decided to try it out for at least a few months. Torres remained disinterested at first, but soon grew devoted to his new line of work. Months turned into years and by October 1953 he was clearly a veteran police officer, ready for the challenge that faced him on Route 85 north of Belen.

A Trial in Pennsylvania

John Wable faced trial in Pennsylvania in March 1954. Valentín Torres was called as a witness to help identify the killer. Torres still recalls the last time he saw Wable in custody. According to Torres, Wable pointed to the Belen patrolman and declared, "I would have killed that Mexican if I had had the chance!"

Wable's trial lasted two weeks. The most damaging evidence against the accused was a watch Wable had stolen from one of his victims and a foreign-made pistol found in his boarding house and identified as the murder weapon. Wable's jury, consisting of seven men and five women, took less than four hours to return a guilty verdict. The Turnpike Killer was sentenced to death and, despite appeals, died in the electric chair on September 26, 1955. Newspaper reports described the killer as calm to the last.

Valentín Torres served on the Belen police force for another nine years before joining the Valencia County Sheriff's department and working in law enforcement an additional sixteen years. He retired in 1980 with much to be proud of. He had worked in the CCC, had played shortstop on several good baseball teams, had served his country well in World War II, had married his wife, Piedad, and had raised a fine family with two sons, Joseph Lawrence and Steven Carl. Even the street where he lives in north Belen is named in his honor. But the moment Valentín Torres can be most proud of came in an instant on October 12, 1953, when he risked his life by pulling his police car in the path of a speeding vehicle. As he told a reporter at the time, he "took a chance," but was never really nervous until it was all over.

Brave people are like that. They are brave by nature, and we only discover the extent of their bravery in times of crisis. In those moments they rise to the occasion, do what most of us would never dream of doing, and then quietly resume their daily lives.

Valentín Torres was like that. Few others can say the same.

Gillie Sánchez:
Master Baker (1947-1987) and
Magistrate Judge (1968-1994)

by Richard Melzer

Gilberto "Gil" or "Gillie" Sánchez was born in Jarales on September 20, 1916, the fifth of six boys and four girls born to Nestor and Carlota Sánchez. Gil learned his strong work ethic at an early age, first on his father's farm and then during high school when he worked at Harrell's bakery, located at the corner of South 6th Street and Becker Avenue in Belen.

From 1931, when he was a sophomore in high school, to 1935, when he graduated, Gil worked at Harrell's Bakery from 4:00 a.m. to 8:00 a.m., before he went to class, and from 3:00 p.m. to 7:00 p.m., after school was dismissed. With full days on Saturdays and Sundays, Gil worked fifty-six hours a week with few days off. He continued to work for Harrell until 1942, completing his "apprenticeship" and becoming an accomplished baker.

Gil also learned about security. One youth, who shall go unnamed, recalls stealing eggs out of the back door of Harrell's bakery in the 1930s. The guilty party remembers that when Gil finally caught him he insisted that the culprit put an egg in his back pocket. When the boy obeyed, Gil promptly smashed the pocketed egg with his hand. No supplies were reported missing thereafter.

During World War II, Gil moved to Hawthorne, Nevada, to manage a huge bakery that provided bread for a nearby navy ammunition depot where thousands of bombs were stored for use on the Pacific front. There was so much work to do at the bakery that Gil's brother, Ted, joined Gil in Nevada and Gil taught his sibling the baker's trade.

Meanwhile, Gil had met and married Priscilla Ursula Sánchez in February 1941, a year after her graduation from Belen High School. The couple had had three children: Raymond, Regina, and Gloria, during the war years in Nevada. (Their last child, Michael, was born in 1950.) The growing family returned to Belen in 1947, where Gil hoped to work for

Harrell again. Finding no work available at his old bakery, Gil decided to strike out on his own.

The Bakery's Early Years

Gil planned to open his own bakery with two of his brothers as partners. Ted would help as a baker and Aurelio (Eddie) would drive the delivery truck, bringing fresh baked goods to grocery stores up and down the valley. Gil applied for a $300 loan to rent space for his new business and buy essential equipment. But the First National Bank of Belen turned him down, an affront he never forgot. Fortunately, Joe Tabet recognized the venture's potential and lent Gil the cash he needed to get started.

Joe Tabet had made a wise investment. Starting as Gil's Bakery and Coffee Shop in 1947, the business was so successful that it began serving meals and became Gil's Bakery and Café in 1952. The enterprise expanded into the adjoining space in the Henry Sachs building and became Gil's Bakery and Restaurant in 1961. Adding a bar (which remained open from 1962 to 1978), the large new addition was made available for gala parties, wedding receptions, "and other social events," according to store advertisements.

Gil became the bakery's sole proprietor a year after the business opened. He bought the property at 239 N. Main in 1978. The bakery was a huge success because Gil was a self-proclaimed perfectionist who demanded hard work from himself and everyone he hired. He kept a spotless operation and closed one day a week (Monday) not to rest but to clean.

Gil's was best known for its excellent baked goods and meals. A breakfast menu from the 1950s listed doughnuts (10¢), sweet rolls (15¢), coffee (bottomless cup, 10¢), hot cakes (3 for 50¢), *huevos rancheros* ($1.10), bacon and eggs ($1.25), and steak and eggs ($1.50). French bread, potato bread, glazed doughnuts, and long johns were popular as well.

Located near the center of town at Reinken and Main, the bakery was a popular social center where residents gathered on a regular basis, including after church on Sundays, and after special events, including the county fair parade and high school football games. The bakery also served as a political center where leaders of both major political parties often met to drink coffee and discuss pressing issues of the day. By 1960, Gil's

Bakery was known throughout New Mexico and as far away as California. Gil Sánchez and Priscilla, Gil's partner in marriage and in business, were clearly in the right place at the right time to make a considerable impact on the history of Belen.

One Attempted Robbery

Remarkably, for all the years that Gil worked in the food service business, he experienced few attempted thefts and only one attempted armed robbery. About 5:15 p.m. on Tuesday, March 25, 1975, a 25 to 30-year old male came to the bakery's back door and asked to speak to Gil. Gil later recalled greeting a slim fellow who stood about five-feet, five-inches tall and wore jeans, a large black hat and a red T-shirt with the word "King" printed on it.

Gil remembered the man saying, "I'm Gino. I want your money." But Gil's daughter, Gloria, had just taken the day's cash deposit to the bank and there was not much left in the cash register or in the office. Angry, the thief shoved a small gun into Gil's ribs and shouted that he'd "blow your head off" if Gil didn't stop "playing around" and hand over his cash.

Fortunately, there were only four customers, two waitresses, Priscilla, Gil, and their son, Michael, in the bakery. The frustrated bandit suddenly panicked and ran from the bakery with Michael in pursuit. Witnesses saw the thief run across the street and behind Caldwell Motors (where Walgreen's now stands). The suspect reportedly jumped into a small tan car and fled. "Gino" was never apprehended, although a man fitting his description attempted a similar holdup in Albuquerque later that same evening.

The bakery was never again disturbed by robbers partly because the business was closely watched by policemen from the time Gil arrived at work early each morning. Police officers drove through the back alley to check on Gil and even put on the heater at Louie Aragón's barber shop next door so the shop would be warm when Louie arrived at work. Of course, the same policemen dropped by later to sample Gil's coffee and freshly baked doughnuts.

Gil's family says that the only other hazard they faced at the store was when drivers accidentally crashed into the front window on more than one occasion. But even this situation improved when the stop sign at Reinken and Main was finally replaced with a traffic light.

Community Service

Gil Sánchez had to be the most active citizen in Belen. Over many years he belonged to the Lion's Club, the Elks Club, the Knights of Columbus, the Chamber of Commerce, the Boy Scouts advisory council, and the advisory board for the University of New Mexico's new Valencia Campus. In each organization he quickly rose to positions of leadership. Priscilla, who would know best, declared, "I've never seen anyone work as hard as Gil has worked." The Belen Chamber of Commerce agreed, naming him its Citizen of the Year in 1981.

Of all his many organizations, Gil was most active as a member of the Belen school board. On October 4, 1954, Gil's brother Ralph, who had been elected to the board in 1949, fell ill and asked Gil to sit in for him at a board meeting. Gil obliged, served out Ralph's term, and ran successfully for his own seat on the board in February 1955.

In the course of the next thirty years, Gil won five additional elections and attended over 350 school board meetings, a record in Belen history. His long tenure put him among the top five school board members in years of continual service in the state. He was inducted into the New Mexico School Board Hall of Fame in 1993.

Gil was proud of many improvements in the Belen public school system during his long tenure in office. Although a life-long Democrat, he strove to take politics out of the hiring of school personnel. Also, the number of schools in the district grew, with building projects or additions at the high school, the junior high, Central School, Jaramillo School, Rio Grande School, Dennis Chávez School, and a new grade school in Jarales.

The elementary school in Jarales was Gil's crowning achievement. He had continuously lobbied for a new school south of town near where he had grown up. The school was built and, in the most controversial vote of his school board career, Gil voted in favor of a motion to name the school after him. Gil believed that "If something is going to be done for someone, it should be done while he's still alive." He nevertheless admitted that his vote was "one of the few things I've had bad feelings about. I'll always call it the Jarales school."

Magistrate Judge

In 1968, New Mexico revamped its local judicial system, eliminating the office of justice of the peace in communities across the state. Many justices of the peace had deservedly earned bad reputations for charging excessive fines for traffic tickets and other minor offenses because their salaries were based on the fines they collected. Tired of this source of corruption, New Mexicans had voted to replace justices of the peace with magistrate judges, chosen in local elections and compensated with set salaries.

Valencia County originally had three magistrate divisions. Recognizing an important new way to serve his community, Gil ran for and won election to the magistrate judgeship in Division 2, based in Belen.

Re-Elect
GILLIE (GIL) SANCHEZ
MAGISTRATE

BELEN DIVISION 2
"Here Comes The Judge"
Your Vote Appreciated

Pd. for by Gil Sanchez

DEMOCRAT
Printed by Vivian's Print & Copy

Gillie Sánchez campaign card (Sánchez family)

Gil knew little about the law when he started his career as a magistrate judge. But he received training, referred to law books, and didn't hesitate to ask questions from legal experts. Mostly dealing with minor infractions, from speeding tickets to domestic disputes, Gil learned quickly and soon much of his work became routine.

Although he dealt with many kinds of cases, Gil always said that his toughest ones involved "family troubles," especially when he saw the same couples and the same abuses over and over. Gil lectured abusive husbands and parents, hoping that he would help change their behavior, but often wondered if they ever did.

In most disputes, Gil simply served as a mediator, winning the trust and admiration of nearly everyone who appeared in his courtroom. Some of the most difficult cases were what Gil called the "your-dog-bit-my-dog kind" where there was no proof of what happened other than each side's recollections and opinions.

Attorney Norm McDonald recalls one such case involving a goat and a chile patch. The owner of the chile patch complained that his neighbor's goat had gotten into his chile and had eaten some of his crop. The goat's owner denied the accusation and went so far as to load his goat onto his truck to bring it to Gil's courtroom to prove the goat's (and his) innocence. No one recalls the outcome of this case, but it is definite that the goat never entered Gil's courtroom, no less appeared as a witness in his own defense.

In June 1971, Gil moved his courtroom to 233 North Main Street, directly south of his bakery. It was said that his was probably the only courtroom in the country with swinging doors leading from a bakery. Despite rumors that he appeared in court in an apron or with baking powder on his suit, Gil was always well dressed as a sign of respect for those who appeared before him. For years Gil wore suits and his famous small bow ties or, later, his large ties, usually worn loosely at the neck.

Gil had definite opinions regarding proper proceedings and behavior in his courtroom. Everyone had to be appropriately attired, respectful, and polite. He tolerated lawyers, although he considered some to be "necessary evils." He always insisted that lawyers speak "plain English" rather than "legalese" that few people could understand and seldom helped achieve Gil's main goal: an amicable conclusion of each case.

John Pope, a young attorney in the 1970s, remembers that he and other lawyers often arrived early to drink coffee and eat a donut in the bakery before proceeding to court next door. Meeting in this informal atmosphere, lawyers frequently negotiated settlements to their cases before Gil even called court into session.

While most observers agreed that Gil was fair and just in his decisions, some believed that he was too lenient, especially with traffic tickets. The judge often deferred the payment of fines or took them "under advisement," meaning they did not have to be paid. Gil's daughter, Gloria, who served as the judge's clerk for over sixteen years, often felt this way, especially when the recipients of her father's largess became ungrateful. Gloria remembers an instance when Gil threw out six or seven tickets for a man, but when he made the culprit pay for just one infraction, the person got so mad that he never spoke to the judge again.

Fortunately, dangerous incidents were rare. In one case, a woman accused of robbery became so incensed that she charged Gil as he sat at his bench. Gloria recalls that it took six men to control the defendant and finally restrain her in a straitjacket.

Attempted bribes were also rare. Gloria says that a man once placed something valuable (probably jewelry) in front of Gil in court. Interpreting the gesture to be a bribe, Gil told the man to get out. The accused claimed that he was only offering the judge a gift. The judge knew better.

Gil's most pleasant moments as a judge were when he officiated at weddings. Some weddings were held in his courtroom, but most took place in private homes. Gil developed a set ceremony and "sermon" with the help of Father Gallegos; the text was typed both in English and in Spanish, depending on the engaged couple's preference. Gil's main problem with wedding ceremonies was when they took place in isolated parts of the county and he got lost, often arriving late and delaying the otherwise blissful event. Even when Gil did not officiate, many wedding receptions were held at his bakery, as when Seferino and Angelina Sánchez were married on October 25, 1958. Of course Gil provided hundreds of well-decorated wedding cakes over the years.

Gil won reelection as magistrate judge six times, always with the help of his family and friends who did everything from placing campaign signs along rural roads to going door-to-door to talk to voters directly. Gloria remembers how popular her father was among most voters. Her only objection to campaigning was when she went to houses with fierce-looking dogs. She simply refused to enter yards with overly aggressive animals on the premises.

Shedding Hats

Gil shed his many hats gradually and, usually, willingly. He retired from the school board after thirty years of dedicated service. A grateful community bid him farewell at a dinner held in his honor at the Tierra del Sol Country Club in 1983.

Unfortunately, Gil was defeated when he ran for reelection to the bench in November 1994. Out of 15,000 votes cast, he lost by a mere thirty. Perhaps it was inevitable that in the course of twenty-six years as a magistrate judge he would alienate at least some voters with his decisions—just enough to influence their votes and cause his defeat. Although described as "saddened" by the outcome, Gil was said to accept his loss with his usual grace and dignity. Five years later the new magistrate court building at 901 West Castillo was named in his honor.

And then it was time to close his bakery. Gil had considered calling it quits as early as 1975 when the demands of both serving as a magistrate judge and running the bakery had become increasingly burdensome. Gil and Priscilla had only taken one real vacation, a ten-day trip to Hawaii arranged by their son, Raymond. Otherwise, the most time they had taken off was on certain holidays (the Fourth of July was his favorite) and to go to the state fair, which Gil looked forward to each year. Maybe it was time to cut back. But the thought of not working at the bakery was worse than working there too much. In Gil's words, the prospect gave him the "shivers."

The decision to close the bakery was finally made in 1987, forty years after its grand opening in 1947. There were several reasons for closing, including competition from supermarkets that Gil said were "taking over with package stuff." Gil remembered when Albuquerque had as many as ten bakeries in the early 1970s, until they were forced to close, one by one, in the face of supermarket competition. The same had happened in Belen a decade later.

Gil also said that good workers were getting harder and harder to find. Employees simply lacked the work ethic and high standards Gil had learned from the German baker Harrell in the 1930s. Reliable bakers were particularly difficult to hire and retain. When a baker called in sick or otherwise didn't come to work, Gil had to jump out of bed and get to the bakery to do the work himself. At 61, he was not as willing and not as able to work 12 to 14-hour days. Priscilla said that after such long days, Gil usually came home so exhausted that he would sit down, soak his feet in Epsom salts, and quickly fall asleep.

And so Gil and Priscilla closed their bakery on July 4, 1987, their own Independence Day. Thirty customers were already there by 8:00 a.m.; they had come to say good-bye and to eat their favorite doughnuts one last time. The place looked much the same as it had for years. Lime-colored stools still lined the long serving counter. Formica-top tables still stood down the center. A famous photo portrait of President John F. Kennedy still hung on the wall beside drawings by Gil and Priscilla's eight grandchildren and ten great-grandchildren.

We can only imagine what went through Gil's mind as he locked his store for the last time after more than 14,000 days in business, regardless of the season, regardless of the weather, and regardless of his physical health. Gil Sánchez died on July 1, 1999, almost exactly five years after that closing; he was 82. His loving wife and partner, Priscilla, died four years later, on November 29, 2003.

A large part of the heart of Belen closed with Gil's bakery in 1987. Other restaurants have attempted to open in the old building, but none have succeeded. Other restaurants in town have come and gone without ever equaling the popularity of the old bakery, no less filling the role Gil's eatery had played for decades.

The corner building at Reinken and Main stands empty now. But as Belen High School's powerful football team won game after game over several seasons, someone thought to paint the team's eagle mascot and the words "win win" on the bakery's front window. It is as if Gil is still rooting for his hometown, cheering on his family, friends, and whole community, just as he had done for so long to the great benefit of all who knew him in the Rio Abajo.

LAWrence Romero's Life as a Lawman

by Jim Boeck

Lawrence Romero was born and raised in the ranching and farming community of Lemitar, New Mexico. He was the oldest of four children born to Joseph and Beatrice Romero. Brother Billy and sisters Lola and Pauline made up the rest of the family. Growing up like most rural New Mexicans, Lawrence did chores and odd jobs to supplement his family's meager income. In his teenage years Lawrence began racing fast cars, an interest that was to serve him well in his future career as a police officer.

Unfortunately, in his younger days he was stopped more than once for speeding with loud open exhaust headers. He laughingly recalls how an Albuquerque policeman once told him, "Lawrence, if you don't close those headers on your car, we are going to weld them shut for you!" It was during this seemingly carefree time of racing cars and dating girls that Lawrence's father passed away at the age of forty-one. Lawrence was heartbroken.

As the eldest child, the heavy responsibility of helping his mother and younger siblings fell squarely on Lawrence's shoulders. He needed a steady job to support his family. His first thought was to get a job in law enforcement. He remembered his uncle, George Romero, dressed in his snappy-looking police uniform with an impressive policeman's badge on his chest. Lawrence was also attracted to a career in law enforcement because of the excitement and adventure it seemed to promise. But it was Socorro County Sheriff Ernest S. Peralta who really impressed Lawrence. Peralta was a big man who wore a large, shiny cowboy belt buckle and exuded an air of confidence that smacked of Wyatt Earp and other Wild West lawmen.

A Young Lawman

Lawrence Romero was hired by the Socorro Police Department in 1965, marking the beginning of a career that spanned nearly forty years. Soon thereafter he married Hazel Moffet. The couple had two children, Lisa and Lawrence, Jr. After serving as the under sheriff of Socorro County for two years, Romero decided to take on the challenge of Albuquerque's

139

South Valley, long known as that city's roughest area. As a rookie in the Albuquerque Police Department, he was assigned to the graveyard shift, from midnight to 8:00 a.m., when most of the violence occurred.

Sheriff Lawrence Romero (Lawrence Romero)

Romero was determined to meet the thugs of southwest Albuquerque head on. But, as he smilingly recalls, the night sergeant on duty had other ideas. The old sergeant told him, "Lawrence, this isn't Socorro with a few bad guys. So, when we get a call about gang activity, turn on your lights and sound your siren long before you arrive at a scene. Then drive thirty miles an hour until you get there."

Dumbfounded, Romero asked, "Why do you want to do that? They might all get away!" With a hint of sarcasm, the sergeant explained, "We do this so most of the cockroaches can get a chance to scatter. We can deal with fifteen, but not a hundred and fifteen." The sergeant's advice fell on deaf ears, because Lawrence was determined to get the bad guys. With grit and determination, he put many of the South Valley's worst gang members behind bars. The training and experience he received fighting southwest Albuquerque gangs would prove invaluable later in his career.

In 1970, Romero moved his family to Belen where he took a job with the Belen Police Department. In 1971, he received his certification after graduating from the New Mexico Sheriffs' Academy. Romero's leadership qualities soon drew the attention of his superiors in Belen, and he quickly rose through the ranks to become Assistant Police Chief.

Becoming Sheriff

One day, while at the Valencia County courthouse, the county clerk took Romero aside and suggested that he would be an excellent Republican Party candidate for sheriff. After talking it over with his wife and many of his friends, the young police officer decided to enter the 1974 race against the Democratic Party candidate, Nick P. Sánchez. Romero ran a hard-fought campaign, but lost the election in the wake of the Watergate scandal, which hurt Republican candidates across the country. As Romero jokingly relates, "Republicans in those days were being knocked down like bowling pins." But meeting people and shaking hands with the voting public was a real delight to a man like Lawrence, with his friendly, outgoing personality. He discovered that he enjoyed the challenge of politics and the chance to make real changes in local law enforcement.

In 1976, Romero felt the people of Valencia County were, as he puts it, "tired of do-nothing political sheriffs." He was ready to reenter the political arena. Campaigning in those days was particularly difficult in a county that included not only present-day Valencia County, but also Cibola County, which was not separated from Valencia until 1981. Romero campaigned, knocking on doors from Belen to Grants. The hard work paid off in this rematch against Sánchez. Thirty-three year old Romero won by nearly fifteen hundred votes. He became the first Republican to win the coveted sheriff's post in Valencia County since 1948.

The situation in the sheriff's office when Romero took over was so bad that most people in a similar situation would have been tempted to throw up their hands and quit. Only one patrol car out of eighteen was in running condition and stacks of legal papers that had never been served and bills that had never been paid were everywhere. Romero could not even get credit to buy light bulbs for the county jail, leaving one entire cellblock in the dark. He recalls that the most embarrassing thing was that there weren't even any badges or uniforms. His deputies wore piecemeal uniforms with badges from such distant, unlikely places as Red River, New Mexico. Not discouraged, Romero forged ahead. He sent his broken-down fleet of police cars to a repair shop where seven were quickly pieced together and the others were eventually fixed for duty.

Two process servers worked diligently serving legal papers, and Romero's motley-looking crew of deputies finally received proper uniforms and badges. He even obtained enough light bulbs for the county jail, after convincing his light bulb supplier that he would finally be paid. Romero soon had the sheriff's department running smoothly and competently.

Lollie Tipton

Within a month after assuming office, Lawrence was involved in one of the most famous criminal investigations in recent Valencia County history, the tragic abduction of Lollie Wood Tipton.

Lollie Tipton (Valencia County News-Bulletin)

A mother of two children, 20-year-old Lollie Tipton worked the graveyard shift at the Circle K store in Peralta so she could be with her young son and daughter during the day. On February 3, 1977, Lollie was abducted from the Circle K store by a knife-wielding maniac. As the five foot, two inch, 110 pound woman screamed and struggled for her life, two customers entered the store and became victims themselves. Felipe Tapia was stabbed in the back and in his arm. The second customer, Dan O'Grady, was held with a knife to his throat. Within moments, Lollie's abductor dragged the small woman to his car and sped away.

Assisted by the FBI and about 1,800 volunteers, Romero's department made an extensive search of the area, but found no sign of Lollie or her abductor. Circle K Stores offered a $1,000 reward for Lollie's safe return or for the arrest of the man who had abducted her.

Searchers on horseback scoured the levees while divers searched the river itself. (Albuquerque Journal)

After many twelve to fourteen-hour shifts, a tired, frustrated Lawrence finally went home to rest. Sitting at his kitchen table, Romero told his wife, Hazel, of his lack of clues and his growing sense of helplessness. All his department had was a crude composite drawing of the perpetrator, but so far no one could identify him, much less tell where he might have taken Lollie. Intuitively, Hazel suggested the possibility that the kidnapper had spent much of the night drinking in a nearby bar, getting drunk, and then looking for trouble. Realizing that this scenario made perfect scene, Romero declared, "I think you're right!"

Following Hazel's logic, Romero's deputies took their composite sketch to the Club 47, and asked the bartender if the man looked familiar. Recognizing the face in the drawing, the bartender's testimony helped lead to the arrest of 24-year-old William T. Altum. A new resident of Bosque Farms, Altum had just been released from a mental institution after having committed a similar kidnapping and armed robbery in Kansas. Sadly, Lollie Tipton did not survive her ordeal. Using a map that Altum drew to show where her body could be found, the police discovered her remains in a culvert in southeast Albuquerque. The young mother had died of a massive skull fracture. But Altum had been apprehended. In a plea bargain agreement, Altum pleaded guilty to second-degree murder and was sentenced to ten to fifty years in prison. Good investigative work by Romero's deputies and his wife's intuition paid off in helping to take a dangerous criminal off the street.

William Altum (Valencia County News-Bulletin)

The Bones in a Boot Mystery

Romero faced a second baffling crime just a year later. A father and son had been digging for rocks east of Belen when they came across a boot with human bones in it. Alerted to the grisly discovery, sheriff's officers soon discovered the rest of the body buried under two-and-a-half feet of dirt. A .38-caliber pistol found near the corpse indicated that the man's death had surely involved foul play. It did not take long to identify the victim. Through a ring found on the body and two slips of paper found with the gun, the man was identified as 73-year-old Fidel Montoya of Bernalillo. But a larger mystery remained. Who killed Montoya and why did they dispose of his body on an isolated mesa so far from his hometown?

Lawmen soon turned to Montoya's much younger wife for answers. Fidel Montoya had married 34-year-old Sofia Salcido just two months prior to his cruel death. Clues led to Sofia and her previous boyfriend, 35-year-old Tito Segura Alatorre from El Paso, Texas. Valencia County detective Joe Chávez and District Attorney investigator Mike Alexander questioned the couple separately in the border town.

Despite tough questioning, Sofia refused to break. But Alatorre broke down rather quickly, confessing to his part in the crime and implicating Sofia in the murder of her elderly husband. The investigation revealed that the young couple had shot Montoya in the back with his own gun, had loaded his body in the trunk of their car, and had buried him at an isolated spot in the desert. Thanks to the persistent work of Romero's department, the "bones in a boot" mystery was solved, with the conspiring couple being charged, tried, and eventually convicted in the murder of Fidel Montoya.

Reelection

It was soon time for Romero to run for reelection. The sheriff confidently pointed out his many accomplishments in office. In addition to solving two highly publicized murders, Romero could boast that he had added ten new patrol cars, a microfilming system to store all records, two radar systems, new shot guns and helmets, a new dispatching room, and a new booking area in the sheriff's department. Romero's deputies had recovered over $74,000 worth of stolen property and had arrested many drug dealers in drug busts across Valencia County.

Lawrence's opponent in 1978 was Billy W. Holliday. In the spirit of friendly competition, Holliday told Romero that he was going to take the "law" out of Lawrence's name so that Lawrence would simply be known as "Rence." As Lawrence jokingly says, "I lost that election to Holliday, but I sure as hell didn't want to go through life known as just 'Rence,' so I had to run against Holliday in the next election, in 1980." With a twinkle in his eye, Romero relates that he ran in 1980 with the slogan "Don't give the crooks a Holliday! Elect LAWrence Romero!" He won the election, and the next one too.

BRING BACK

LAWrence Romero

as
SHERIFF

LAWrence Romero campaign card (Lawrence Romero)

Personal Tragedies

Meanwhile, in his personal life, Romero went through a divorce and later married Carol Thomas. The couple was blessed with a baby girl, Lawren. In business, Romero purchased The Westerner bar. But a serious problem had gradually crept into Romero's life. Drinking was slowly taking over his life, damaging not only his body, but also his mind, his soul, and, most tragically, his new marriage. He soon found himself in a hospital bed with a serious liver ailment. His doctors warned him never to drink again.

After being released from the hospital, Romero was closing his bar late one night. With everyone gone and the lights low, he felt a strong urge for a drink. Seeing his image in the bar mirror, a feeling of overwhelming guilt swept over him as he thought of his little girl and how he wanted to live to see her grow up. He knew that goal would not be possible if he kept drinking. His desire for alcohol was gone in an instant. He never drank again. Romero has been sober since then, and he thanks God every day for that victory.

Romero resumed in his law enforcement career. But along with his many successes, there were disappointments. The most disappointing case he ever worked on involved the disappearance of Tara Calico. Tara was an active 19-year-old student at the University of New Mexico's Valencia Campus in the fall of 1988. Living at home with her parents in Rio Communities, she liked to exercise, riding her bike for up to thirty-four miles a day. On September 20, 1988, Tara left on one such bike trip, but failed to return at her usual time. Lawrence led the massive hunt for Tara Calico in a nationally publicized case. Lawrence says, "We put a lot of man-hours into the search without success. But what is really sad is that there is no closure to her parents' heartache and grief."

Tragedy struck a young person in Romero's own family on May 19, 1991, when his son, "Little Lawrence," was killed under suspicious circumstances. Romero still maintains that his 21-year-old son's death was a homicide. When he learned of his son's death, he felt as if his heart had been torn out. Going outside his ranch home and leaning on an old cottonwood tree, he looked up to heaven with tears streaming down his face. Just then 6-year-old Lawren came running up to Lawrence and said, "Don't cry, Daddy. I'm here." Lawrence picked her up gently and told her, "You are so precious." Grateful to his daughter, he has called her Precious ever since.

After the tragic death of his son, Romero decided to return to his career in law enforcement, having taken time off to run his horse ranch and manage his bar. He went to work for the Torrance County sheriff's department and later joined the Socorro Police Department. After serving five terms as the sheriff of Valencia County, Lawrence is sometimes asked if he'd be interested in a sixth run. With a sly grin, he says, "Never say never, troop."

The Ultimate Sacrifice: Valencia County Lawmen Who Died in the Line of Duty

by Don Bullis

Ten Rio Abajo law enforcement officers have given their lives in the line of duty. We have discussed several of them in other chapters in this book. Daniel Bustamante, Vicente Wuerro, and Frank X. Vigil were all killed by "Bronco Bill" Walters and "Kid" Johnson in a shootout along the Rio Salado after the Great Belen Train Robbery of 1898. J. A. McClure was killed by Frank B. Howe and his sons in 1911 during the investigation of the Abo Pass Gang. Charles "Casey" Cunningham was killed by Bonifacio Torres during the 1930 shootout at Torres's grandmother's house in Jarales.

The other five--Luis Abeita, Andres Chávez, Louis McCamant, Damacio Montaño, and Charles Wasmer—also deserve mention for their dedication and sacrifice.

Louis Abeita

Louis Abeita was 38-years-old, married, and the father of five children. He had served as a deputy sheriff and special agent for the Santa Fe Railway for Isleta Pueblo for six years. Prior to his service for the Pueblo he had been a federal Indian police officer for ten years.

In January 1921, Abeita was sent to arrest a 19-year-old janitor and shoeshine boy from Albuquerque who had shot and badly wounded another teenager during a dust-up in the Alvarado Hotel. The reason for the squabble is not known, but the fugitive, James Mackey, escaped to the Pueblo where he shot at the wife of the Isleta postmaster and also shot and fatally wounded Deputy Abeita. A posse from Isleta tracked Mackey to a swampy area just northeast of the village of Isleta where another Isleta deputy, Pablo Lujan, shot and killed him. Louis Abeita died from his wounds a few days later. He was remembered as a man who "had been in the service for a number of years and was considered one of the most trustworthy and invaluable of the force."

Andres Chávez

Andres Chávez was a Valencia County Deputy Sheriff and resident of Belén with two young children. On January 6, 1934, he was assigned to provide security at a dance being held in Jarales. During the festivities a fight broke out inside the dance hall and then moved outside. When Chávez went outside to break it up, he was shot four times—once in the abdomen and three times in the leg. Before he died he told Sheriff Abelicio Sánchez that another deputy, Diego Trujillo, was the person who had shot him.

Sheriff Sánchez investigated the killing and soon arrested four (of Valencia County's twenty-two) deputies: Trujillo, Edmundo Lovato, Matías Chávez, and Tomas García. The four were tried and three of them were convicted of second-degree murder; only Matías Chávez was acquited. A subsequent retrial ordered by the New Mexico Supreme Court resulted in a hung jury.

Andres Chávez's grave in the Belen Cemetery (Richard Melzer)

Louis McCamant

Railroad Special Police Officer Louis McCamant, 24-years-old, boarded an eastbound freight at Gallup on April 25, 1934, heading for Belen. Crossing into Valencia County, the train stopped at Wall to take on coal. Three men, J. L. Berry, James Carlton, and John Edwards, asked if they could board without tickets, but McCamant denied their request. As the train pulled out the three jumped aboard anyway. When McCamant confronted them on top of a car, one of the transients threw a large metal bolt, striking McCamant in the head and knocking him off the car. The officer fell onto the tracks and was run over by the train, leaving his body mangled and dismembered. After an investigation, Berry was released, and Carlton and Edwards were indicted for murder.

Damacio S. Montaño

Deputy Sheriff Damacio "Moss" Montaño and his brother, Eric, a

New Mexico State Police officer, were off-duty in a Los Lunas restaurant at 1:30 a.m. on Sunday, October 6, 2002. When a fight broke out, the two brothers identified themselves as police officers and assisted bouncers in escorting two suspects outside. Out in the crowded parking lot a known gang member opened fire on the unarmed siblings, wounding Eric and fatally shooting Damacio when he went to his brother's aid.

Valencia County Deputy Sheriff Damacio Montaño (Valencia County Sheriff's Department)

In August 2003 the shooter, Michael Armendáriz, was convicted of murder in the death of the 31-year-old deputy sheriff and of attempted murder in the case of his brother. Armendáriz was sentenced to life in prison; an accomplice was sentenced to four years as an accessory to murder. Valencia County's Fraternal Order of Police Lodge 14 created the Damacio Montaño Officer's Choice Award to honor police officers who make it their daily mission to assure that drunk drivers are taken off the streets. The local FOP also dedicated its lodge to the brave young deputy. In addition, the sheriff substation in Jarales is named in his honor.

Charles Wasmer

Charles Wasmer was an officer in the newly constituted Bosque Farms Police Department. He was married with two sons. In the early evening of August 18, 1977, Wasmer and citizen patrol officer Rick Switzer were on routine patrol on the Bosque Loop when a vehicle recklessly rounded a curve, nearly sideswiping their patrol car. Quickly turning around, the officers stopped the car, but before they could begin their traffic stop procedures, another driver stopped and reported that the same vehicle had just sideswiped her pickup truck and then fled the scene.

Wasmer identified the driver of the car as Ruth Manus and noted that she had obviously been drinking. As the officers were continuing their investigation, Manus's husband, William Manus, a 58-year-old retired air traffic controller, came up with a 12-gauge, double-barreled shotgun and shot Wasmer in the chest and face. Wasmer managed to lurch to his car and call for help before he died. Patrol Officer Switzer shot Manus, although not fatally.

Manus was subsequently convicted of first-degree murder for killing Wasmer and of attempted murder for shooting at Switzer. He was sentenced to life in prison. His wife was also convicted of DWI, reckless driving, and leaving the scene of an accident.

Charles Wasmer and the Memorial at the Bosque Farms Village Complex (Valencia County News-Bulletin; John Taylor)

Not Forgotten

All officers killed in the line of duty are honored each May in Law Enforcement Memorials held in towns across the state.

Courthouses of Valencia County

by John W. Pope

Picture, if you can, a crude building of adobe and uneven planked lumber, forty feet by fifteen feet, two windows with cloth drawn over them to keep out the wind and elements. Picture a mud-packed floor with a crude metal heater that provides smoky heat against the early spring chill. Maybe as many as three chairs are accorded the judge, attorney, and sheriff, with rough-hewn benches provided for everyone else. Oh, yes—one concession to comfort—a couple of boards are placed under the judge's feet to afford him a little additional status. This is the setting on April 29, 1852, in Tomé, New Mexico, county seat of Valencia County, when the first capital murder sentence was pronounced under the newly created laws and legislature of the U.S. Territory of New Mexico.

Early Sites

The year 1852 was not the earliest date for a courthouse in Valencia County. In fact, Valencia County had had two county seats before Tomé. And by 1852, it was about to build for that time a very fine courthouse in Tomé. The first county seat for Valencia County was designated at Valencia in 1846 after a petition was filed by the wealthy sheep owner and merchant, Juan Otero of Valencia, in 1844. The county building was known as the Casa Consistorial de Valencia and was located on the east side of one of the two Valencia plazas, this one near or just north of the intersection of today's State Road 47 and North El Cerro Loop. In 1848, the county seat was moved to Peralta, the headquarters of a younger faction of the Otero family who were known to be more pro-American. Remarkably, the courthouse was lodged in the Otero family chapel.

By 1852, the county seat came to rest in Tomé. The new building consisted of one *salón*, or large room, three regular-sized rooms, and a *calavoso* (jail). The *salón* functioned as the courtroom for the probate judge, who served as the modern magistrate, and for the visiting circuit-riding judge. The other rooms were for essential county business. The district judge, who also served as a Supreme Court judge six months of the year, rode circuit from Albuquerque through Tomé, down to Socorro, and across the Jornado del Muerto to Mesilla. Tomé must have been a welcome reprieve on the way south and on the way north for the judge. The court and jail were built by order of the probate judge to Sheriff Lorenzo Labadie. This courthouse served the county for twenty years.

In 1872, Belen became the fourth town in Valencia County to host the county seat and courthouse. The move was probably initiated by movement of the river and flooding in Tomé. Belen's courthouse ended up at the site of the old Catholic Church at Plaza Vieja after the new church had been constructed about a mile to the west. The courthouse in Belen lasted for only two years, being destroyed by flooding and heavy rains in 1874.

In 1874, the very transitory county seat and courthouse moved back to Tomé. Probate Judge Manuel A. Otero, widely recognized as one of the most powerful men in the county, wanted to have a modern courthouse. The courthouse he commissioned in Tomé looked remarkably like the Lincoln County courthouse. It was a two-story adobe structure with a shingle roof. Court functions were held on the second floor, and county administrative functions were on the first floor. The second floor was reached by an outside stairway located on a balcony in the center of the building. A very sturdy jail was attached. This was a building for all the ages, or for one year, whichever came first.

Los Lunas

In 1875, the territorial legislature voted to move the county seat of Valencia County to Los Lunas. The new courthouse in Tomé functioned as a courthouse exactly one year! Of course, the courthouse did have its uses. The jail was used for several years until one was built in Los Lunas. And, according to a county ordinance banning them, the courthouse was apparently rented out for dances and shows for a number of years. According to family stories, the courthouse in Tomé had a fairly lively, if not ribald, life after decommissioning. Traces of the jail still exist, and children played on the floor of the courthouse into the 1950s.

The move to Los Lunas is thought to reflect the growing power of the Luna family, the shift of fortunes to the west side of the river, and the eventual arrival of the railroad. When the county seat was moved to Los Lunas in 1875, a new courthouse was built of adobe and wood, basically along the same lines as the one left behind in Tomé. Interestingly, there was no jail built in Los Lunas for several years, so prisoners continued to be quartered in the Tomé jail. The Tomé jail of 1875 was and is a remarkable structure.

A cloud of controversy seemed to hover over the first Los Lunas courthouse, which may have been Tomé getting its revenge. First there was the notorious 1881 jailbreak led by Elfego Baca. Later, in 1886, Manuel Otero of Tomé was the acting county clerk. It was his custom to take his work home with him. Unfortunately, his route home took him across the Rio Grande, and, in this particular instance, the river was unusually swollen. He and the public records he was to complete that evening were swept off his horse. Fortunately, Otero survived, but the records did not.

By the turn of the century, the courthouse was starting to show its age, and Valencia County was prospering, with Belen being a railroad hub and the Lunas of Los Lunas being a political power. People believed statehood was around the corner and no one really liked being saddled with an aging, territorial-style courthouse. Providence also struck in the matter of losing the area that became Torrance County. In 1909, the legislature compensated Valencia County $25,000 for its loss and this money was then dedicated to build a new courthouse and jail.

Los Lunas or Belen?

In 1909, Belen was a bustling commercial center. It had a bank and many more retail establishments than Los Lunas. It even had two newspapers, the *Belen News* and the *Belen Tribune*. Belenites could be quite dismissive of their county cousins to the north. Basically, what Los Lunas had was the county seat and some agriculture. Belen decided it should have the county seat and courthouse it had been denied these many years and have its pre-eminence sealed permanently. The timing was right since a new courthouse was in the offing. There was a small hitch: a statute passed in 1897 made it a requirement that to remove a county seat, the new county seat had to be at least twenty miles from the present seat. Belen wasn't twenty miles from Los Lunas. There has been some opinion that this was a forethought by Solomon Luna, but it is more likely that it had to do with another county's fight. Officially on August 18, 1909, money was allocated to build the courthouse and jail, but would it be in Belen or Los Lunas?

On August 15, 1912, the issue came to a head when the courthouse in Los Lunas burned virtually to the ground and the cause was never determined. The citizens of Belen were quick to point the finger and say that Los Lunas burned down the courthouse for its benefit so that a new one had to be built before the law could be changed. Los Lunas pointed south, saying that with no courthouse there was no impediment to moving it north. As early as April 1912, three months before the fire, there had been a petition to move the jail to Belen preliminary to moving the courthouse. Colonel Berger, editor of the *Belen Tribune*, was the party supporting the move, backed by a substantial body of Belen citizens. The real battle was joined on October 5, 1912, when the county commission met to consider the courthouse problem in light of the fire. Belen was represented by Felix Lester, an attorney with the Rodey law firm from Albuquerque. Rodey was the largest law firm in the state and represented powerful railroad and commercial interests.

According to the minutes of the meeting, a petition was presented, signed by a large number of qualified voters, and

> … recited that in their opinion, the town of Belen would be the most advantageous place for the County Seat to be located and asked that action be delayed until such time as the now existing laws could be changed to permit the removal of said County Seat.

In reply, José G. Chávez of Los Lunas responded, according to the minutes of the meeting, that

> owing to the destruction by fire on the 15th day of August of the Court House and Jail of Valencia County, the records of said County were in an unprotected condition, and the business of the County was being interrupted and delayed on account of the officers of said County not having proper offices for the administration of the said business of the county and requested the

board to proceed immediately with the erection of a new
Court House and Jail at the County seat, Los Lunas.

Chávez also came armed with petitions from a large number of qualified voters.

The commissioners took a five-minute recess and then returned and announced that they had decided "after due consideration" to proceed with the building of the courthouse and jail at Los Lunas. A Mr. Jacobson of Belen asked for an individual vote on the questions, which was taken. All three commissioners voted affirmatively.

This being Valencia County, a lawsuit quickly ensued seeking to enjoin the action of the county commission. The suit was assigned to Judge Merritt Mechem, a great friend of the late Solomon Luna. Needless to say, the suit was soon extinguished, and the building of the new courthouse was promptly embarked upon.

The Los Lunas Courthouse in 1936 (Los Lunas Museum of Heritage and Arts)

The new courthouse, built in the Federalist style, was dedicated with much pomp and circumstance on September 1, 1913. After a Mass at San Clemente Catholic Church, the speechmaking commenced with presentations by Governor William McDonald, Secretary of State Antonio Lucero, and Ralph Twitchell, probably the foremost New Mexico historian of his time. Following the oratory, a barbeque and baseball game rounded out the ceremonies.

The new two-story building with a complete basement was the pride of Valencia County. It included court facilities and offices for county officials from the county nurse to the rural school supervisor.

Over the years surprisingly few modifications were made to the venerable brick structure, but by 1960 it had become seriously overcrowded and the county commission razed the old building. A modern new courthouse, costing $700,000, was dedicated in Los Lunas on September 4, 1960.

The First Execution
in Valencia County, 1852

by John W. Pope

Valencia County has the dubious distinction of having one of the first murder trials and one of the first legal executions held in New Mexico under U.S. Territorial rule from 1850 to 1912. These events occurred in Tomé in 1852, a few short months after the first U.S. Territorial legislature met and established New Mexico's county boundaries, including Valencia's.

Despite many misspellings, court records show the indictment and the verdict in the murder trial of Felipe García:

> That Phillipi García, late of the County of Valencia, laborer, not having the fear of God before his eyes, but being moved and seduced by the instigation of the Devil, on the Twenty-third day of April, in the year of our Lord, One Thousand Eight Hundred and Fifty-Two—at Tomé—upon Thadeus E.C.S. Canter with a certain large stick of no value—two mortal wounds three inches in length and one in depth—and with a certain case knife, made of iron and steel of the value of fifty centers—feloniously, willfully, and of his malice aforethought did strike and cut and give unto Thadeus E.C.S. Canter two mortal wounds of the length of two inches and of the depth of five inches of which said mortal wounds the said Thadeus E.C.S. Canter languished and languishingly did live for three hours and die.

> We the juoro find Felipe Garsilla gilte of murder and worthery of deth.

Felipe García was tried on April 29, 1852. The verdict was returned on the same day, and García was sentenced to be hanged on the 25th of May 1852. The sentence was duly executed in Tomé on the appointed day by Lorenzo Labadie, Sheriff of Valencia County. García was buried in the Tomé parish cemetery.

It will be noted that the crime was committed on the 23rd of April; the grand jury met and returned its indictment on the 27th of April; the trial was held on the 29th of April; and the sentence was carried out on the 25th of May. Within one month and two days, the crime was committed and the defendant was executed.

The Old Tomé jail (Baldwin G. Burr)

It is generally assumed that Felipe García's trial was conducted in both Spanish and in English. It must have been interesting to hear the old Anglo-Saxon legalism translated into Spanish, particularly given that the previously used Spanish legal system was completely different than the American system used in 1852. Despite this, there never has been a suggestion that justice wasn't done in this landmark case.

Felipe García was the first of seventy-nine men who have been legally executed in New Mexico under U.S. rule. Like García, most (86 percent) died on the gallows, the legal means of execution in New Mexico until the 1920s. Another 9 percent died in the state's electric chair, in use from 1933 to 1956. David Cooper Nelson, convicted for murder in Valencia County, was the only prisoner executed in the gas chamber, succumbing in 1960. Terry Clark, the last person to be executed, and the first prisoner to die from lethal injection, died in 2001. New Mexico joined fourteen other states in banning capital punishment in 2009.

The Hanging Trees of Los Lunas and Belen

by Richard Melzer

The Los Lunas Hanging Tree (from These Also Served, Susan E. Lee, 1960, p. 190)

There is a legend about an old cottonwood tree in Los Lunas. No one remembers when the story got started or if it's even true, but it's a good legend, especially when told during the Halloween season. According to this eerie tale, a stranger arrived in Los Lunas by train one dark evening in the late nineteenth century. Not familiar with the town, he walked from the railroad station in search of a friend's house somewhere near the old Simon Neustadt store on Main Street.

As the stranger passed under a tall tree, he felt something brush against his face. He pushed the mysterious object aside, only to discover that it was not a branch or some other natural obstruction but a man's dead body. The stranger had accidentally bumped into the latest occupant of Los Lunas's infamous hanging tree.

Understandably terrified, the stranger fled. As he ran, he felt another object brush across his face. Fearing that all the trees in this macabre community might have dead bodies hanging from their ominous limbs, the man raced back to the train station at top speed. The horrified stranger huddled in the train station all night, anxiously awaiting the next train out of town. With daylight, he had regained much of his composure, although his previously dark hair had reportedly turned pure white in the course of his night of terror.

Dr. William F. Wittwer supposedly had a similarly frightening experience when he first visited Los Lunas a few years later. Arriving by train one morning, he was aghast to see a corpse dangling from a limb of the town's hanging tree. The vigilantes who had killed the accused outlaw had deliberately left him hanging to serve as a public notice to others who might consider a life of crime in this normally peaceful community.

Dr. Wittwer was unnerved by the scene he witnessed, but local leaders, eager to have a resident physician in town, reassured him that he had nothing to fear if he remained to practice medicine. Solomon Luna went so far as to have a fine house built for the young doctor to alleviate his fears and entice him to stay. (Luna's house is, of course, the Luna Mansion, while Dr. Wittwer's house, across the street, is now Teofilo's Restaurante.)

In the most gruesome legend regarding the hanging tree in Los Lunas, three accused criminals were "jerked to Jesus" on a single night, March 7, 1882. Guarding, housing, and feeding accused criminals until the next court session was scheduled could be expensive for local taxpayers in those days (as it is today). Fed up with the burden of their overcrowded jail, Los Lunas vigilantes had solved their problem by simply lynching every prisoner in custody that night, long before any of them could exercise their legal rights as American citizens. Other multiple hangings took place in 1881 and 1893.

It is even possible that prisoners were lynched simultaneously from not one, but three adjacent hanging trees, known collectively as the Gallows. According to various sources, the Gallows represented the "end of the rope" for as many as thirteen accused prisoners in Los Lunas history. The existence of such a morbid grove of trees helps explain how strangers (like the one whose hair had turned prematurely white) could bump into multiple hanging bodies while trying to find their way through town on dark, ghoulish nights.

Unfortunately, Los Lunas wasn't the only village in Valencia County with a hanging tree—or trees. Belen had its own designated tree, although it was never quite as active as its counterpart ten miles to the north. For some unknown reasons, Belen's tree, also a large cottonwood, was located in the enclosed yard west of Don Felipe Chávez's house off North Main Street.

Belen's vigilantes were far less bold, compared to those who took the law into their own hands in Los Lunas. Writing about his boyhood memories, W. E. Goebel recalled a sad event involving a young black man who was accused of raping a local girl near Belen. A posse chased the youth to the Rio Grande, apprehending him only after shooting him in the leg. The man was dragged to a nearby saloon, where its reckless patrons appointed themselves both judge and jury in the interest of administering immediate "justice." Those present handed down their hurried verdict: the accused was sentenced to be hanged as punishment for his alleged deviant behavior. The sentence was to be carried out at once.

The vigilantes unceremoniously hauled the wounded man to a telegraph pole in front of the John Becker Store, if only because the cottonwood tree at Don Felipe's home was probably reserved for legal executions. The black man was only spared from immediate death because, in Goebel's words, "nobody had the nerve to pull the rope."

At that moment, the county sheriff arrived at the scene, drew his six-shooter and ordered the crowd to disperse. The sheriff took the injured prisoner into custody, choosing the Los Lunas jail as a debatably safer place to hold the man until true justice could be served. Unfortunately, justice was never served in this case. Before the prisoner could stand trial, his wound became seriously infected. Without proper medical attention, the young man died in his cold, lonely cell.

Of course, hanging trees (or street poles) were not unique in Los Lunas or Belen in the late nineteenth century. With scarcely enough lawmen to deal with the wave of violence that swept New Mexico, many large- and small-town residents took the law into their own hands, fighting fire with fire to protect themselves, their families, and their entire communities from the ravages of contemporary criminals. Las Vegas and Socorro were especially known for their late-night brand of frontier justice. In fact, in Las Vegas the question people asked each morning was not if someone had been killed the previous evening, but who had died at the hands of angry citizens.

Vigilantes from Las Vegas went so far as to circulate a poster with a less-than-subtle message to a long list of undesirable characters:

NOTICE! TO THIEVES, THUGS, FAKERS, AND BUNKOSTEERERS,

Among whom are:

J.J. Harlin, alias "Off Wheeler," Sawdust Charlie, William Edges, Billy the Kid, Bill Mullin, Little Jack, The Cutter, Pockmarked Kid, and about twenty others:

If found within the limits of this city after ten o'clock p.m., this night, you will be invited to attend a GRAND NECK-TIE PARTY, the expense of which will be born by 100 substantial citizens.

As in Los Lunas, the vigilantes in towns like Las Vegas and Socorro preferred to leave their victims hanging until the following morning, the better to serve as deterrents for would-be troublemakers. In Las Vegas, citizens often awoke to the scene of bodies hanging from the tall windmill located in the very center of their community plaza.

After a period of intense activity in the 1870s and 1880s, many vigilantes began to realize that their methods were no more just than the actions of the men they accused. Many came to this conclusion when they discovered that many of the men they had executed had been innocent after all. Other vigilantes abandoned their illegal methods when they finally appreciated the importance of due process in the American legal system.

Vigilantes also realized the bad example they had set for the next generation of New Mexicans. This was especially true in Las Vegas, where parents found grotesque evidence that they had gone too far in their frenzied quest for law and order. To their alarm, parents discovered that children had begun lynching pet dogs and cats in an attempt to emulate nocturnal "adult" behavior.

Vigilante activity declined in New Mexico as a whole when the law was more strictly enforced and, eventually, more respected. The total number of known lynchings in the territory fell from eighty-seven in the 1870s and 1880s to just three in the 1890s and none in the first decade of the twentieth century.

The hanging tree still stands in the backyard of Felipe Chávez's ancient hacienda in Belen. If three hanging trees existed in Los Lunas, only one survived by the mid-twentieth century, albeit with major changes. A severe windstorm on May 26, 1959, so damaged the surviving tree's largest branch that the limb had to be removed. Workers cut down the entire tree, located on Main Street about where the new middle school has been built, when the road was widened and improved in the 1960s.

Before this last cottonwood was eliminated, a Los Lunas author named Susan Lee wrote of seeing an elderly man stagger down Main Street. Intoxicated and hardly able to stand, he nevertheless stopped beneath the hanging tree, removed his hat, and bowed his head in silent prayer. Moments later, he donned his hat and continued on his way.

No one knows why this man—and probably others—offered up a prayer below the hanging tree. Perhaps a friend or ancestor had been killed there. Perhaps he himself had participated in a lynching and was praying fervently for God's forgiveness. Or perhaps this man uttered a prayer of gratitude that law and order had finally come to his community, leaving the cottonwood as a daily reminder of a violent past that was long gone and largely forgotten.

What had once been a grim symbol of crime and violence had, with time, become a benign symbol of restored justice.

When Elfego Baca Liberated His Father from the Valencia County Jail, 1881

by Jim Boeck

Elfego Baca was one of the most fascinating characters in New Mexico's long history. His was a diverse, colorful life, dating from February 1865 to his peaceful death on August 27, 1945. Rough-hewn from his frontier birth in Socorro, Elfego was almost equally capable with his six-shooter as he was as an attorney, even arguing before the U.S. Supreme Court. As the sheriff of Socorro County, Elfego was bold enough to send standard letters to even the most dangerous outlaws. A typical letter of this kind read as follows:

> Dear Sir,
>
> I have a warrant for your arrest. Please come in by March 15 and give yourself up. If you don't, I'll know that you intend to resist arrest, and I will feel justified in shooting you on sight when I come after you.
>
> Yours truly,
>
> Elfego Baca, Sheriff

Most recipients of such a letter turned themselves in without incident rather than test Elfego's blunt threat and reputation.

Elfego had earned his reputation as a fearless lawman when, as a young man, he had single-handedly held off eighty rowdy Texas cowboys for thirty-three hours, wounding eight and killing four on October 29-31, 1884. Miraculously, Elfego survived the long fight in Reserve unscathed. This and other heroic stories about Elfego were immortalized by Walt Disney in a 1950s television series (filmed in Cerrillos, New Mexico) called *The Nine Lives of Elfego Baca.*

Elfego Baca's fame extended throughout the Southwest, but one of his most famous exploits took place in Valencia County in May 1881 when he was only 16-years-old—three years before his legendary shootout in Reserve. Elfego's family had left Socorro, bound for Topeka, Kansas, when the young man was just a year old. His father, Francisco, was a tough New Mexican, quick with a gun and proficient in the manly art of fisticuffs. But Francisco was also a concerned father who wanted his children to benefit from a good education in Topeka where Francisco worked as a contractor to support his growing family.

Elfego Baca (Museum of New Mexico, #75265)

Francisco moved his family back to New Mexico following the death of his wife, Juanita. While Francisco wrapped up his business in Topeka, Elfego and his brother Abdenago moved to Socorro to live with their uncle.

Returning to Socorro, Elfego felt like a foreigner in his native land. Speaking only a smattering of Spanish, he had difficulty conversing with his fellow Hispanics. However, his Kansas education gave him a distinct advantage, since he was one of only a few Hispanics who spoke English fluently and could relate to the increasingly large Anglo population of the territory. Francisco rejoined his sons a year later. He was hired to serve as the town marshal in Belen, thirty-five miles north of Socorro.

A prominent citizen of Los Lunas had challenged Francisco to a horse race, which Francisco had easily won. Becoming quite irate, Francisco's defeated competitor shouted insults and threats in a tirade. In response, Francisco's temper flared, and he responded by rearranging the contours of the man's face with his fists. Francisco's twice-defeated foe and his powerful clan resented the beating and plotted revenge.

An opportunity for revenge came in December 1880, when Francisco, in his role as town marshal, killed two brothers Eutimio and Ternuno Baca (no relation) for a disturbance they caused in a local store. To Francisco's surprise, he was arrested and placed in the Los Lunas jail. After an unusually quick trial, Francisco was found guilty of murder in his first trial. Sure that his powerful antagonists had unfairly influenced the outcome of his trail, Francisco awaited his second trial for murder without much hope for justice, much less acquittal.

Elfego and his family were outraged by this travesty of justice. Fearing the outcome of the second trial, Elfego vowed to rescue his father from the Los Lunas jail. He knew that the best time to attempt such a rescue would be during the Feast Day of St. Theresa, when local lawmen would be distracted and local residents would be celebrating with much food and drink. With the help of a young man known only as Chávez, Elfego traveled from Socorro to Los Lunas to execute the daring rescue mission. Once in Los Lunas, Elfego and his friend reconnoitered the courthouse, noting that the local jail was located on the first floor of a two-story building. The second floor was used as a courtroom.

As anticipated, the jailer was gone for the night, attending the *fiesta*. Elfego found a ladder and climbed it to reach the second floor. As good fortune would have it, Elfego and Chávez also found a saw and an auger which they used to cut a hole through the wooden floor directly above Francisco's jail cell. The prisoners were shackled, but one of them had found a key that the jailer had lost several weeks before. He quickly freed himself and his companions. A tall fellow named Thacker, accused of murdering his wife, was chosen to hoist the others up through the small hole in the ceiling. Thacker was left behind, perhaps because even criminals could not stomach a man who had killed his wife in cold blood.

With the escapees free at last, Elfego conscientiously returned the ladder to its previous location. In the process, he noticed a clothesline covered with jerked venison, enough food to sustain the men while enroute to their respective destinations. Deciding not to make their final getaway until the following night, the escapees hid in a high, grass-covered field across from the jail. The field also had a bountiful crop of ripe watermelon, good snacks to eat while they watched events unfold at the jail.

Throughout the next day, vigilantes, deputies, and posses searched everywhere in Valencia County for the desperados. No one dreamed that the escapees were watching from a vantage point so close to the place where they had once been held. The escapees filled their stomachs with jerked venison and watermelon while quietly laughing at the search teams as they returned empty-handed and exhausted. The search was finally discontinued.

At dark, the small band of fugitives parted ways. Elfego, Francisco, and Chávez headed south, while the two other former prisoners went north to Albuquerque. At Escondida, a small farming community just north of Socorro, Elfego and his father left Chávez, obtained three horses, and recruited a guide familiar with the long route south. Their destination was Ysleta, Texas, just east of El Paso, where Francisco's brother ran a general hardware store. Francisco worked for his brother in self-imposed exile for seven years before returning to Socorro County, where he thereafter led an exemplary life, unhindered by old or new trumped-up charges.

Safely delivering his father to the security of his brother's store in Texas, Elfego returned to Socorro. Having experienced the sting of injustice, he began to contemplate a career in law enforcement in hopes of ensuring fairer treatment for families like his own. Three years later, Elfego made his heroic stand in Reserve. He was well prepared for this most famous incident in this life, having first proven his great courage and asserting his strong sense of justice in Valencia County.

Bonifacio Torres's Shootout
in Jarales, 1930

by Matt Baca

On Saturday, March 1, 1930, 19-year-old Bonifacio Torres engaged in a long, bloody shootout with law enforcement officials at his grandmother's house, two-and-a-half miles northeast of Jarales. Those who knew Bonifacio say that he stood about five feet, six inches tall. With an attractive smile, he radiated intelligence and a kind of thoughtfulness found only in a few. He was said to be an easy-going young man who liked music and played the guitar. But Bonifacio is most remembered for the tragic events of early March 1930.

It all started about 7:00 on that Saturday morning when Valencia County sheriff Ignacio Aragón y García, two of his deputies, and Belen city marshal Daniel Sánchez arrived to take Torres into custody. Torres, who had been staying with his grandmother, had recently become abusive, especially when he drank. Responding to his family's complaints about his behavior, local lawmen had declared Torres to be "incorrigible" and had made arrangements to escort him to reform school.

Bonefacio Torres (far right with guitar) (Torres family)

At first it appeared that Torres was willing to surrender peacefully on that Saturday morning. But then, in an act of sudden defiance, the young man drew a pistol and shot Marshal Sánchez in both the hand and thigh. Torres also shot Sheriff Aragón in the left lung as the sheriff fled from the line of fire. A deputy managed to get both wounded lawmen into a waiting car. The vehicle sped to Belen to get Sánchez and Aragón emergency medical attention. Meanwhile, Torres rushed into the attic of his grandmother's one-story adobe house. An eerie silence followed. Three other lawmen cautiously approached the structure.

Accompanied by deputies Dennis Gabaldón and Joe Gabaldón, deputy Charles "Casey" Cunningham was heard to declare that he could flush out this "Mexican" as easily as he could flush out a jack rabbit. These were to be Cunningham's last words. Firing from the attic through a ceiling hole previously used for a stovepipe, Torres shot the deputy in the shoulder. Deputy Joe Gabaldón caught Cunningham as he fell. Fellow deputy Dennis Gabaldón exchanged fire with the fugitive for the next thirty minutes.

Alerted, deputies from as far away as Albuquerque and Grants began arriving at the crime scene. Valencia County district attorney Fred Nicolas came as well. A crowd of curious spectators grew in size to as many as three hundred as the hours passed. But what could be done to dislodge Torres without further bloodshed? Many strategies were discussed. Some lawmen suggested that they burn the house down to force Torres out, a notion the district attorney opposed because it would leave the boy's grandmother homeless. At a time before SWAT teams and negotiating experts, the authorities were at a loss on how to proceed.

About noon, the police settled on a plan to use tear gas to drive Torres from his adobe fortress. A large "tear bomb" was thrown into a window, but proved ineffective when drafts caused by air blowing through broken windows blew the gas back into the open.

Next, the police tried to force Torres out by using dynamite that might damage, but not completely destroy the adobe home. Blasting powder and other needed materials were purchased from stores in Belen and brought to the crime scene in Jarales. A local plumber, who had worked with dynamite before, volunteered to carry out this dangerous mission. Using a barrage of bullets for cover, F. W. Reinkhardt approached a side of the house, dug a hole, and carefully planted seven sticks of explosives.

After lighting a two-minute fuse, the plumber ran for protection and awaited the expected blast. But little happened. In fact, the blast failed to do more than blow a small hole in the structure's thick adobe walls.

In another attempt to end the standoff, Valencia County deputy Raymendo Lovato, armed with a borrowed Army rifle, crept to another side of the house, took position, aimed, and pulled the trigger. Nothing happened. Retreating to a safe distance, Lovato examined his weapon only to discover that in his haste he had failed to release a safety catch. Yet another strategy had been stymied. But now time was running out. Night would soon fall, providing young Torres with an opportunity to escape in the darkness.

Despite his earlier objections, District Attorney Fred Nicolas now agreed that the best thing to do was to set fire to the house and thereby force Torres out into the open, hopefully to surrender. Siphoning gasoline from nearby cars, the police saturated a gunnysack with the flammable liquid. Under another barrage of gunfire, a volunteer approached the adobe house, lit the sack, and lobbed it into a window. It was 5:10 p.m.

This time the plan worked. Fire spread quickly through the building, driving Torres into the only room left undamaged. According to an *Albuquerque Journal* reporter at the scene, "flames from the burning flooring and furniture at last penetrated Torres's last place of refuge."

Forced out by the smoke and flames, Torres, making a sound like a rodeo rider leaving a chute, hurled himself through a glass window and into the yard. Getting to his feet with both hands raised, it appeared that the fugitive was ready to give himself up, as he had promised to do ten hours earlier. However, as before, Torres chose to resist arrest, making a final bid for freedom. Dropping his arms, Torres ran about 100 feet toward an open field, turning to shoot his two revolvers as he fled. When lawmen returned his fire, a single bullet struck the young man's heart. Torres stumbled another 50 feet before he finally fell. The police surged forward, surrounding the fugitive and keeping the crowd of onlookers at a safe distance.

According to witnesses, Torres breathed spasmodically for several minutes. A small hole in the breast pocket of his overalls revealed the fatal bullet's point of entry. His half-open eyes stared upward. His lips formed a slight smile, and he uttered a few words before he "drew his last, gasping breath," according to the *Journal* reporter.

The long standoff was over. It was 5:40 p.m. and nearly dark. The crowd and deputies began to disperse, jamming the narrow dirt road with cars and trucks. An inquest was quickly held. The coroner's jury found that "Bonifacio Torres came to his death from a gunshot wound fired at the hands of a posse of the sheriff's office of Valencia County while the said Bonifacio Torres resisted arrest." Torres's body was turned over to the boy's father. He was unceremoniously buried in the Belen Catholic cemetery the following day.

Deputy Charles Cunningham also died of his wounds the following Monday. Fortunately, Sheriff Aragón and Marshal Sánchez survived, although they required prolonged care at St. Joseph's Hospital in Albuquerque. On April 10, 1930, the *Belen News* reported that Sheriff Aragón, the more seriously wounded of the two surviving lawmen, had returned home and was expected to be back on the job soon.

The standoff had been expensive in dollars as well as in lives. According to the *Belen News*, the county paid $683.75 in medical expenses for the care of Sheriff Aragón, Deputy Cunningham, and Marshal Sánchez; $439.75 for Cunningham's funeral expenses; $26.10 at the Becker Dalies and Feil and Ellermeyer stores for fuses and cartridges; and $83.90 to compensate ten deputies for their services. The total bill, as of May 1, 1930, equaled over $1,200, or over $13,000 in today's money.

Should Bonifacio Torres be remembered as a hero or as a villain in local history? Some said that Torres reminded them of 21-year-old Billy the Kid because both men defied the law and both were killed by a lawman at an early age. Others think of 19-year-old Elfego Baca who heroically held off dozens of gunmen from a shack in Reserve, New Mexico, over a period of thirty-three hours in 1884. But how can Torres be called a hero when he defied his grandmother, deceived the police, resisted arrest, and shot three police officers, including one fatally?

The tragedy of Bonifacio Torres has been eulogized in at least two *corridos*, or epic ballads, including one by Adolfo Silva of Torres's home village of Jarales:

On the first of March of 1930
Bonifacio Torres died.
Don't let this tale be lost.

In the village of Jarales,
New Mexico,
in the annals of history
they treated him like a man.

He chose freedom,
not to suffer slavery,
and, not to see himself enslaved,
he preferred to die.

This boy, whose poverty
led him to act badly,
and for this they called
the reform school.

And when Ignacio Aragón,
the sheriff [of Valencia County],
went to arrest Bonifacio,
[the sheriff] wanted to play with
[Bonifacio's] life.

When [Bonifacio] saw the sheriff
who had come to arrest him,
at him and his assistants
he started to shoot.

With the first shots
he made Aragón his target,
and from those moments
the confusion began.

After fifty men
gathered there
the result was that
two others were wounded.

They were Charles Cunningham
and [Daniel] Sánchez, policemen,
who went there warm
and left there cold.

To see from all sides
the large number of bullets
to be witnessed at that conflict,
they came from everywhere.

Soon two hundred people
did not come because of a man,
[but as the police] fired at the youth
[Bonifacio] gave them lessons on
how to be a man.

Fearing a single man
for his extraordinary defense,
they entered timidly
to drive him out with dynamite.

They set a cartridge
to try to kill him,
but the cartridge was bad
and he continued being strong.

Then they thought to draw him out
with tear gas,
but the boy continued
shooting as before.

A while later, a plumber
and a county deputy
were credited with an act
of bravery for exposing themselves
to danger.

And although it was an inhumane
act
which those men committed,
they stayed there without revealing
anything.

Perhaps the best we can say is that Torres was a confused young man whose troubles escalated far beyond his control. Lacking wisdom and experience, he reacted poorly to his desperate circumstances. Having shot three lawmen, including the sheriff, Torres probably did not expect to be shown any mercy by the deputies who, in the course of ten hours, employed every means of violence at their command. Although all but one of their plans failed, the police gave no indication that they were about to allow Torres to simply surrender peacefully. Put this way, Torres's actions can at least be understood, if not condoned.

"I Have No Hard Feelings Toward Anyone:" The Trial and Punishment of David Cooper Nelson, 1956-1960

by Richard Melzer

David Cooper Nelson displayed some of the most bizarre behavior ever witnessed in a Valencia County courtroom during his 1956 trial for murder. At various times during his eight-day trial, Nelson had moaned, sang, or sat hunched in his chair with his eyes closed and his fingers placed securely in both ears.

On two occasions, the 35-year-old defendant had had to be forcibly restrained following violent struggles with sheriff's deputies sent to guard him. Carried from the courtroom, Nelson had been placed in a straitjacket back in his cell. Moments later he had looked bewildered and had asked Deputy Sheriff Luciano T. Sánchez, "What happened? What happened? I'm sorry!" To prevent future outbursts in court, guards placed Nelson in arm and leg irons during much of the rest of his trial. Based on such irrational behavior, many observers believed that Nelson must surely be insane.

But others were not as easily convinced. They noted that Nelson had pleaded insanity as his defense and had undergone several hours of psychiatric testing, conducted by two Albuquerque doctors before his trial began. Nelson had told the psychiatrists that he was a "weapon of God" who had simply carried out God's command to serve as "His executioner." Despite this assertion, the doctors had concluded that Nelson was "bright," "alert," and sufficiently sane to stand trial and assist his court-appointed counsel in his legal defense.

If Nelson's behavior and assertions were a charade, he was strongly motivated to give an Academy Award performance. After all, he had been accused of first-degree murder, and if found guilty, faced almost certain death in the gas chamber. Nelson had, in fact, confessed to the murder in which he was charged shortly after his arrest in early February 1956. Calmly smoking a cigar, Nelson had displayed a cool detachment as he described the brutal crime he had committed on January 9, 1956, close to the small town of Budville in western Valencia County.

Confession

According to the five foot, six inch, 175-pound drifter, he had been hitchhiking en route to Chicago when 48-year-old Ralph H. Rainey had given him a ride near Flagstaff, Arizona. The trip went well until Nelson claimed that Rainey wanted to leave him off in the middle of nowhere, in the dead of night. Nelson had accused Rainey of wanting to steal the bag of processions he carried in his travels. Angered, Nelson had reached into his bag and retrieved a .38-caliber gun. Brandishing the weapon, he had forced Rainey to stop the car and let him drive. In Nelson's words,

> I got behind the wheel and stuck the .38 between my knees. He made a lunge for the gun, and I gave him a judo chop.... He made another grab for the gun, so I shot him. I drove on down the road. He was gurgling and gasping and trying to talk. There was blood everywhere. It was enough to make a man sick. So I shot him again and dumped him [in an arroyo along Route 66].

As if this confession wasn't damaging enough, Nelson also admitted to a similarly grizzly murder committed less than two weeks later. Nelson confessed that on January 22, 1956, he had shot 36-year-old Kenneth Short after Short had given him a ride, much as Ralph Rainey had done in Arizona. Given a ride in Oklahoma, Nelson had shot Short, dumped his body near Amarillo, and driven his car west to Nevada. Nelson told Valencia County Sheriff Medardo Sánchez that he'd decided to confess to both crimes because "I can't get hung any higher for two [murders] than I can for one." Put another way, he offered that the police couldn't "fry me more than once."

New Mexico tried Nelson first with the understanding that the State of Texas was ready to prosecute him if he was found innocent or otherwise escaped the death penalty in New Mexico. But the odds of being found innocent or escaping the death penalty did not look good for Nelson at his May 1956 trial. Despite his plea of insanity and absurd courtroom behavior, he had been judged sane enough to stand trial. And, despite the efforts of his court-appointed defenders, including M. Terry Boucher of Belen, District Court Judge Paul A. Tackett had allowed Nelson's full confession to be admitted as testimony in his trial.

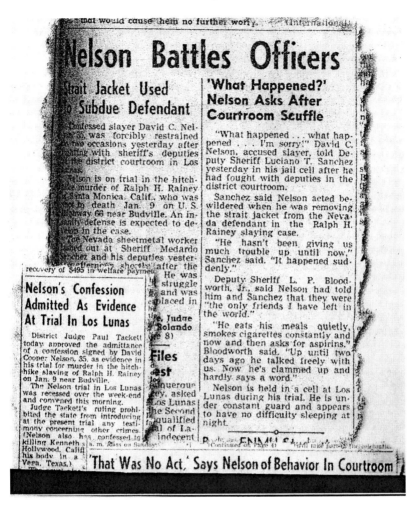

Nelson Battles Officers

Strait Jacket Used to Subdue Defendant

Confessed slayer David C. Nelson, 35, was forcibly restrained on two occasions yesterday after fighting with sheriff's deputies in the district courtroom in Los Lunas.

Nelson is on trial in the hitchhike murder of Ralph H. Rainey of Santa Monica, Calif., who was shot to death Jan. 9 on U. S. Highway 66 near Budville. An insanity defense is expected to develop in the case.

The Nevada sheetmetal worker cried out at Sheriff Medardo Sanchez and his deputies yesterday afternoon shortly after the recovery of $495 in welfare payments he was struggling and was placed in ... Judge Bolando ge 8)

Files est buquerque ey, asked Los Lunas the Second qualified al of La- indecent a. m. Mass on Sunday.

'What Happened?' Nelson Asks After Courtroom Scuffle

"What happened . . . what happened . . . I'm sorry!" David C. Nelson, accused slayer, told Deputy Sheriff Luciano T. Sanchez yesterday in his jail cell after he had fought with deputies in the district courtroom.

Sanchez said Nelson acted bewildered when he was removing the strait jacket from the Nevada defendant in the Ralph H. Rainey slaying case.

"He hasn't been giving us much trouble up until now," Sanchez said. "It happened suddenly."

Deputy Sheriff L. P. Bloodworth, Jr., said Nelson had told him and Sanchez that they were "the only friends I have left in the world."

"He eats his meals quietly, smokes cigarettes constantly and now and then asks for aspirins," Bloodworth said. "Up until two days ago he talked freely with us. Now he's clammed up and hardly says a word."

Nelson is held in a cell at Los Lunas during his trial. He is under constant guard and appears to have no difficulty sleeping at night.

(Continued on Page 4)

Nelson's Confession Admitted As Evidence At Trial In Los Lunas

District Judge Paul Tackett today approved the admittance of a confession signed by David Cooper Nelson, 35, as evidence in his trial for murder in the hitchhike slaying of Ralph H. Rainey on Jan. 9 near Budville.

The Nelson trial in Los Lunas was recessed over the week-end and convened this morning.

Judge Tackett's ruling prohibited the state from introducing at the present trial any testimony concerning other crimes. (Nelson also has confessed to killing Kenneth Vern Hollywood, Calif., his body in a Vern, Texas.)

'That Was No Act,' Says Nelson of Behavior In Courtroom

Newspaper reports of David Cooper Nelson's trial

And so David Cooper Nelson stood trial for the murder of Ralph Rainey. Aware that the odds were not in his favor, Nelson had caused trouble outside as well as inside the courtroom. The former sheet metal worker smoked constantly, pounded on his cell walls, often screamed, and spoke to himself, according to the man who occupied the cell next to Nelson's. The accused murderer also received a black eye and several cuts on his nose during a jailhouse fight. Increasingly desperate, he even attempted to escape from the jail in Los Lunas. In response, Sheriff Sánchez had had Nelson transferred to the lockup in Albuquerque and, later, to the state prison in Santa Fe for safekeeping.

Nelson's murder trial ended on May 20, 1956. As his 8-man, 4-women jury retired to deliberate, the defendant told one of his guards, "I'm glad that's over. Now I can quit this act. One more day and I would have [gone] nuts." The jury's verdict was a foregone conclusion. Having been found guilty of first-degree murder, Nelson walked calmly to the bench to hear Judge Tackett sentence him to death.

Setting the execution date for August 13, 1956, the judge added, "May God have mercy on your soul," to which Nelson replied, "and [on] the rest of us, too." Leaving the courthouse in chains, Nelson praised his attorneys for doing a "great job," but claimed that the psychiatrists who had declared him to be sane were liars and that Judge Tackett had been prejudiced against him from the start.

En route to the state prison in Santa Fe, Nelson went so far as to boast that the death penalty was "just what I wanted. If that New Mexico jury had come up with anything else, I would have laughed at them." Nelson even claimed that he welcomed death and would refuse a pardon from the governor even if he "came to my cell and said, 'Dave, I'm freeing you.' I wouldn't leave. I don't conform to society, and….I'll be glad to [die]. I can't get along with anybody on the outside."

Despite such statements, Nelson's lawyers attempted to prevent his execution by appealing his case to the New Mexico Supreme Court. The lawyers based their appeal on Nelson's claim that the police had reneged on their promise of leniency if he confessed to murdering Ralph Rainey. Nelson's lawyers could certainly not hope for mercy for their client based on his life and criminal record prior to his latest crimes. Nelson had, in fact, been arrested for armed robbery as early as the age of 11. After serving time in juvenile detention centers, he had been released as an adult only to be convicted of additional felonies in Michigan and Montana. He was, in short, a life-long, hardened criminal long before he killed Ralph Rainey in Valencia County in early 1956.

To the surprise and dismay of many, the New Mexico Supreme Court struck down the verdict in Nelson's first trial based on the broken promise of leniency that the police had offered the accused in exchange for his confession.

A Second Trial

Nelson's second murder trial before Judge Tackett began in Los Lunas almost two years to the day after his first. But some things had changed in the intervening two years. For one, jury selection was more difficult in this second round because so many Valencia County residents had already formed on opinion about the case and Nelson's guilt.

Nelson's appearance and demeanor was also quite different in his second trial. Although clearly nervous, the defendant came neatly dressed in a suit and tie, carrying a Bible and two law books into the courtroom. Nelson's legal strategy had changed as well. This time Nelson entered a plea of not guilty and dropped all pretext of insanity. His only unorthodox behavior involved a request to defend himself, with his court-appointed lawyers available for legal assistance. Judge Tackett granted the request.

But, true to character, Nelson changed his mind on the third day of his second trial. In a confusing five-minute courtroom speech, the accused demanded that his attorneys be dismissed, but then suddenly asked them to remain. Exasperated, the two Albuquerque lawyers asked the court to excuse them from defending Nelson. Their request was undoubtedly appreciated, but denied. Judge Tackett seemed eager to move the proceedings along, especially given the high cost of such a high-profile trial in Valencia County.

The eight-man, four-women jury seemed equally eager to bring things to a close. After a week-long trial, ending on May 23, 1958, Nelson's jury returned a guilty verdict in less than two-and-a-half hours. Before a packed courtroom, Judge Tackett summoned Nelson to the bench and for the second time handed down a mandatory death sentence. The execution date was set for August 1, 1958. Nelson remained calm and even smiled as his guards led him away. A *Valencia County News-Bulletin* reporter interviewed Nelson shortly after he was returned to his isolated cell in the Los Lunas jail. Showing neither anger nor remorse, the twice-convicted slayer referred to the jury, declaring, "God bless them! I have no hard feelings toward anyone."

Although he refused to testify and called no witnesses in his own behalf, Nelson now told the *Valencia County News-Bulletin* reporter that a third party had accidentally shot Rainey while Nelson was lying in the back seat of the murdered man's car. But Nelson refused to identify the mysterious third party, saying, "I'm no stool pigeon. I'd rather die than tell on the other fellow, a nice guy with a wonderful family."

The New Mexico Gas Chamber (Richard Melzer)

Nelson's Fate

Nelson's tactics had now covered the entire legal gamut, from a full confession in the hope of gaining leniency to a plea of insanity to a plea of not guilty to the role of an innocent bystander. But nothing had worked. Having exhausted all routes, the convicted killer awaited his destiny in a tightly secured prison cell in Santa Fe.

Nelson had few complaints while awaiting his final execution date. He objected to not getting "enough fresh air and sunshine," in his words, but he appreciated the use of a typewriter on which he claimed to have written two novels and five short stories. One can only imagine the perverse fictional plots developed by such a perverse criminal mind.

Nelson's lawyers dutifully appealed his conviction to the U.S. Supreme Court, but the high court refused to hear the case. Only an act of clemency by Governor John Burroughs—which Nelson had already claimed he would refuse—could save the convict from his fate. Governor Burroughs did not offer clemency, and David Cooper Nelson's legal clock finally ran out on August 11, 1960. He died in the gas chamber, the first person in New Mexico history to be executed in this supposedly more modern, merciful fashion.

Neither David Cooper Nelson nor his victim, Ralph Rainey, were residents of Valencia County. Only fate brought them to a deserted stretch of highway that would not even be part of Valencia County by 1981 when Cibola County was created. But the residents of Valencia County, including Judge Tackett, defense lawyer Terry Boucher, District Attorney John Murphy, Sheriff Medardo Sánchez, and the men and women of two separate juries did their best to see that justice was served in this case. They performed their civic duty, despite the tragic nature of the crime committed, the high cost of the proceedings, and the often-absurd legal maneuvers and behavior of the accused.

Valencia County and the Worst Prison Riot in New Mexico History, 1980

by Richard Melzer

On February 2, 1980, inmates at the state penitentiary south of Santa Fe staged the worst prison riot in New Mexico history and the second worst prison riot in all of American history. Many residents of Valencia County were directly or indirectly drawn into the 36-hour nightmare. Some were inmates. Others were caseworkers or guards. Many were members of the National Guard or State Police, called on to help control and, eventually, end the bloodshed. Regardless of his role, each person has his own story about what he saw, heard, and felt on that terrible weekend. After many years, a few are now willing to share their memories of early February 1980.

Bob White was a young caseworker at the prison when the riot broke out. Living near the prison in one of several mobile homes made available for support staff and correctional officers, White remembers a neighbor urgently knocking on his back door to report that a riot had broken out in the prison. It was about 2:00 a.m. Not knowing what danger lay ahead, White drove his wife, Marguerite, and their young son, Travis, to safety in Santa Fe, fourteen miles north. Leaving his wife and son with Marguerite's family, White raced back to the prison and the horrors playing out within it.

Eager to help in any way he could, White was put on traffic control to sort out who should or should not be allowed onto the prison grounds. He recalls Governor Bruce King's black limousine arriving on the scene, the governor waving from the back seat as he sped by. King was about to face the worst crisis of his record-breaking three terms as New Mexico's chief executive.

Members of inmate families rushed to the prison gate from nearby homes. Distraught and nervous, they were soon joined by hundreds of other concerned friends and relatives who drove from miles away, including from Valencia County. All but essential personnel were turned away, left to wait out the riot from along State Road 14. Rumors spread, but little reliable information was available. A young state legislator named Manny Aragón circulated in the crowd, handing out business cards and offering his assistance to the anguished families.

Corrections Officer Bob White Outside Cell Block 6 of the New Mexico State Penitentiary (Bob White)

Causes of the Riot

Bob White stayed at his post for the next five hours. He remembers the bitter cold and growing fear. As the caseworker for Cellblock 4, White was familiar with chaos and fear. Filled with as many as 150 inmates in need of protective custody, the notorious cellblock suffered continuous tension, reflected in a "constant roar" of noise every waking hour of the day. Inmates were locked in their cells with only a few hours out for showers and use of the recreation area each week. Some were too frightened to leave their cells on even these limited occasions.

White knew everything there was to know about the men in Cellblock 4, from their prison numbers (which he still remembers) to their criminal records and the reasons why they were in need of special protection. Most were physically or emotionally weak, unable to defend themselves in the general prison population. Some were pedophiles or rapists, detested by other inmates for their hideous crimes.

Many in Cellblock 4 had been branded as snitches for having shared information about their fellow inmates in exchange for favors from the prison staff. Inmates hated informants not only because they were considered traitors, but also because the information they offered often led to new charges and longer prison terms for those they implicated.

The prison had become so overcrowded prior to the riot that guards and members of the administration had relied on snitches to know what was going on in the prison and what trouble lay ahead. Built to hold no more than 974 inmates, the prison housed 1,157 by early 1980. Overcrowding became especially bad when an entire cellblock was closed for repairs and its inmates were transferred to already cramped dorms and cellblocks. Small 6-foot by 9-foot cells meant for two men often housed four.

Ironically, the $8 million prison south of Santa Fe had been built to replace New Mexico's antiquated first prison, opened in 1885, on Cerrillos Road in Santa Fe. A prison riot in June 1953 had proven how small and outdated the 104-cell first prison had become. It took another riot, in 1976, to prove that even worse conditions existed at the "modern" facility built in 1956.

In many ways the prison had never recovered from the disturbance of 1976. Windows smashed in the disturbance had never been replaced or repaired, making much of the prison extremely cold in the winter and extremely hot in the summer. Flies swarmed through the broken windows. The electrical system was often broken. Visiting the prison as part of a Catholic ministry, Joan Artiaga remembers it as a dark, dismal, angry place. Prisoners had little communication with friends or relatives. There were no phones and all mail was censored. Inmates resorted to listening to an "oldies" radio station in Santa Fe to receive coded messages through requested song dedications.

Inmates also complained about the food they were served. Food was notoriously poor and infested with bugs, as Bob White observed when meals were brought to Cellblock 4 where inmates were not permitted to eat with the general population. White recalls that prisoners who served food in the prison cafeteria were seldom screened for contagious diseases.

White also recalls that hardened, high-security-risk prisoners were housed with or near first-time offenders. The latter included "60-day diagnostics," or men sent to the pen for two months prior to their final sentencing. Long-term inmates had little to do to occupy their time and prepare themselves for eventual reentry into society. Prison work programs were rare and often involved only part-time labor. Educational opportunities and drug and alcohol counseling had been cut back. Inmates with time on their hands drank homebrew liquor, known as Raisin Jack, complained about their plight, and schemed of staging a major revolt.

Not all prisoners were willing to resort to violence. In 1977, Dwight Durán and two of his fellow prisoners attempted to force changes through legal recourse. In a class action suit Durán sued the state of New Mexico, the prison warden, and then-governor Jerry Apodaca for the horrible conditions inmates endured at the state pen. After negotiating a settlement in 1979, a U.S. district court ordered that improvements be made as soon as possible. But significant improvements were not made as soon as most inmates had hoped. According to Bob White, it was a matter of too little too late because the prison lacked the staff and the funding to implement the court order. Ironically, by causing additional frustration, the Durán Consent Decree may have fueled the riot it was meant to help prevent.

According to one former prison official, the prison "had become a time bomb of human rage ready to explode." Bob White and others had hoped that a mass escape by eleven of the prison's most dangerous inmates on December 9, 1979, would be a wake-up call for prison authorities. Instead, little changed. By 1980, the prison lacked not only adequate conditions, but also an adequate staff. With only fifteen guards on many shifts, the ratio of inmates to guards was a dangerous eighty to one.

To make matters worse, guards were poorly paid and seldom trained beyond elementary instructions. White remembers that his training by a lieutenant in September 1977 consisted of a tour of the prison, followed by some instruction with a handgun, although guards never carried weapons when among the general population. White was then assigned to a veteran guard he was supposed to shadow the rest of the day. The lieutenant told the experienced man to let White follow him during his shift, but to keep possession of his keys at all times. Despite this stern warning, the older guard handed his keys over to White and announced that he was going to lunch just moments after the lieutenant departed.

Other than a course on defensive driving, this was all the training White ever received during his ten months as a correctional officer and his two years as a caseworker. But at least White was 27-years-old and well-educated, lacking only one course to complete his college degree, which he subsequently received from the University of North Carolina. Some rookie guards were as young as 18 and lacked even high school diplomas. White recalls that almost every male who walked into the state personnel office in Santa Fe was asked if he had ever considered a career in corrections. Those who were unqualified to do anything else would always be offered a job at the prison.

Some of those who were hired were so illiterate that White had to write their daily reports for them. Sometimes arriving to work drunk, intoxicated guards were assigned to tower duty to sober up. White says that these men often had trouble even climbing the towers' stairs in their inebriated condition. Lax guards did not show up to work at all, leaving many shifts shorthanded. The turnover rate among guards was predictably high. As many as 70 percent of all guards quit each year, often shortly after they had been hired. About 40 percent of the guards still employed in early 1980 had less than one year of experience.

Poorly trained and badly outnumbered in an incredibly stressful job, some guards resorted to brutal methods to keep control of the inmates in their charge. According to a former inmate, it felt as if harassment was part of the guards' training. "You were never right, no matter what you did. You were always wrong and being punished" for trumped-up charges. The guards' ultimate harassment was disclosure to other inmates that a man was a snitch, whether such disclosures were accurate or not. The hint that a prisoner had ratted on his fellow inmates led to brutal retaliation, including beatings and even death. Guards were particularly brutal with prisoners who dared threaten or attack other guards.

Without sufficient guards to provide adequate protection, inmates often harassed one another, creating a "pall of fear" and tension, in the words of a former convict. "Bulldogging," or violently forcing another prisoner to comply with a bully's demands, ranged from taking a man's money or property to forcing him to perform sexual acts. Some men were labeled as snitches simply because they had identified those who had bulldogged them. Inmates often joined cliques or gangs to seek protection that the guards could not or would not provide. Hispanics, blacks, and whites often clashed, with deadly results.

The cruelest guards were the most feared and hated. Rioters targeted these men when the riot started early on Saturday morning, February 2, 1980. Sixteen guards and a medical technician were on duty that fateful morning.

The Riot Begins

A poorly trained, 18-year-old guard with only four months' experience played a pivotal role at the outset of the riot. A team of four guards had approached Dormitory E-1 for a final inspection at 1:30 a.m. Three guards went inside the dorm, telling the rookie to stand outside and lock them in until their routine inspection was complete.

But instead of locking the dorm door shut, the rookie simply put his foot in the door and awaited the older guards' return. Seeing the young man's mistake, inmates closest to the door grabbed the 18-year-old, took his keys, and easily captured the other guards, including Captain Greg Roybal, a twenty-year veteran and the commander of the graveyard shift that critical night. Forced to strip, all four guards were handcuffed and blindfolded. Inmates confiscated the guards' keys and opened locks to other dorms and cellblocks. Hundreds of freed prisoners ran wild through the south side of the facility. Other guards were quickly captured, abused, and dragged down the main corridor.

Within moments as many as seventy-five rioters stood outside the prison's main control center. If they gained entry to the center they would have access to every square foot of the prison. Until weeks before the riot, the control center's glass wall had been encased in 10 inch square steel bars. Even if each pane of glass had been broken, the steel bars would have effectively prevented access. But the control center's wall had recently been replaced by a new, reportedly shatterproof single-sheet of glass. Prison officials had hoped to improve visibility by removing the steel bars from the all-important control center. White remembers seeing an inmate looking at the new glass wall shortly after it had been installed. Not believing what he saw, the man had stood there, laughing. White calls the installation of the glass wall at the control center the prison administration's "greatest blunder." Despite warnings to prison officials by White and other staff members, the new glass was still in place when the riot began.

And so the rioters stood before the poorly defended control center and simply smashed it in with a fire extinguisher. Panicked, the two guards on duty fled for their lives. Rushing into the center, the prisoners confiscated every key in the prison plus many dangerous weapons.

Twenty-five minutes after the riot had begun, the inmates had taken complete control of the prison.

Rioters gained access to two coveted areas in particular. The first was the prison's infirmary, where they consumed every drug they could find in the prison pharmacy. Not stopping to check the contents of pharmacy bottles, the rioters took uppers and downers and, overdosing, became even more of a danger to themselves and to others.

The rioters' second targeted area was Cellblock 4 where the most vulnerable prisoners were held. The killers arrived at their destination about daybreak. According to one Valencia County resident housed in the cellblock, rioters broke into his cell and brutally stabbed his cellmate. John Smith (not his real name) saw his cellmate die within minutes of the assault. Rioters kicked, tied, and forced Smith to accompany them to the gymnasium, where he saw several burned bodies laid out in a row. Smith somehow managed to climb through a broken window and jump to the yard below. He was taken by ambulance to St. Vincent's Hospital in Santa Fe where he was treated for fractured ribs. A total of 106 convicts were treated in the emergency rooms at St. Vincent's and the Indian Health Service Hospital, filling the halls with casualties ranging from smoke inhalation and lacerations to stab wounds and bone fractures.

White says that an inmate's fate was often sealed by being in the wrong place at the wrong time during the riot. In one case, while a Cellblock 4 inmate was away at court his cell was occupied by another man when the riot began. Brutally killed, the second man may well have been attacked by rioters who had simply confused him with the cell's usual occupant.

While some prisoners committed acts of unthinkable violence, others simply tried to protect themselves and the friends or relatives they often knew long before they had been sent to prison. A former Valencia County resident told of men defending themselves with make-shift weapons and hiding out in cells until the time seemed right to make their escape out into the yards. An inmate from Socorro County later described how he protected an obese elderly prisoner who seemed to have suffered a stroke. With the help of six other inmates, "We threw a blanket on the man and carried him out through the smoke-filled halls" and into the yard where he was rushed away by ambulance.

Meanwhile, crazed inmates continued to set fires throughout the facility. Wrecked plumbing caused extensive flooding. Once in the prison's administration offices, rioters destroyed their prison records, hoping to avoid future punishment based on documentation of previous poor behavior. Fueled by hate and drugs, the riot raged long into Saturday afternoon.

The National Guard Arrives

Additional Valencia County residents were drawn into the mayhem by Saturday afternoon. Battery B of the New Mexico National Guard's 3rd Battalion had spent much of that fateful Saturday conducting regular drills at their armory in Belen. Justly proud of their skills, the soldiers of Battery B had recently earned high honors for their proficiency. Their high proficiency might well have been the reason they were called to serve in the current crisis.

Kenny Griego, a National Guardsman with nine years of experience by 1980, recalls the moment when his company received orders that it was to proceed to Santa Fe. Not realizing the extent of the trouble that awaited them at the prison, the ninety-four guardsmen relaxed en route, often joking and kidding one another as their vehicles sped north.

But the atmosphere changed abruptly when the National Guardsmen arrived for a briefing at the armory in Santa Fe, just miles from the prison. Although reassured by a state police officer that "everything was going to be OK," the men suspected trouble when they were issued live ammunition and were shown a map of the prison with details of how they would be deployed. The mood became even more somber when some officers ordered their men to cover the name tapes on their uniforms so inmates in the riot could not identify them and later seek retaliation against them or their families.

National Guardsmen from Belen were no strangers to crises and danger. In the spring of 1970, their company had been ordered to the University of New Mexico's Albuquerque campus to break up anti-Vietnam war protests. The guardsmen considered their operation a success; the protest was broken up and no one was seriously injured or killed, as had happened when a National Guard unit had been deployed to Kent State University that spring. But six protesters and bystanders had filed charges against the National Guard, claiming that the guardsmen had wounded them with their bayonets. After a high-profile trial the guardsmen were found innocent, but memories of the controversy lingered long after the jury announced its favorable verdict. The guardsmen sent to the Santa Fe prison in 1980 hoped that they would perform well and avoid controversy in this new crisis. Most members of the company had joined the National Guard since 1970, but all knew that they would be watched and carefully evaluated.

The soldiers from Belen were among the first National Guardsmen to reach the prison, arriving at the gates and taking their positions by afternoon. Kenny Griego remembers that there were several opportunities for guardsmen to assist at critical moments. With fires blazing throughout the prison, veteran guardsmen offered to help extinguish the flames. Later, guardsmen offered to help remove the bodies of inmates killed in the bloodshed. In each case, veterans hoped to assist in volatile situations that less experienced men might not have been able to handle as well. In each case, the guardsmen's assistance was declined. It was still too dangerous for anyone to enter the prison to fight fires or remove bodies. Instead, prisoners removed the bodies as the death count steadily rose. Sgt. Tony Sánchez recalled the "brutal sights" of mutilated bodies. The fires were left to burn themselves out. Smoke from the prison could be seen from one hundred miles away in eastern New Mexico.

The soldiers from Belen stood guard as inmates fled the prison to seek shelter in outside yards. As Kenny Griego describes it, he and his fellow soldiers formed a human wall, standing elbow to elbow along the outer parameter, their M-16s at the ready. Hungry, thirsty, and shivering in the bitter cold temperature, inmates called out for food, water, and blankets. Rupert Baca, who had left his daughter's wedding in Belen to accompany his National Guard unit to Santa Fe, recalls that prisoners were given sack lunches prepared by his company's mess sergeant. Inmates were also issued blankets to stave off the extreme cold. But violence continued even in the outer yards. Kenny Griego saw one inmate suffer convulsions and die on the ground. A second convict placed his foot on the dead man's neck and challenged the guardsmen to shoot him because he had nothing to lose except the rest of his life in prison. According to Griego, few rioters showed remorse of any kind.

The Riot Rages On

Meanwhile, Bob White remained busy at various tasks. When some prisoners attempted to negotiate an end to the riot via telephone, White was asked to help identify convicts' voices so others could judge if they could be trusted as spokesmen. The prisoners communicated eleven demands, ranging from better food to better educational programs. The authorities negotiated in order to buy time in their efforts to free the guards still held hostage. No concessions were made.

Ironically, communication with inmate negotiators was often clearer than among law enforcement groups at the scene. Describing the situation as "horrendous," White says that people often spoke over one another on their radios, preventing the coordination of efforts. Adding to the mass confusion, each group, from the prison administration to the state police, acted as if it alone was in charge.

By Sunday morning, more and more prisoners had fled from what was left of the prison. Many of these men had gathered in the recreation yard to the west of the prison where they proceeded to fight one another with anything they could lay their hands on. Anglo, Hispanic, and black inmates battled one another, while temporary prisoners, known as 60-day diagnostics, were often caught in the middle. In White's understated words, the situation had grown "nasty" in the yard. White, a Hispanic lieutenant, and a black correctional officer were ordered to tower #3 to separate the groups and restore order. Armed with rifles and shotguns, White and his colleagues warned the inmates that they would open fire if the fighting continued.

Fortunately, the inmates respected the three staff members and responded to their commands. Black inmates and temporary prisoners retreated through a hole cut in a chain-link fence to gather at a distance from the Anglos and Hispanics. A tense situation had been defused without additional injuries or loss of life.

The Riot Ends

Bob White was still in tower #3 on Sunday at 1:10 p.m. when the last hostages were released and the rioters' last line of defense was eliminated. Fifteen minutes later National Guardsmen and a 22-man state police SWAT team stormed the prison with no resistance by the hundred or so convicts who still remained inside.

Rather than retaking the prison, the authorities simply occupied the burned shell of what remained once the riot had literally and figuratively burned itself out. The time was 1:55 p.m. Often wading through water mixed with human blood, guardsmen and state policemen later testified that they had never seen such horror and destruction. Noxious smells were everywhere. Walls, darkened by the fires, were still hot to the touch.

The smoke was so thick that a National Guardsman remembers moving through the prison "in a line formation, one hand holding our M-16s and the other hand on the shoulder of the guardsman in front of you, not knowing what lay ahead or behind." According to National Guardsman Rupert Baca, "Anything that could be broken was broken, anything that could be pulled out was pulled out, and anything that could be burned was burned." Only the prison's law library and Catholic chapel were left undisturbed, although the communion wine stocked in the Catholic chapel was gone. The rest of the prison lay in shambles. Worse, the death toll had reached thirty-three by 3:00 p.m. on Sunday, with thirteen of the victims found in Cellblock 4, including two young brothers from Bosque Farms.

While many believe that rioters targeted Cellblock 4 to kill men rightly or wrongly branded as snitches, Bob White believes that men in the cellblock were targeted because they were the least able to defend themselves against predators who roamed the prison in search of easy prey. White helped identify the dead from pictures taken of their often-mutilated bodies and, in one case, by a man's bad teeth. White remembers working round-the-clock during and after the riot, getting little sleep and only one quick shower in the course of several days.

All sixteen guards held hostage were released, and, while the most detested had been tortured by convicts, other guards had been protected by less violent inmates. The latter went so far as to disguise one or two of the hostages in inmate uniforms so they could flee with convicts to the yards outside. Eight of the hostages were treated for severe injuries. Their lives were probably spared not out of mercy or a sense of humanity, but because the rioters knew that the National Guard would have been ordered to storm the prison if word had spread that even one hostage had been killed.

National Guard medic tends to wounded inmates (R. Melzer's collection)

The National Guard unit from Belen left the prison on Tuesday, February 5. In one of their last assignments, the men stood in formation to separate the prisoners from their relatives as most of the convicts who survived the violence were put on buses and transferred to prisons in

Arizona, Colorado, Kansas, Oklahoma, and Georgia. Suffering from "riot trauma," thirty prisoners were escorted to the state psychiatric hospital in Las Vegas.

Back in Belen by Tuesday night, the guardsmen told a local newspaper reporter of the catastrophe, relating "horror stories likened to those from old prison movies." Rupert Baca recalled their four difficult days in Santa Fe, eating at his battery's mobile mess kitchen, enduring the cold, and rotating shifts to allow guardsmen to sleep at a nearby Army Reserve building.

Four days after the riot, Capt. Bernardo G. Iorio wrote a letter to the *Valencia County News-Bulletin* to praise the men of Battery B for conducting themselves "with professionalism and compassion" during the riot. "They were firm when circumstances dictated, but acted with maturity and good judgment." Each guardsman received a citation for excellent service, as did their unit as a whole.

The Riot's Impact

The Santa Fe prison riot had ended, but its impact lasted for years. Of the sixteen correctional personnel on duty that dreadful weekend, none remained on the prison's payroll a year later. Eleven of the twelve guards taken hostage received disability compensation. Many suffered significant personality or physical changes. White has noticed a high incidence of cancer among the former guards and rioters.

Bob White remained in institutional corrections until 1985, when he became a parole officer based in Albuquerque. He recalls suffering terrible nightmares for months after the riot, dreaming that he was trying to help the men he knew in Cellblock 4, but could not.

Although unable to view the emotionally troubling images of the riot for about ten years, White is able to describe its events in considerable detail. The best he can say about the experience is that when he faces a bad situation in life today, "I can always think that I had faced a far worse one and survived."

The riot also had a lasting impact on the ninety-four National Guardsmen sent to Santa Fe in February 1980. In addition to Rupert Baca and Kenny Griego, those who served in Battery B included Fernando Baca, Ramón Baca, Elias Castillo, Tom Esquibel, Herman Kaneshiro,

Salomon Moya, Frank Ortega, Joe Peña, Jerry Sánchez, Tony Sánchez, Ronald Sinclair, and Joe Trujillo. These brave men came from all walks of life, including teaching, welding, farming, banking, and working for the Belen city government.

Griego remained in the National Guard for another eleven years, retiring after twenty years of service in 1991. He is also retired from the Belen Public Schools where he worked as a teacher, a coach, the superintendent of schools, and in other administrative roles. Griego suffered difficult episodes immediately after returning to his teaching and coaching duties at Belen High School. He does better now, although he and his old friends from the National Guard seldom discuss the horrors they faced in 1980. As Griego recalls, witnessing the riot and returning to his normal life was "like being thrown into the dark side of the world and coming back to deal with its memory."

Another guardsman, from a different unit (who wishes to remain anonymous), recalls months of nightmares and sleepless nights after returning from Santa Fe. When he did sleep he often woke up thinking he was still at the prison and desperately "running around the house trying to find my fellow guardsmen." Good friends and strong faith helped him recover from what he now realizes was a clear case of Post Traumatic Stress Disorder (PTSD). He retired from the guard after twenty-eight years.

Rupert Baca served in the National Guard for a total of twenty-three years. Fortunately, he did not suffer from nightmares about the riot, although he is still saddened by the memory of convicts who had so little respect for human life. "They would just as soon kill you as look at you," says Baca. Only the state police SWAT team intimidated these cruel men and brought order to the prison after hours of chaos.

State district court judge Tibo J. Chávez played a role in the aftermath of the riot as well. Two of the young men he had sent to the prison for sixty-day diagnostic evaluations returned to his courtroom just five days after the riot had ended. One of the two was John Smith, the convict who had seen his cellmate brutally stabbed to death in Cellblock 4. Judge Chávez told the men that when he had heard that the prison riot had broken out he had uttered a prayer that "nothing would happen to you fellows." The judge said that he was relieved that the two had survived, especially because Smith had been a Marine and "I didn't feel you were the type of person who should be in the penitentiary. I had sent you only for evaluation." Hearing of Smith's terrible experience in Cellblock 4, Chávez sentenced him to one-to-five years in prison, but suspended the sentence and placed him on probation for five years for his crime of contributing to the delinquency of a minor.

The second prisoner's crimes were far more serious, but he had helped put out fires during the riot and had volunteered to help clean up the mess when the riot subsided. Although assistant district attorney Jonathan Zorn asked the judge not to "rush into sentencing as a result of what happened at the state penitentiary," Chávez proceeded to sentence the man to one-to-ten years. As with Smith, his sentence was suspended and he was placed on five year's probation. Judge Chávez hoped that what the men had experienced in the riot was enough to deter further bad behavior. "If nothing else," Chávez declared, "the riot should awaken you to responsibility and reality."

But any hope that the riot might have served as a deterrent to further violence at the Santa Fe prison was not realized. In fact, the post-riot level of violence among prisoners far surpassed the pre-riot violence whether New Mexico convicts were housed at in-state or out-of-state prisons. And, despite millions of dollars spent on investigations and trials, few inmates were found guilty of riot-related crimes. Having already been sent to the prison to serve life terms, those who were found guilty were often simply sentenced to additional life terms.

Valencia County as a whole was affected by the riot when a new 288-bed medium-security prison was built and opened later in 1980. At last prisoners would be evaluated and classified as minimum, medium, or maximum security risks, rather than be mixed together in a single pressure cooker, as had happened before the riot began.

Los Lunas now had two prisons: a minimum-security facility, or honor farm, opened in 1939, and the new medium-security facility located about a mile northwest of the farm. A new prison in Grants (still part of Valencia County until mid-1981) was also opened. New inmates were evaluated in the Grants facility, eliminating the need to send men to the state pen for 60-day diagnostic evaluations. In addition to alleviating major problems in the state's correctional system, the new prisons in Los Lunas and Grants offered new job opportunities for hundreds of Valencia County residents. Correctional officers now received better training and better pay, leading to longer careers and more consistency in their profession.

Within the prisons the Durán Consent Decree was carried out, providing generally improved conditions and more education and job training for inmates interested in changing their lives. The UNM-Valencia Campus offered such training at the medium-security facility in Los Lunas for many years. Unfortunately, the Durán Consent Decree expired in 1999. For better or worse, over 40 percent of the inmates in New Mexico's prisons are now incarcerated in privately run facilities, compared to a national average of 6 percent per state.

And what of the old prison, the scene of so many atrocities in February 1980? Using what remained of the facility, the state housed 400 to 500 inmates in the prison until it was completely closed in 1997. A new maximum-security facility was built nearby, with two control centers, thereby reducing the odds of a control center takeover, as happened in 1980. The old structure still stands. Suggestions for its fate have ranged from making it into a museum, favored by former Governor Gary E. Johnson, to bulldozing it, favored by former Governor Bruce King.

In 2002, a group called the Southwest Ghost Hunters visited the old prison and reportedly detected considerable evidence of paranormal activity, from the slamming of old cell doors to the turning on and off of lights in cellblocks without electricity. In another strange use of the prison, an Albuquerque radio station sponsored a contest in which contestants were challenged to spend time (minutes, not years) in such places as the prison's old gas chamber, its solitary confinement cell, and its notorious Cellblock 4. Contestants of this bizarre reality show returned home with only hair-raising memories as "prizes."

Even New Mexico's expanding movie industry has made use of the prison. Several movies have been shot at the location, including *And God Created Woman* (about a women's prison) in 1988 and a remake of *The Longest Yard* (about an inmates' football team) with Burt Reynolds and Adam Sandler in 2005. At one point the state even offered the prison to any moviemaker who needed a place to blow up in an action scene. No movie companies have taken the offer--yet. Instead, movie props, from giant piñatas to coffins, are now stored in a large shed on the old prison grounds.

It is natural to prefer to forget the prison riot of 1980. Second in deaths only to the Attica, New York, prison riot of September 1971, where thirty-nine prisoners died, the Santa Fe riot is a black mark on the history of New Mexico. But even our darkest history should not be ignored if we are to learn from it and hope not to repeat it. With so many of our residents directly or indirectly tied to the events of February 1980, it is especially important that the people of Valencia County work to ensure that the explosive conditions that caused the Santa Fe riot never occur again, be it in our state prisons, our private prisons, or our local jails.

"Nothing to Lose:" The Helicopter Escape from the State Penitentiary to Mid-Valley Air Park, 1988

by Richard Melzer

The sound of a ringing telephone broke the silence at Charles Bella's Bear Helicopter Corporation office in El Paso, Texas, in early July 1988. Bella's wife Carol took the call, hoping it might be a request for Bella to take someone up in either of the two helicopters in the company's small fleet. The Bellas were especially proud of their five-seat Aerospatiale Gazelle helicopter, purchased from a man in Clovis about three years earlier.

The helicopter chartering business had been good but not always consistent for the ten years Bear Helicopter had been in operation. Most requests for the company's flying services came from TV news reporters on special assignments or from real estate agents wanting to show isolated sections of land to prospective buyers. The price for a chartered flight: $450 per hour in 1988, or $820 per hour in today's money.

This time the call was from a woman who gave her name as Diana Lane. The caller said that she represented a real estate company that wanted to show some ranch land outside Santa Fe. Carol Bella scheduled the trip for Monday morning, July 11, never guessing that this call and a seemingly routine flight would change her and her husband's lives forever.

On Monday, July 11, 43-year-old Charles Bella went through his regular routine in preparation for taking off in his yellow and bronze helicopter to meet his scheduled client in Santa Fe. Bella was proud of both his French-made Gazelle and his own flying skills, based on at least 7,000 hours of flight time accumulated over fifteen years. He had learned to fly in the Army and, later, on his own. Bella's helicopter had recently become famous, thanks to its "supporting" role in the Sylvester Stallone thriller, *Rambo III*. Shot mostly in Arizona in late 1987, the movie featured a high-octane action scene in which Stallone escaped from a Russian prison camp by commandeering a helicopter. Later in the movie Stallone shot down a Russian helicopter (Bella's Gazelle) with an "atomic arrow." Bella served as the stunt pilot.

An Aerospatiale Gazelle Helicopter similar to that owned by Charles Bella (Sud Aviation)

But most of Bella's jobs were not nearly as exciting. A charter flight in Santa Fe certainly seemed routine to an old pro like Bella. The pilot took off at 5:00 a.m. Bella arrived at the Santa Fe Municipal Airport about 7:00 a.m. He refueled with forty gallons of gasoline, good for about two hours of flight, more than enough for the job ahead, or so he thought. Charles Bella drank some coffee, watched some TV in the charter service lounge, and waited for Diana Lane to arrive.

Take-Off from Santa Fe

The first hint that Charles Bella's chartered flight was anything but routine came when he met Diana Lane, an alias for 41-year-old Beverly Shoemaker. Arriving in a Capital City taxi rather than in a company vehicle, the woman hardly looked like a Santa Fe real estate agent. Shoemaker wore a loose-fitting white blouse and red slacks, rather than a business suit; she carried a large, blue duffel bag, rather than an attaché. Bella grew even more suspicious when Shoemaker insisted on sitting in the helicopter's back seat rather than beside him in the front, as most passengers did for a better view and to communicate over the loud sound of the machine's engine and rotor.

And then, about ten minutes into the flight, Charles Bella saw a gun. Shoemaker had taken a .357 Ruger handgun out of her duffel bag and was pointing it directly at the pilot's head. In a husky voice she announced that the real estate she needed to see was located in the exercise yard at the state prison ten miles south of Santa Fe. Three convicts, including Shoemaker's boyfriend, 30-year-old Daniel Mahoney, eagerly awaited the helicopter's arrival. They were planning to escape.

Shoemaker forced Bella to head for the penitentiary, explaining that Mahoney just "couldn't do the time" any longer. Mahoney would turn 31 the next day, and Shoemaker planned to give him his freedom as a birthday gift that went far beyond the proverbial file in a birthday cake. Bella was sure that Mahoney, like so many convicts, had conned this vulnerable woman into a jailhouse romance to curry favors, including the ultimate favor, scheming and assisting in a prison escape.

The odd couple had met through a "pen pals wanted" ad printed in a country western magazine. It was not long until Shoemaker claimed that Mahoney had become her entire life, although she admitted that her "lover" was a "hot-blooded Irishman" with a "quick temper." Like a loyal camp follower, Shoemaker moved from state to state as Mahoney was transferred to prisons in Florida, Arizona, and, by July 1987, New Mexico. In Santa Fe she worked as a nurse's aide when she was not writing Mahoney letters, receiving his frequent phone calls, or visiting him at least twice a week at the prison.

It was during her prison visits that Shoemaker had helped Mahoney plan the bold helicopter escape. If Mahoney or Shoemaker had seen *Rambo III*, with its use of a helicopter in a prison break, they clearly hoped to make life imitate art two months following the movie's May release. Shoemaker had booked the helicopter, had reserved a small plane at the Double Eagle II airport in Albuquerque, had gathered a long list of supplies, and had stolen not one, but two guns from her roommate, leaving her a note that "I need them worse than you do." Everything had gone as planned with the exception of the small plane in Albuquerque, whose owner cancelled at the last minute.

Now the helicopter was heading straight toward the prison. With a gun pointed at his head, Charles Bella saw few options but to fight. He and his female passenger struggled as Bella's helicopter banked dangerously to the left. Bella regained control of the helicopter, but lost control of

Shoemaker's weapon. The prison, with about a hundred inmates in its exercise yard, was now clearly in view.

Daniel Mahoney, inmate #35893-0826, was a desperate man with little to lose by trying a daring escape. Convicted of second-degree murder, armed robbery, and sexual assault in Maryland, he was serving a life plus sixty-year sentence in New Mexico as part of a state-to-state prisoner exchange program. He had already escaped from prisons in 1980 and 1983; his 1980 escape had lasted nearly a year and had included an incredibly violent crime spree in Florida. In each escape Mahoney had been recaptured and incarcerated, but he never tired of planning and attempting new "exit strategies." As he put it, there "ain't nothin' else to do in prison."

The two inmates who waited with Mahoney for Bella's helicopter to arrive were equally desperate characters. Francis Preston Mitchell and Randy Mack Lackey faced long prison terms with little hope for parole. Mitchell, 27, was serving a life sentence for a drug-related murder he'd committed in Utah in 1984; he'd been transferred to Santa Fe in June 1986. Randy Lackey, 36, was serving a nine-year sentence for larceny; he had stolen a small plane in Clovis and had flown it over 400 miles to his hometown in Muleshoe, Texas, where he was captured and returned to New Mexico to face charges in 1986. Having served time for auto theft, Lackey listed his occupation as "race car driver." Found guilty of stealing the small plane in Clovis, Lackey was sent to the minimum security section of the Central New Mexico Correctional Facility in Los Lunas to serve his sentence. A year later two books, entitled *Flying the Helicopter* and *Mexico Flight Plan*, had been found in Lackey's possession. Now considered an escape risk, prison officials had reclassified Lackey and had sent him to the state penitentiary in Santa Fe in late 1987. With or without his confiscated books, Lackey continued to scheme his escape.

Mahoney, Mitchell, and Lackey had planned their daredevil escape while living in adjoining cells among sixty convicts housed in Cell Block 5, a medium-security section of the state penitentiary. The three undoubtedly planned their group escape less out of friendship than from a need to eventually divert searchers in three directions rather than just one.

Daring Escape

At approximately 10:50 a.m., pilot Bella cleared the prison's ten-feet-high razor wire-topped double fence and followed Shoemaker's directions to land near first base on the exercise yard's baseball diamond. Waiting at this designated spot, Mahoney, Mitchell, and Lackey jumped on board the moment the helicopter touched down.

But the combined weight of a pilot, four passengers, and Shoemaker's heavy duffel bag was too much for the helicopter to lift off easily. One escapee jumped out to reduce the weight, running alongside the helicopter until it gradually began to climb, when he leapt back on board. Seeing a once-in-a-lifetime opportunity, a fourth inmate grabbed the rising helicopter's skids, but was gruffly pushed off as the helicopter gained altitude.

Taken by surprise, guards in two watch towers opened fire on Bella's helicopter and the escaping convicts. But the guards' marksmanship and weapons were ineffective. One fatigued guard on his second sixteen-hour shift later recalled that he "attempted to fire, but there wasn't a round in the chamber and I guess I froze." Another guard did not fire because she feared she might hit other inmates in the crossfire. To this day, Bella says that he is thankful that the prison guards had poor weapons and were such "lousy shots."

Only one shot hit its mark, causing little damage to Bella's helicopter. Prison-issued weapons were clearly meant to deter escapes on the ground, not in the air. Ironically, new electronic equipment and additional fencing had recently been installed at the prison in reaction to a ground breakout that had occurred almost exactly one year earlier, on Independence Day, 1987. Recalling the well-executed helicopter escape on July 11, 1988, correctional officer James Salazar declared, "It was the smoothest thing I've ever seen. It was just like a movie."

Once airborne, the escapees quickly handcuffed Bella to the controls of his helicopter and ordered him to fly south. Their plan was simple: to land at a small airport, steal a plane, and fly it to freedom in Mexico. With few small airports to choose from, the convicts forced Bella to fly eighty miles south to Mid-Valley Air Park in Valencia County.

Events Unfold at Mid-Valley Air Park

Jack Wood had built Mid-Valley Air Park on his own Los Chávez farmland, starting in 1968. Two years later he had completed two landing strips, some hangers, and an office, with plans to build thirty homes in a residential community where plane-owning families could live, house their small aircraft, and, in Wood's words, "taxi right up to their front doors." By 1988, the quiet community, located between the Rio Grande to the east and the Santa Fe Railway tracks and State Road 314 to the west, had become exactly what Wood had envisioned two decades earlier.

The air park was built directly across from the New Mexico Honor Farm and within three miles of a new medium-security prison, built in 1980. Some observers wondered why an air park had been built so close to the honor farm. Law officials pointed out that inmates at the farm were classified as low security risks and far less likely to escape than medium or maximum security inmates. Escapes from the honor farm occurred, but escapees were most likely to flee as fast and as far as they could, seldom lingering in the prison's immediate residential area.

The trio of convicts who escaped from Santa Fe in 1988 had had nothing to do with the honor farm, although Randy Lackey undoubtedly remembered Mid-Valley Air Park from his days at the nearby Central New Mexico Correctional Facility. He and his cohorts knew that if they got as far as Mid-Valley they might confiscate a plane that Bella or Lackey could use to fly them to freedom in Mexico.

Learning of the daring, mid-morning helicopter escape from Santa Fe, state policemen were ordered to watch all local airports. Three state policemen were already at Mid-Valley when Bella's helicopter appeared in the sky and came in for a landing about 11:00 a.m. All three convicts fled from the plane, heading in different directions. Mahoney fled on foot, heading east into the thick bosque along the Rio Grande. Lackey searched for an escape vehicle near the hangers on the east side of the airport's runway. Gerald Arnold and his 8-year-old son Daniel saw Lackey by their Ford F-150 and asked what he needed. Replying "just looking," Lackey proceeded across the road, found a beat up old pickup belonging to W.B. "Mack" Makison, spotted keys in the ignition, and sped off.

Lackey, who still fancied himself a race car driver, headed north on old

Highway 85 and then east on Courthouse Road in Los Lunas. With the police in close pursuit, the escapee turned north on Los Lentes and east on Main St., traveling as fast as ninety miles-per-hour. Weaving through traffic while trying to run police cars off the road, Lackey finally sped out of control near the southwest corner of the Los Lunas bridge over the Rio Grande. Police cars converged on the spot, cornering Lackey's stolen pickup and shooting two rounds into the old truck's radiator to disable it permanently. Ordered out of the vehicle and onto the ground, Lackey was back in custody just moments after his car race to freedom had begun.

Meanwhile, back at Mid-Valley, Francis Mitchell had jumped back into the helicopter and had ordered Bella to takeoff. But Bella's takeoff was blocked. A U.S. Customs Service Blackhawk helicopter had arrived and now attempted to prevent Bella's departure by hovering about a hundred feet above his helicopter's takeoff path. A Customs Service agent on board the Blackhawk fired his automatic weapon at the Gazelle, its pilot, and its convict passenger. Somehow Bella maneuvered below the Blackhawk and lifted off with only inches to spare in a scene that might well have appeared in another Rambo action flick.

With Mahoney racing through the bosque and Mitchell and Bella flying north in Bella's Gazelle, the convicts' bold escape seemed like it might actually succeed for at least two of the three fugitives.

Chase Over Albuquerque

Joined by a state police Huey helicopter, the Blackhawk pursued Bella's Gazelle in a wild aerial chase over Albuquerque. At one point, Bella landed at Coronado airport, but, seeing policemen on the ground, Mitchell ordered the pilot to take off again. Desperate about the safest course to take without drawing more gunfire, Mitchell even asked Bella if he had enough fuel to fly back to Santa Fe to drop him off in the same prison yard from which he had fled just hours before. Bella replied that their fuel tank was nearly empty.

In perhaps the strangest pursuit in New Mexico criminal history, the renegade chopper crisscrossed over Albuquerque's two malls, downtown district, and eastern foothills. TV news helicopters joined law enforcement vehicles in the increasingly crowded sky. Bella flew as low as fifty feet above the ground. Many watched the spectacle from below. Bob White of Belen recalls seeing the aircraft racing by windows at the old Bernalillo courthouse.

Chased at dangerously close range by the state police Huey to his left and the Customs Service Blackhawk to his right, Bella finally landed at the Albuquerque International Airport. Major John Denko, a thirteen-year state police veteran who piloted the Huey, recalls that he and the Blackhawk's crew "hung close" to Bella. "We knew he had to set down because he was running low on fuel."

According to Bella, Mitchell was so concerned for his safety that he had Bella land near the passenger terminal so the convict's surrender would "at least be in front of witnesses in case the police tried to gun him down." Once landed, Mitchell quickly exited the helicopter, threw up his hands, and assumed a prone position as eight police officers closed in. The time was 11:38 a.m. The forty minute chase from Mid-Valley Air Park was over. Mitchell and the previously captured Lackey were back in Santa Fe—in maximum security lockdown—by nightfall.

Chasing Mahoney

Back in Valencia County, a huge manhunt had been organized to search for the last escapee on the loose, Daniel Mahoney. State policemen were joined by as many as 150 officers from seven police agencies, including Bosque Farms, Los Lunas, Belen, and the county sheriff's office. National Guardsmen were deployed, as were a SWAT team and New Mexico state corrections personnel. Seven roadblocks were set up on routes as far south as Socorro. Alerts were broadcast on police radios across the state.

Lawmen in Valencia County searched in police cars and on horseback. Others scoured the region in three helicopters and two small planes. An airboat was launched to patrol the Rio Grande and bloodhounds were set loose, although reporter Ernie Mills factiously suggested that birddogs might have been more appropriate in finding a convict who had used aerial flight to make his dramatic escape.

Mahoney was armed with the same Ruger handgun his girlfriend had used to hijack Charles Bella's helicopter hours before. Mahoney stood 6 feet tall, weighed 175 pounds, and sported two tattoos: a marijuana leaf on one hand and the word "Mom" on an upper shoulder. Photos of the suspect were distributed to all law enforcement officers employed in the hunt.

Hearing of events at Mid-Valley Air Park, nearby residents were on high alert. Eleanor Love, who lived at the air park with her pilot husband John, recalls going to her backyard vegetable garden and suddenly realizing that the escapee might well be hidden in the bushes by her fence. Eleanor backed all the way to her kitchen door, "not daring to turn my back to anyone who might be there." She wisely remained indoors the rest of the day. Her neighbors were equally prudent. Police created a special phone number for people to call if they observed suspicious behavior.

Residents reported sighting Mahoney at various locations throughout the afternoon and evening. A man fitting Mahoney's description caused alarm when he was spotted near the Tomé Community Park. It turned out to be a false alarm when a sheriff's reserve officer identified the suspect as a local resident. Across the river in Los Chávez neighbors reported hearing gunshots about 3:00 p.m., but the police thought the sound might have been made by boys shooting bottle rockets. Forty-five minutes later another man was seen hiding under a car, but he was not Mahoney. A hitchhiker was also picked up on I-25, although his ID verified that he was from out-of-state and was just passing through.

Meanwhile, Mahoney's girlfriend, Beverly Shoemaker, was found hiding in a hanger at Mid-Valley, but refused to talk to police about her lover's whereabouts, if she in fact knew it. She later vowed that her love for Mahoney was so deep that she would aid in his escape all over again.

In the most comical episode of the day, a Camaro sped through a roadblock on Route 47. Police cars pursued, following the sports car into a parking lot south of the old Ranchers State Bank at the Valencia Y. The police discovered that the car belonged to a female bank employee who was apparently speeding because she was late returning to work after taking an afternoon break.

When no leads had panned out before sunset, authorities kept twenty-five searchers and two helicopters with search lights on duty well into the night. The searchers' luck began to change on the Los Lunas bridge shortly after midnight. Patrolman Roy Creek of the Los Lunas Police Department and Marc Lee of the New Mexico Mounted Police had been assigned to watch the bridge and the river bank below it. Creek, a fifteen-month veteran of the local police force, heard rustling in the brush before seeing Mahoney dash under the bridge. Creek chased the fugitive several hundred yards before he finally subdued the convict. Fearing for his life, Mahoney shouted that he no longer had a weapon. Creek reported that Mahoney "didn't give me any problem." He was easily handcuffed and was soon handed over to correction officials for transit to Santa Fe. Hailed as a hero, Creek modestly told reporters, "I think the mosquitoes and the heat got the best of him." Ironically, Mahoney was captured close to where fellow escapee Randy Lackey had been apprehended following his car chase through Los Lunas earlier in the day.

And so one of the boldest prison escapes in New Mexico history was over some fourteen hours after it had begun. Local newspapers covered the escape in great detail, with maps, timelines, photos, editorials, and even political cartoons in the *Albuquerque Journal* and the *Albuquerque Tribune*. The incident also drew considerable national attention, including TV coverage by Dan Rather on the CBS evening news and by Tom Brokaw on NBC. Reporters interviewed Beverly Shoemaker from jail in an eight-minute segment of Maury Povich's TV show, *A Current Affair*. (Shoemaker later married Daniel Mahoney, but they eventually divorced.)

Newspapers from as far east as New York and as far west as Los Angeles carried the story, as did legendary radio journalist Paul Harvey. Harvey mistakenly reported that the escape took place in Arizona, perhaps forgetting that New Mexico exists, as many out-of-staters are prone to do.

Bella Charged

A strange case became even stranger when state police went so far as to arrest Charles Bella, charging him with several counts of conspiracy and assisting in an escape from the state penitentiary, all felony crimes in New Mexico. The authorities simply did not believe Bella's account that his helicopter had been hijacked and that he had been an unwilling participant in both planning the escape and carrying it out. Outraged by these charges, Bella insisted that he was innocent. The pilot protested that "I never got so much as a parking ticket in New Mexico." In fact, he had just recently worked for the police, using his helicopter to help search for marijuana farms in Catron County. Catron County Sheriff Vern Mullins, now retired in Belen, remembers that Bella had found an enormous farm with about 15,000 marijuana plants, a large water tank, and a circus-sized tent.

Eager to clear his name in the prison escape case, Bella hired the best legal talent he could find. Bella secured the services of the world famous lawyer—and fellow helicopter pilot—F. Lee Bailey. In an aggressive defense, Bailey argued that Bella had been forced to participate in the escape and was, in fact, handcuffed to his instrument panel through most of the ordeal. In Bella's admiring words, Bailey "really slammed it to them."

After a nine-day trial, the jury deliberated just three hours before returning a not-guilty verdict on August 24, 1989. To this day Bella claims that the jury would have come back sooner but stayed out long enough for one last free meal. Bailey was so sure of the trial's outcome that he left town before the verdict was read. Bella traveled home to El Paso, making sure that he flew his helicopter over the Santa Fe state pen for spite.

Infuriated that the government had brought him to trial, Bella eventually sued two Custom Service agents for their use of excessive force against a victimized citizen. Bella contested that government agents had endangered his life by firing at his helicopter with semi-automatic weapons when they could plainly see that he was being held captive and was handcuffed as he attempted to take off from Mid-Valley Air Park. Bella lost his case in 1992, but still insists that government agents should be made more accountable for their dangerous actions and damaging accusations.

The day prison convicts hijacked a helicopter and escaped to Mid-Valley Air Park will long be remembered in the annals of New Mexico penal history. While not as famous as Billy the Kid's escape from the Lincoln County jail on April 28, 1881, the helicopter caper was listed by the *Albuquerque Journal* as one of New Mexico's 112 worst blunders or mishaps of the twentieth century.

Reporter Dana Bowley was one of many Valencia County residents who vividly remembers the incident. Bowley recalls that the foiled escape occurred on his first day working at the *Valencia County News-Bulletin*. After several hectic hours covering the story, Bowley told his new boss that "if it was going to be like this every day they were doing to have to pay me more." Bowley didn't get the pay raise, but then no day was ever as exciting or as exhausting while he remained at the *Valencia County News-Bulletin*.

Perhaps someday someone will see fit to place a historical marker at the Mid-Valley Air Park to commemorate the events of 1988. If that day ever comes, the marker might read:

Mid-Valley Air Park

Here, on July 11, 1988, three convicts, one girlfriend,
and a hijacked pilot landed in a helicopter following a bold
escape from the New Mexico State Penitentiary in Santa Fe.
All three convicts (and the girlfriend) were captured
within fourteen hours. The bizarre ordeal remains one of the
most famous aerial escapes in American history.
It is certainly among the most exciting days in the
colorful history of the Rio Abajo.

Section II—Miracles, Mysteries, and Disappearances

The Los Lunas Mystery Stone

by John Taylor

The Los Lunas Mystery Stone (Thorton Schwenk)

There is an eighty-ton boulder in a small hollow on the southeast side of Hidden Mountain looking out over the Rio Puerco about sixteen miles west of Los Lunas. The flat face of the boulder is covered with nine lines containing 216 carved characters. This bit of epigraphy has puzzled historians and researchers for more than a century.

Was this inscribed in a Greek-Phoenician script in 500 B.C by a Greek traveler to North America named Zakyneros? Or is it a combination of Phoenician, Hebrew, and Cyrillic inscribed around 2000 B. C. by ancestors of the Navajo or Acoma Indians who may have been fleeing an eruption of Mount Taylor? How about a version of the Ten Commandments written by one of the Lost Tribes of Israel in Paleo-Hebrew? Or is it simply a clever forgery perpetrated by a linguist named Muñiz during the 1776 Domínguez-Escalante expedition or by a college student who came through in the early twentieth century? Each of these has been suggested as an explanation for the mysterious carvings.

The site itself has been documented by the State of New Mexico as the location of a fourteenth-century pueblo with living structures, kivas, and petroglyphs; but the first written documentation of the stone is in 1933 when Professor Frank Hibben, a University of New Mexico archeologist, wrote about it. He stated that he had been led to the site by an Indian who had first found it as a child in the 1880s. Local legend (perhaps from the same source that Hibben used) said that the first identification of the stone was in the 1850s, although some have said that the stone was first noticed by Mexican settlers around 1800. There are also reports that the landowner Franz Huning knew of the site as early as 1871.

Hibben himself espoused the Ten Commandment thesis, but his somewhat shady reputation for archeological fraud tended to discount his writing on the subject. Because of repeated visits and well-intentioned attempts to "clean" the engraving, there is no in-place patina or evidence to help modern-day scholars accurately date the engraving.

Suggestions of Pre-Columbian travel to North America are not unique to New Mexico. There are a number of other stone carvings across the United States that have been variously associated with Viking explorers, travelers from the Mediterranean cultures, and others. According to the proponents of the Zakyneros theory, this native of Samos in the eastern Mediterranean, was perhaps an exiled citizen who somehow found his way to North America and then New Mexico during a time when the area was much more verdant and tree-covered than the high desert of today. Advocates of this theory translate the message on the stone as describing Zakyneros's struggles to escape those who apparently killed his companions and of his harvest of plants and fish from in and around a "swiftly flowing" Rio Puerco. Their translation is:

> I have come to this place to stay. The other one met with an untimely death one year ago, dishonored, insulted, and stripped of flesh; the men thought him to be an object of care, whom I looked after, considered crazed, wandering in mind, to be tossed about as if in a wind; to perish, streaked with blood. On Samos I was respected and honored, of blessed lot or fortune, with a body of slaves, and so many olive trees; also, and I planted them, a peg to hang anything upon. Men punished me with exile to exact retribution for a debt, meanwhile I remain or stay a hare. I, Zakyneros, just as a soothsayer or prophet, out of reach of mortal man, I am fleeing and am very afraid. I am dross, scum refuge, just as on board ship, a soft effeminate sailor is flogged with an animal's hide or all who speak incorrectly or offensively are lashed or beaten with a cane; but after a little, or a very short time, the hurtful and destructive ones may be sated; at an unseasonable time I remain to protect from the west, many south or southwest winds, the ravine. Very much harvest is gathered in, very much in the woody dell and glen, very many bags of young deer. Very many bands or hides with delicate, luxuriant hair, by the channel of a river, swift flowing. Very much is given by the gods for again and again, at the unreasonable time I become gaunt from hunger.

Skeptics argue that there is no supporting evidence of encampment or occupation of the area that would lead one to believe that the area was occupied by Greeks—no pottery shards, no bronze points, etc.—but, admittedly, it has been a very long time since his purported visit!

The Paleo-Indian proponents translated the text by reading it aloud in the Phoenician dialect and noting similarities to the Navajo language. They then translated the Navajo language to get a text that describes a battle and its aftermath around Hidden Mountain and the Rio Puerco. This "translation" reads as follows:

> We retreated while under attack, continually moving ahead; then we traveled over the surface of the water, then we climbed without eating. They surrounded us from above, some hiding among rocks, scattered and alone, while part of them remained together, and took us by surprise. We found that they were afraid, so we did a fearful thing to them, for their coming against us. Just when we were greatly in need of water, we had rain. They were surprised to see us wearing shoes for crossing the land along the trail behind us. It is good hanging down the meat and it was soon ready. We were grateful for what they gave us to carry away. Although we were afraid, we proceeded to the river, throwing our bodies and feet in the water, and bringing water back to the others who carried the burdens in the hot sun as they climbed the side of the hill. Then an omen or sign in front of us on the slope or lodge, pointed at us to stop and camp. Then we found something still farther on. It was on the shore of the river. It was discovered that they were all meeting us to help us build and get our dwellings ready. In the water we sat down and camped on the surface above where we took land. We were about to run away, but found they went about the land, and we found there was a change of weather on the land.

This theory is unsupported by archeology relative to the Paleo-Indians in the southwest. First of all, the last eruption of Mt. Taylor is dated to between 1.5 and 3.3 million years ago; and, the Athabascan nomads (Apaches and Navajos) did not appear until the fourteenth century. In addition, there is no evidence for any form of writing for earlier Native

Americans. Pictographs and petroglyphs are common, but nothing else of the runic or alphabetical variety has been found in the area.

Those who refer to the engravings as the Ten Commandments or Decalogue suggest that the text contains an abbreviated version of the precepts from the Old Testament, perhaps written by one of the Lost Tribes of Israel, by exiled Samaritans, or by some of the peoples whom the Mormons believed populated the continent in ancient times. Advocates of this interpretation of the text translate it as follows:

> I am Yahweh thy God who brought thee out of the land of Egypt, out of the house of bondage. There shall not be unto them other Gods before me. Thou shalt not make unto thee a graven image. Thou shalt not take the name of Yahweh in vain. Remember the day of the Sabbath to sanctify it. Honor thy father and thy mother that thy days be long on the soil which Yahweh thy God giveth thee. Thou shalt not kill. Thou shalt not commit adultery. Thou shalt not steal. Thou shalt not testify falsely against thy neighbor. Thou shalt not covet thy neighbor's wife.

One theory is that King Solomon used some of his enormous wealth to underwrite a Hebrew-Phoenician world exploration and that some of his explorers wound up here in the Land of Enchantment. Although the prevailing opinion among experts is that the language is a form of ancient Hebrew, an argument against the great antiquity of the engraving is that some of the word order and apparent punctuation on the engraving are inconsistent with the rendering of the Decalogue in ancient Hebrew and that textual errors and apparently modern insertions suggest a more recent origin for the inscription.

Of course, the easy answer is to simply cry forgery. But why would a linguist-forger clever enough to craft such an engraving put it in such a remote location? Wouldn't he or she want the world to find and read his or her work? That question notwithstanding, there are at least four credible possibilities for forgeries. The first of these is a linguist and translator named Andres Muñiz who came from Bernalillo, New Mexico, and traveled into the Great Basin with the 1776 Domínguez-Escalante expedition. Frustrated at his treatment by other members of the expedition, Muñiz may have carved the inscription from the Old

Testament rather than the New as a subtle way of getting back at the friars who had annoyed him. Alternatively, it is possible that Muñiz may have been one of many so-called *conversos* or "crypto-Jews," individuals that had nominally adopted Catholicism to avoid the perils of the Inquisition but who maintained their Jewish faith and practices in secret. This is suggested because the surname Muñiz, a variant of Muñoz, is among surnames of Jewish families in Spain and Portugal in the fourteenth and fifteenth centuries. In any event, Muñiz's presence in the area is suggested by his initials, "A.M.," carved in a rock about fifty feet away from the Mystery Stone itself.

A second possibility is that a member of the 1847 Mormon Battalion who traveled through the area during the Mexican-American War carved the inscription as a way of perhaps enhancing the possibility that it would someday be discovered and used to support the tenets of Joseph Smith and Brigham Young as written in The Book of Mormon. However, to date, no member of the battalion has been identified as a scholar of ancient Hebrew; and the Mormon church has rejected this theory.

A third possibility is that a scholar of ancient languages from an eastern university, perhaps Harvard or Yale, traveled to New Mexico in the late 1920s or early 1930s and forged the inscription on the isolated rock. He or she then "bought off" a local Indian to lead Hibben to the site (after enough time had lapsed for the engraving to age a bit) and told him to tell the archeologist about "finding the site as a child." Hibben would have been predisposed to accept an "ancient explanation" and so would be susceptible to the inference of great antiquity. This fraud could also have been perpetrated by a professional "enemy" of Hibben or by a disgruntled student at the University of New Mexico.

Finally, there is the possibility that Hibben himself created the inscription to further his own career and reputation. He knew the language and script and could have created the "backstory" to support it. The reports of earlier sightings could simply refer to the petroglyphs which are at the site.

Frank Hibben (University of New Mexico)

Whatever the explanation, the Mystery Stone remains a strange and mysterious sentinel in Rio Abajo history. Its origin remains one of the most often asked questions by tourists to the area to this day.

Isleta Pueblo and the Lady in Blue

by John Taylor

The Spanish friars at Isleta were confused. Jumano Indians from east of the Manzano Mountains, whom they had never seen before and who they were sure had never been visited by other Franciscans, were at the gates of the Church of San Antonio — rebuilt later as St. Augustine — asking to receive the sacraments and requesting priests to come and establish a mission in their lands. How did they know that sacraments even existed?

When queried, the Indians said that they had learned about these things from "the Lady in Blue." This woman, they said, was dressed in brown and cream-colored robes with a blue cape. She came to them on several occasions, telling them stories from the Scriptures and urging them to go to the mission and ask to receive the sacraments. Word had also percolated through the Spanish Catholic and political hierarchy about a cloistered nun in a small convent in Ágreda, Spain, who had told her confessor about ecstatic visions in which she was "bilocated" and transported to the New World to preach to the Indians. Her confessor, unable to keep this secret, told others, and the story spread like wildfire.

The nun, Sister María de Jesús de Ágreda, was born in 1602 and donned the veil of the Catholic order of Conceptionists at the age of 16. She later told of a play she saw at age 7, based on *The New World Unveiled by Christopher Columbus*, by playwright Lope de Vega. From then on, she felt a great missionary zeal to journey to the New World to preach. Instead of traveling, however, she decided to devote her life to Christ.

Inside the convent, María de Ágreda's enthusiasm for the New World combined with her deep contemplative prayer life seemed to lead her across the ocean where she met the people and places she had longed to visit. Interviewed afterwards, she noted specific details of the terrain, weather, and a people called the Jumanos. She said there was no language barrier between her and the Jumanos, and described a particular Jumano chief named Tuerto, so named because he had only one eye. Her sisters at Ágreda reported that during some of her ecstatic trances she actually levitated in her cell. The nuns also confirmed that she had never left the convent.

The Lady in Blue preaching to the Jumanos in their own language (Convent of the Conception, Ágreda, Spain)

In 1626, the Franciscan Minister General in Spain wrote to the Archbishop of México, Don Francisco de Manso y Zuniga:

> It is very probable that in the course of the discovery of New Mexico and the conversion of those souls, there will soon be found a kingdom including the Chillescas, Jumanos, and Carbucos, more than four hundred leagues from the city of Mexico to the west and north, between New Mexico and La Quivira. It will be of assistance to learn if there is any knowledge of our holy faith, and in what manner our Lord has manifested it.

Archbishop Manso was familiar with the Jumanos. He also knew that many explorers had searched for a legendary place called "Quivira." As Manso had heard it reported, Quivira's distance from Mexico City was about four hundred leagues to the northwest, the same approximate location the Spanish nun had identified to her confessor. Manso was keen to investigate the nun's visions. In 1628, he appointed Padre Estéban de Perea to head the New Mexico mission work, a post most recently filled by Alonso de Benavides. Archbishop Manso prepared a letter of inquiry to Benavides, dated May 18, 1628. In it, Manso ordered Benavides and the missionaries to inquire among the natives from Texas, which Sister María had called "Tixtlas," to see if they showed previous knowledge of the faith, and, if so, to research these claims.

Perea hand-carried this letter to Benavides in 1628. Ironically, Benavides, too, was familiar with the Jumanos from the plains to the east. Each year he had visited Isleta, they had presented themselves at the mission of San Antonio requesting baptism and the establishment of a mission at their encampment many days' journey away. "I didn't have enough clerics, and so I continued to put off the Jumanos . . . until God should send me more workers," Benavides reported later to his superiors.

In July 1629, fifty Jumanos arrived at the mission and restated their request. Although Benavides had not yet left, Perea, as the new *custos*, received them this time. Recalling the archbishop's inquiry, Perea asked them why they had come. For baptism, they answered, at the urging of the Lady in Blue. To further reinforce María's visions, the leader of the Jumano delegation was named Tuerto!

Immediately, Perea and Benavides sent a delegation to the Jumano pueblos where they were received with a procession led by a cross garlanded with flowers. The natives explained that this was the way the Lady in Blue had told them to greet the priests. Within a few weeks the priests had baptized several thousand Indians.

Although María's "visits" to the New World ended in 1623, interest in her bilocations continued. She was visited and severely questioned twice by members of the Inquisition who eventually cleared her of any witchcraft or wrongdoing. She also established a twenty-two-year correspondence with King Phillip IV of Spain. She was promoted to abbess of her convent and wrote a number of treatises, including a lengthy work entitled *The Mystical City of God—A Divine History of the Mother of God*. This volume, controversial at the time because of its strong advocacy for the doctrine of the Immaculate Conception, continues to be revered by Catholic theologians the world over.

Sister María de Ágreda, the Lady in Blue, died in her beloved Ágreda in 1665. Her legacy lives on in the Rio Abajo.

Father Padilla's Mysterious Rising Coffin at Isleta

by Richard Melzer

Interior of the Church of San Agustín at Isleta circa 1900, showing the altar (Museum of New Mexico, #015590)

There is a mystery in Isleta. It's a mystery that has persisted for more than two centuries and has yet to be completely solved. It is the mystery of Father Padilla's grave near the altar of St. Augustine Church.

Cause of Death

Actually, there are several mysteries involving Father Padilla. The first has to do with Father Padilla's true identity and the cause of his death. According to some sources, the Franciscan missionary buried to the right of the altar at St. Augustine is Father Juan Francisco Padilla who accompanied Francisco Coronado when that intrepid explorer led a Spanish expedition through today's Southwest in the 1540s. After two years of finding much Indian resistance and little in gold and silver,

Coronado returned to Mexico, leaving three missionaries to continue their efforts to convert the native population to the Catholic faith.

Father Juan Francisco Padilla was one of the missionaries who willingly stayed behind. But without Spanish soldiers to protect them, Father Padilla and his fellow Franciscans became the first Catholic martyrs in New Mexico history. According to legend, Father Padilla was killed by nomadic Indians and unceremoniously buried in an isolated cave in the mountains. Years later, after the Spanish had returned to conquer and settle New Mexico, the Indians of Isleta Pueblo reportedly suffered a severe drought. Remembering the story of Father Padilla's fate, Isleta Pueblo leaders met in council and decided that Father Padilla's spirit may have caused the drought because his body had never been properly buried in the holy ground of the Catholic Church. To placate the priest's spirit and end the drought, Father Padilla's remains would have to be found and brought to Isleta for a formal Catholic burial among Christians. Father Padilla's body was therefore found in its primitive resting place, dug up, and transported down from the mountains to Isleta for burial.

Until the nineteenth century, many Catholics in New Mexico were buried in the holy ground of church interiors. Those buried closest to the altar were especially blessed—for a slightly higher fee. The floor nearest the altar was reserved for deceased priests, clearly deserving of the holiest of holy ground. And so it was that Father Padilla's recovered remains were buried by the altar at St. Augustine on the side closest to the church's pulpit. The drought reportedly ended shortly thereafter.

But some contend that this account of who the buried priest at Isleta was and how he died is simply a myth. According to a second version of the story, the Father Padilla who was buried by the altar at St. Augustine was Father Juan José Padilla, a priest assigned to the San Juan Mission at Laguna Pueblo from 1733 to 1755. But why would a priest from Laguna be buried in Isleta? Some believe that Father Padilla was simply traveling through Isleta when he became ill and died of natural causes. Or perhaps the priest had grown ill and gone to Isleta to seek the care of a fellow Spaniard, Father Pasqual Sospedra, the Franciscan then serving at the Isleta mission. In either case, Father Padilla did not recover. He expired on February 5, 1756.

Others believe that Father Juan José Padilla may have faced a more insidious end. Supposedly, he had ventured out on a snowy night to hear the confession of a man who may have been close to death. Losing his way home in the winter storm, the priest stopped at a house and was welcomed by a woman who offered him a cup of coffee. He was drinking the warm coffee when the woman's husband arrived, drunk and angered that he had lost at a game of cards. Taking his anger out on his wife and Father Padilla, the man reportedly cursed the woman and stabbed the priest with a knife. Terrified, the woman screamed, "¡El Padre! El Padre!" Now more frightened than angry, the man carried Father Padilla's body outside and put it on his saddled horse. The murderer tied the priest's boots in the stirrups and his hands to the saddle's pommel. Slapping the horse's rump, the man sent the animal and its lifeless rider into the night.

On the following morning, a woman in Isleta was out drawing water from a well when she noticed a strange horse standing idly by the gate to the churchyard. Father Padilla's slumping body was still tied to the horse's saddle. Told of this horrific sight, Father Sospedra hurried to the church gate to untie his fellow priest and bring his corpse into the church. Father Sospedra dutifully prepared the body, said a funeral Mass, and buried Father Padilla at the side of the altar in St. Augustine that same day. Without mentioning the cause of death, Father Sospedra carefully noted the burial in his church record book.

The Rising Coffin

Father Padilla's true identity and manner of death are mystery enough, but this is only where our story begins. The important historical questions we have asked dim in comparison to the larger mystery of Father Padilla's cadaver and coffin. It seems that Father Padilla's coffin developed a habit of rather regularly rising from the ground where it had been buried!

The coffin reportedly rose from the ground at least five times—in 1775, 1819, 1889, 1895, and 1914. Those who witnessed one or more of these levitations have wondered if they should be considered religious miracles, natural phenomena, or symbolic messages from the dead priest and his unsettled spirit. Many residents of Isleta believed the last interpretation. They felt that, regardless of which Father Padilla is buried in their church, he died a violent death. As a result, his spirit remained restless, causing it to wander through the streets of Isleta at night and to force the dead priest's body to rise to the surface quite regularly. The priest's body was likely to rise when Father Padilla's spirit was most upset with the pueblo for one reason or another.

On at least two occasions, Father Padilla's spirit reportedly grew upset with the people of Isleta when some residents entered St. Augustine and performed their ancient traditional dances in the church. Witnessing one such event on Christmas Eve in 1889, Pablo Abeyta and others from Isleta said that they heard a loud noise from beneath the altar while the Indians danced. It was someone kicking from below the wooden floor. The noise grew so loud and shook the altar so violently that the dancers fled from the church in fright.

Investigations

With time, church leaders grew curious about Father Padilla's mysterious behavior. They launched two official investigations, about seventy-five years apart. The first of these occurred in 1819 when Father Francisco de Hozio, the leading Franciscan in New Mexico, visited St. Augustine. Inspecting Father Padilla's burial site, Father Hozio described how the priest's corpse was "by slow degrees … raising itself up from the very depth in which it was buried." In fact, by the time Father Hozio arrived on the scene, Father Padilla's coffin, made from the hollowed-out trunk of a cottonwood tree, was clearly showing through the surface of the floor.

Eager to investigate, Father Hozio ordered that Father Padilla's body be exhumed as soon as possible. To help in this morbid task, Father Hozio called on no fewer than six fellow priests and five leading *vecinos* (settlers) of the Rio Abajo. Placing Father Padilla's exhumed body on a table, those present found the corpse dressed in the blue woolen habit of the Franciscan order. The habit was so old and decayed that "it became dust at the touch." However, upon close examination the group discovered that the body itself was so well preserved that a wound behind one ear was still noticeable and thought to be the cause of death. This observation added credence to the theory that the body belonged to Father Juan José Padilla and that he had been murdered with a knife to his neck in 1756.

Father Padilla's body was reportedly in such good condition and gave out such a "pleasing smell" like "the earth smells when it is watered" that "even the women and children … admire it without terror." Unwilling (or unable) to offer his opinion of why Father Padilla had risen to the surface, Father Hozio saw to it that Father Padilla was dressed in a new habit, given a solemn Mass, placed back in his coffin, and reburied in the same spot with a note of explanation placed on his chest. Translated from Spanish, Father Hozio's note read:

> This is the body of Father Juan José Padilla, Religious Priest, former Missionary in-charge of the Mission of St. Joseph of Laguna; seventy-six years, a little more, are counted since his passing, up to this date, and with this one it is the third time that he is buried, being the second that he has risen to the surface of the ground.

After more than two months on public display, Father Padilla's body was buried once more. Isleta's church bells announced the solemn occasion.

After several more mysterious "uprisings" in the nineteenth century, church officials ordered another exhumation of Father Padilla's remains in 1895. Archbishop Placido Luis Chapelle gathered a special committee for the new inspection, including eight priests, four local residents, and the "very able" Dr. William Ruben Tipton. With Dr. Tipton along, it appeared that the church sought a more scientific explanation for Father Padilla's restless behavior over the decades.

But if scientific conclusions were its goal, Archbishop Chapelle's committee of 1895 was no more successful that Father Hozio's of 1819. Although Dr. Tipton was requested to record his observations, his report has yet to be found. The committee was only more objective in its measurements of Father Padilla's corpse (5 feet), the size of his feet (7 inches each), and the dimensions of his coffin (6 feet, 7 inches by 17 inches). The group also interviewed six Isletans who had witnessed Father Padilla's strange comings and goings on one or more occasions in the previous years.

The Chapelle committee finished its work by reporting its findings in writing and placing a copy of its report in a metal box to be buried along with the priest. Pablo Abeyta later said that several people also wrote notes and placed them in the coffin along with a pencil so that

Father Padilla could explain his actions for future investigators to read and finally understand.

Father Padilla's last appearance occurred seventeen years later, in 1914. Father Anton Docher, the Isleta priest and a member of the 1895 committee, did not see fit to call for another church investigation. Instead, Isletans recall that Father Docher simply ordered the coffin to be reburied with stronger boards nailed over the altar floor covering Father Padilla's grave. Apparently, no one checked to see if Father Padilla had explained his movements on the notes left in his coffin, as hoped by those in attendance in 1895.

Father Padilla never resurfaced of his own volition. However, his coffin was exhumed and reburied by workers in 1948 and 1962 when St. Augustine was twice remodeled. If his spirit had been restless or upset before, it appears to have resigned itself to rest in peace at last. Or, as the more scientific among us might insist, the high water table that might have previously pushed Father Padilla's tree-trunk coffin to the surface in the past may have declined by the mid-twentieth century due to large-scale conservation and damming along the Rio Grande.

Whatever explanation one favors, we can draw at least one clear conclusion: Father Padilla may have died by the late eighteenth century, but his legend has persisted and has done much to assure that this seemingly humble Franciscan priest will never be forgotten among residents and historians of the Rio Abajo.

The Healer: Francis Schlatter in the Rio Abajo, 1895

by Richard Melzer

Valencia County has had many famous—and infamous—visitors in its long history. Many traveled on wagons down the old Camino Real. Others arrived by train after the Santa Fe Railway reached the region in 1880. Most recently, motorists speed through Valencia County on Interstate 25. But probably the most unusual, most mysterious traveler to ever visit in the Rio Abajo simply appeared in early July 1895.

First Seen on Tomé Hill

Francis Schlatter was first seen in Valencia County on the top of Tomé Hill. By one account, two boys discovered him lying on the hill, hands outstretched to the sky. Another version of the story attributed the discovery of Schlatter on Tomé Hill to a posse out looking for an escaped prisoner. A third, more mystical version of Schlatter's sudden arrival had him simply falling from Heaven onto Tomé Hill, a place of enormous religious significance in our history.

Regardless of his means of arrival, contemporary reports agreed that Schlatter was a man like few had ever encountered in Valencia County. He was said to have stood about 6 feet tall and have weighed about 160 pounds. He wore simple clothes, but seldom any shoes on his 13-inch long, 4 1/2-inch wide feet, although he was a shoemaker by trade.

Born and raised in Alsace-Lorraine, France, Schlatter had migrated to the United States when he was about 28-years-old in the mid 1880s. After spending several years in New York, he moved to Denver in 1892. He began his religious odyssey the following year, traveling through the West, including across the formidable Mojave Desert.

More mysteriously, Schlatter reportedly resembled artists' renditions of Jesus Christ in every detail. With piercing blue eyes, he wore his long dark hair parted down the middle. Comparing Schlatter to a picture of Christ that hung on an adobe wall, a New Mexico reporter found the likeness to be "startling…every line and touch to be found in the picture were the same in the man." Francis Schlatter also resembled Christ in much of his behavior. He deferred to God (who he called "the Master") in making even the smallest decisions. He often fasted for weeks, refusing food and drinking only small amounts of water. He also refused money, insisting that it held no value for him.

Francis Schlatter (Museum of New Mexico, #51264)

But Schlatter was most like Christ in his ability to heal the sick. He had no sooner arrived in Valencia County than his remarkable power was demonstrated on a blind man named Jesús M. Vásquez of Peralta. Although Vásquez had consulted many doctors and had spent much money on attempted cures, nothing had improved his vision until Schlatter's arrival. Vásquez recalled how this stranger "took my hand in his and said something which I could not understand. Almost immediately, I felt my sight coming back." Three days later, Vásquez took delight in seeing and describing the style and color of a carriage driven by reporters sent to the scene by an Albuquerque newspaper.

Not far from Vásquez's house, "The Healer," as Schlatter was soon called, visited the home of Silverio Martín. There, he reportedly healed Martín's aging mother, a woman who suffered paralysis in both arms. According to her son, Schlatter "simply touched her hands, and today she is working out in the fields." Andres Romero, one of the oldest and most prominent men in Peralta, confirmed that Vásquez, who had not seen for three years, was no longer blind while Silverio Martín's mother, who had not been able to use her arms for sixteen years was as fit as any woman her age. Romero concluded that "the work of this man is something inexplicable and wonderful."

Juan José Chávez, another leading citizen of Valencia County, agreed with Romero's observations. He attested that all who had been cured by Schlatter were doing well days later "without a single exception." Chávez himself had been cured by Schlatter. He recalled being "so drawn up with rheumatism that I was bent nearly double, and it was impossible for me to straighten my back, but now look at me."

The Healer's greatest miracle occurred in Los Lunas. There, he reportedly brought a boy back from death not once, but twice. Hearing of such miracles, many implored Schlatter to visit their homes to treat those who could not travel to him. When a grateful man in Tomé insisted that The Healer accept his money, Schlatter reluctantly took it, but quickly distributed it to needy onlookers. Large crowds gathered as news of The Healer's work spread through Valencia County and beyond. Throngs of no less than five hundred people, representing all social classes, sought him out as he traveled by foot in Peralta, Los Lunas, Tomé, and Isleta.

To Albuquerque and Denver

It was not long before Schlatter was urged to go to Albuquerque to continue his work in that larger community. After consulting with his Master, Schlatter agreed to go, leaving Tomé in a buggy driven by Jesús Lucero and arriving in Albuquerque in the early morning hours of July 20, 1895.

The Healer's fame grew even greater in Albuquerque where crowds met him at every turn. Staying in a home in Old Town, Schlatter treated hundreds of visitors, ranging in age from small infants to the oldest residents. Most claimed that they had been cured. Those who were not cured were simply told that they needed additional time with The Healer. Schlatter took no credit himself, saying that he was simply an instrument of the Master.

While he had suffered little if any criticism in Valencia County, Schlatter faced many skeptics in Albuquerque. A leading Catholic priest announced that the church did "not sanction or approve of such proceedings." A businessman called Schlatter a "humbug of the first order." Others declared that Schlatter must be an imposter at best and insane at worst, especially after he declared that he was, in fact, Christ, the Son of God. At least one judge thought that he should be arrested for vagrancy, as he had been in Arkansas and Texas before arriving in New Mexico.

But most Albuquerqueans disagreed, quickly coming to Schlatter's defense. According to the well-respected Perfecto Armijo, "There is not a large enough police force in Bernalillo County to arrest this man when he is in the midst of a crowd. Anyone who would lay hands on him would be torn to pieces." Those who did not call him "The Master" often preferred to call him "El Gran Hombre" or even St. Francis.

Schlatter was soon commanded by his Master to return to Denver where his ministry had begun two years earlier. An immense crowd came to see him off at the Albuquerque depot on August 22, 1895. While The Healer waited for the train to take him to Colorado, an ailing Isleta Indian came to see him and ask for help for his chronic pain. The man knelt before Schlatter and kissed his hands and feet. Embarrassed (Schlatter seldom let people kneel at his feet), The Healer asked the sufferer if he had a handkerchief. When the man answered that he did not, a woman offered hers. After holding the handkerchief in his hands for several minutes, Schlatter gave it to the Isletan, instructing him to place it where the pain was and he would be relieved. The press reported that "it was with great difficulty that the Indian was taken away." The Healer finally boarded his train with the help of a policeman who cleared a path through the large crowd. As Schlatter's train moved northward, large numbers assembled at each stop, including at Bernalillo, Lamy, and Las Vegas.

Back in New Mexico

But The Healer's departure did not mark his last visit to New Mexico or Valencia County. After ministering to crowds of up to three thousand in Denver, Schlatter suddenly left Colorado in mid-November 1895, writing in a note he left behind that "my mission is finished. The Father takes me away." Riding a large white horse named Butte, Schlatter was seen near Santa Fe by mid-December. He was later spotted in Valencia County, where he was escorted by dozens of followers from Isleta, Tomé, and other nearby settlements. Finally, in a moment that one contemporary described as "a scene reminiscent of…Biblical days, The Healer bade his followers farewell, blessed them, and …struck out across the county" to the southwest.

After an exhausting trip in rough winter weather, Schlatter eventually arrived at the Morley Ranch near Datil, New Mexico. The Morleys welcomed him and invited The Healer to stay until he could recover his strength. For three months, he spent his days swinging a long copper rod for exercise and dictating his thoughts, later published in a book entitled *Life of the Harp in the Hands of the Harper*.

But it was simply a matter of time before local residents learned of The Healer's presence and began arriving at the Morley Ranch to see him. Refreshed and eager to avoid crowds, Schlatter headed south again in April 1896. Days later, he was observed crossing the international border into Mexico.

Francis Schlatter died in Chihuahua, Mexico, sometime in 1897. His body was found near a white horse, undoubtedly Butte. A weather-faded Bible inscribed with his name was discovered in the horse's saddle bag. A long copper rod lay nearby. His Master had called Schlatter home, although the cause of his death was unknown.

While most would agree that Francis Schlatter was not Christ, many saw his ministry as a gift from God in an age when human faith was shaken by worldly crises. It is well to value The Healer's faith and remember it as a gift from God, and not merely good history, in our lives today.

Belen's Miracle Window, 1926–present

by Richard Melzer

Ramón Baca y Chávez and his family were well known and well respected in Belen in the 1920s. Don Ramón had served as the community's justice of the peace and police judge for many years. Judge Baca and his wife Eulalia Castillo Baca had raised seven fine children and were active members of Our Lady of Belen Catholic Church. One of their five daughters, María Lucía, had become a nun, serving at Loretto College in El Paso.

Always eager to improve their well kept home on Gilbert Avenue off South Main Street, the Bacas had bought a new windowpane from the Becker Dalies store in December 1926. Measuring 20 inches by 32 inches, the window had cost only $1.15, or roughly $13.50 in today's money. Sixty-three year-old Ramón and 59-year-old Eulalia had not noticed anything unusual when they had installed their new window.

But that had all changed on June 1, 1927. On that Friday morning Eulalia had returned from attending daily Mass and was cleaning her backyard when she glanced up at her east-facing attic window. To her surprise, an image of Christ ascending into heaven was clearly evident in the window in colors of soft blue, green, red, and brown.

Belen's Miracle Window and Judge Ramón and Eulalia Baca (Baca family)

Eulalia called Don Ramón to come see the breathtaking vision. Devout Catholics, they were sure they were witnessing a miracle, especially because the image of Christ had appeared in their window shortly after the Lenten season had ended. Word of the miracle window soon spread through Belen and beyond. Men, women, and children flocked to the Bacas' home to see the image for themselves. By June 27, the *Belen News* reported, "Thousands of people from different parts of the state have motored to Belen to see the strange apparition."

Many more visitors came by the Bacas' house during the Belen *fiestas* later that summer. Believers prayed at the window, asking for special blessings for those who had traveled from far and wide to attend the famous *fiestas*. The Bacas' window became so well known that the Southwestern Indian Detours Company made it a special destination by 1928. The Detours offered Santa Fe Railway passengers opportunities to interrupt their train travel to take excursions by car to local attractions, including Indian pueblos, Spanish mission ruins, and now the miracle window. Driven to Belen from Albuquerque, Detour passengers stood in awe at the Bacas' humble dwelling (located just north of the China King restaurant today).

Southwestern Indian Detours may have profited from the miracle window, but the Baca family never did. Many people offered to buy the window, and a showman promised the Bacas thousands of dollars if they would allow him to build a fence around the family's property and sell tickets for the chance to see the image. But the Bacas never considered selling tickets, souvenirs, or refreshments, although these commercial ventures may well have made them rich. Instead, the Bacas graciously displayed their window free of charge. Like custodians of a sacred shrine, they believed that it was their religious duty to share their miracle and their faith with others.

Many priests and nuns now joined the crowds of reverent visitors. In fact, so many visitors arrived to see the image that the Bacas began to board up the window at night, for fear that someone might hurl a stone or otherwise damage the miracle left in their care. Visitors soon realized that the image of Christ could only be seen in daylight and could not be seen from the attic's interior. Located about 12' above ground level, the image could be viewed from any angle in the yard below. Some said that if they gazed long enough they could see the Christ figure's arms move.

Observers saw as many as three images in the Bacas' window. Visiting the site on July 1, 1927, Jim Whittington of Santa Fe reported that when he stood below the window he could see "a figure of the Christ child seated in a chair with a basket of roses nearby. Standing further from the window the figure of Christ, the man, could be seen. Standing still further away the figure of Christ's mother is clearly outlined."

Of course, there were skeptics among those who came to see the window. Doubting Thomases wanted to examine the window from inside the house to see if the strange phenomenon was caused by light reflecting off an image on the attic's wall. No such image was found in the vacant attic. In fact, a black cloth was placed over the window's interior surface, but rather than eliminating the image, the dark background just made it clearer.

Others wondered if the image was a reflection of an object in the surrounding area. After careful scrutiny no such object was discovered. Despite Eulalia Baca's objections, glass experts arrived from Albuquerque to test the window, cleaning it inside and out with various chemicals, acids, and even gasoline. But nothing altered or affected the image.

According to another theory, advanced by a Santa Fe newspaper, "pictures may have been put in the glass by some process similar to that used in making stained glass windows and through an error this picture glass was sent to Belen."

Countless visitors attempted to photograph the apparition from the Bacas' yard or roof. A movie company even tried to film the scene for a newsreel to be shown in movie theatres. But not even the most sophisticated cameras could capture the image. Once developed, pictures and movies always came out blurred.

Over the years, only one person ever photographed the window successfully. Using a simple, low-cost camera Fernando Gabaldón of Albuquerque had accomplished what all others had failed to do. An invalid, Gabaldón made his unique photograph into postcards and asked Judge Baca to sell them to visitors for 25 cents each. The judge agreed, giving all proceeds to the impoverished photographer.

Like many others, Fernando Gabaldón had come to see the Bacas' window in hopes that a miracle might cure his illness. Some visitors were cured, although others, including Gabaldón, were not. The window was never known as a healing site like the legendary Santuario in Chimayó or other holy sites in New Mexico or the world.

With time the image was said to have faded and the number of visitors declined. The Great Depression of the 1930s limited travel for many would-be pilgrims from beyond Belen.

The Bacas brought the miracle window with them when they eventually moved to a house on Dalies Avenue. Tragically, the window cracked in the move, but the pane was not shattered and the image of Christ was untouched. Many considered the window's survival a miracle in itself. The Bacas installed the glass in the second floor window of their new home so that visitors could still see it from the street below. When Don Ramón and Eulalia died in 1950 and 1951, respectively, their daughters, Ana María and Beatrice, continued to live in the house and display the famous image of Christ.

Meanwhile, the house on Gilbert Avenue was sold to Bob Garley in 1967. After water damaged the property in the terrible flood of 1969, the Garleys remodeled the building and have lived there ever since. Until a local historian came by, no one had ever asked them about the miracle window. The only unusual phenomena the family has experienced is when Bob's daughter, Lydia Pino, and other relatives sometimes hear strange knocking on doors and inexplicable footsteps on the staircase.

Many Belen residents still remember seeing the miracle window at its Dalies Avenue location. Some recall uttering prayers of devotion as they passed by, especially if they had loved ones in the military during times of war. Some prayed as they walked to class in the old high school several blocks away, especially when they faced difficult exams or other personal challenges.

The miracle window was moved for a third time when Ana María and Beatrice moved to Albuquerque and put the glass into storage in the early 1970s. In the mid 1980s, Phil Baca, Ramón and Eulalia's grandson, brought the window to his home in Longmont, Colorado, for safekeeping. Leaders of the Valencia Country Historical Society learned of the window's long history, discovered its location in Colorado, and helped negotiate its return to the Rio Abajo in 1999.

As generous as ever, the Baca family lent the window to the historical society, which kept the priceless item in a vault in the local Wells Fargo bank until its recent move to an equally safe place in town. The Valencia County Historical Society displayed the miracle window at a large reception in the Wells Fargo bank building on February 27, 2000. Anthony Baca presented a brief history of his grandparents' window and led the singing of "De Colores," a song he called a "reflection of the colors and visions that have been seen in this window" for over seventy years.

For many, Belen's greatest mystery remains a mystery. What a *New Mexico Magazine* author wrote in June 1941 remains true today: "To date, no one has given a satisfactory [scientific] explanation concerning the vision." For others, Belen's greatest miracle remains a miracle. The image may have faded with time, but the faith it inspired in thousands remains as strong and as lasting as ever.

Ghosts of the Rio Abajo

by Sandy Battin

Sometimes it's possible not only to read about historical figures but to meet them. Of course, they may not acknowledge you – and you might be able to see right through them.

Like most places, the Rio Abajo can boast a number of ghosts in its population, many of them in its most historic buildings. Beautiful adobe homes, old buildings that serve as a library and a museum, an old-time hotel, and even one of the West's storied Harvey Houses along the tracks of the old Santa Fe Railway are said to carry more than echoes from the past. Apparitions – full-body spirits – of people from another time help tell the stories of the structures in which they still dwell.

The Luna Mansion

The Luna Mansion today (Luna Mansion)

Probably the most well-known ghost in the Rio Abajo is said to haunt the historic Luna Mansion on Los Lunas' Main Street, once part of that American classic highway, Route 66. The ghosts – there are said to be three or perhaps even four – help tell the story of this once sleepy little village that has grown into the thriving suburban home of many commuters eager for life in a small-town atmosphere that is still close to the jobs of Albuquerque.

The most famous is Pepe, the nickname for the quite historic Josefita Manderfield Otero, once the lady of this elegant mansion. As the tale is told, she sits in the rocking chair that she once – or perhaps still does – own placed just past the stairwell on the second floor of the mansion, now turned into a fine restaurant. She watches the patrons, sometimes makes an appearance, and every now and then, causes the seemingly empty chair to rock.

Josefita, who lived from 1874 to 1951, lived in and loved the mansion for many years. The house was built in 1881 by Don Antonio José Luna with money paid by the Santa Fe Railway for a right-of-way through the land on which his *hacienda* stood. Don Antonio passed away before it was completed. His son, Tranquilino Luna, Tranquilino's wife Amalia, and their son, Maximiliano, were the first to reside in the mansion. Among those who inhabited the mansion was Don Solomon Luna, one of the fathers of the New Mexico constitution. The mansion passed down to Don Solomon's nephew, Eduardo Otero, who brought Josefita there as his wife.

Josefita loved the mansion and gave it its distinctive Southern look, complete with a portico and high white columns. She painted murals on its walls and added a solarium to bring in the bright New Mexico sunshine. Current owners Pete and Hortencia "Tensie" Torres have lovingly remodeled the building, hung Josefita's paintings on the wall, and created a welcoming atmosphere that is probably quite similar to that the former lady of the house maintained.

Several long-time employees have quite a history of encounters with Pepe, who seems to enjoy interacting playfully with them. Chef Thomas Shook began coming to the mansion as a child when his parents worked at the restaurant. He has seen Pepe in her white 1920s-style clothing and her somewhat unruly red hair.

"Since I've been back with Tensie and Pete, there seem to have been a few different things that kind of jolt you," he said, sitting in the old parlor with a good view of a self-portait of Pepe painted with her dogs and a herd of sheep. "I was standing at the computer ... and I could see a white dress. I saw her walking up to the double door. She had red frizzy hair. I stayed out of this side of the house for a while. She made her presence known. ... I think she knows me; I don't know to what extent."

Interested customers, as well as local school children exploring the historic building, always ask: "What did she look like?" "Whatever I saw walking by those two doors was solid. You couldn't see straight through her, but you could tell she wasn't flesh," Shook said. She seems to enjoy making her presence known. Early one morning, waiting for a former owner to meet him at the mansion, Shook found "the stereo upstairs was on full blast." When the owner arrived, Shook told him about the stereo. "When we came back in, it was playing nice and quiet and soft .... We decided to let her listen to her music that day," the chef said.

Cindy McCloskey, another longtime employee, says the music levels are played with quite frequently. "It's not that easy to change. You have to climb on a ladder. It's not like someone walks by and turns it on. It's very inconvenient." A couple of weeks earlier, she said, the music was playing and, when she went back upstairs, the speakers on both floors were off.

Another time, after business hours, Thomas and his wife were chatting with a bartender in the second floor's aptly named Spirit Lounge. "There's a door that faces the south. There's a push handle. The lever started going up and down. ... Then it just stopped. We checked the door. On the other side, there's only a push button and it doesn't bring the lever down," he said.

Thomas even recalls a story that his mother told him about what happened when Pepe's rocking chair was, ever so briefly, moved. A waitress, his mother reported that one Saturday evening was especially busy. The former owner told her to move Pepe's chair into a nearby storeroom so that a "two-top" table for a pair of diners could be added to help deal with the crowd. "My mom said, 'I'm not moving that chair.' He told her to and she said again she wouldn't move it. He went up and moved the chair into the storeroom. ... He came back downstairs and they were talking. That big 6-foot-tall mirror came off the wall, landed face up, made the curve in the stairs, and slapped him right in the back of his ankles – and it didn't break," Thomas said with a chuckle.

Cindy jokes that she believes Pepe "doesn't like me very much. ... When people ask about her, I point to her picture and say it's the lady with the bad perm." While she may have been snubbed by Pepe, Cindy says she has seen the other ghost in the mansion – Compadre Cruz, believed to one have been a groundskeeper.

"It was a Sunday and it was very quiet. I didn't have anybody upstairs (in the lounge) and I was visiting with everyone downstairs. I thought I'd better go back up and check. There was a gentleman sitting in one of the big rockers," Cindy said. "I turned around … to pick up a napkin and he was gone. He was in dark clothing. It was quick, and I only saw the back of his head and his shoulders. "What startled me the most is that there was a man at the bar and I hadn't known it – my only customer and he just disappeared."

Sometimes customers have reported seeing Cruz sitting at dining tables. In life, when Cruz became ill, his employers set up a bed for him in one of the downstairs room and nursed the quarantined man until his death. While Pepe seems to almost acknowledge the presence of the newcomers to her home, Cruz seems not to notice. "I get the impression … that he's not aware," Cindy said. "He's in his own world. Cruz is just carrying on his duties." He may still be working. One passerby asked who the man in the long coat was working on the grounds one night. No one – except, possibly, Cruz – was on duty at the time.

And when the Torres family was remodeling the restaurant in preparation for its reopening, Hortencia says, her grandson was upstairs one day while the work was being done. "He came down and said, 'Who's that man who's up there?' He said he saw this man stand up and walk," she said; no one could be found.

Tranquilino Luna's second wife, Lola, is said to also be continuing her sojourn in the mansion. "I've never seen Lola either," Cindy said, "but I know people who feel they're sensitive and they've said they feel or see her. She's mainly in the basement."

Of late, another apparition has apparently found its way to the mansion. Cindy relates the story: "It was a Friday evening … and a friend of mine comes out of the men's room and said, 'You've got a shoeshine boy in there.' I said, 'Whatever.' He said the boy 'had a shoeshine kit and asked me if I wanted a shoe shine.' I thought maybe I would have to oust a neighborhood kid trying to make a little money. … Finally, my friend convinces me he's not a neighborhood kid, [that] there's a picture at the back of the men's room and my friend ID'd the middle child as the shoe shine boy. Two days later, I hadn't talked to [another employee] … and she told me another man had gone into the men's room and asked when he came out whether we had a shoeshine boy. And he'd identified the same kid in the picture."

Meanwhile, other unexplained events keep happening. "The only time I was ever a little creeped out was last spring," Cindy said. "I was upstairs at 4:00 in the afternoon ... and I heard a lot of noise, like 20 people were coming up the stairs. It was so loud that it was bouncing off the back wall. No one was there. And then the dishwasher starts. ... The hair on my arms stood up."

Thomas says that the dishwasher in the kitchen has also come on by itself a couple of times.

Teofilo's Restaurante

Teofilo's Restaurante (Teofilo's Restaurante)

Across the street from the mansion is Teofilo's Restaurante, another fine-dining establishment owned by the Torreses. The old adobe, once the home and office of Los Lunas' long-time physician, Dr. W.F. Wittwer, is also said to be haunted.

Decorated with colorful paintings, serapes, and New Mexican folk art, Teofilo's is treated with such loving kindness by its owners that they built an expanded dining room around a tree rather than cutting it down. Once again, Hortencia says she hasn't seen a ghost in the restaurant that she's owned for a couple of decades.

"But one family was sitting at a table and one of the waitresses took a picture of them. ... They left, and when they checked the picture, there was this whole figure standing behind the family. No one had seen it when the photo was taken," she said. A shadowy figure has also been seen near the fireplace, prompting chills in a spot that's usually warm and cozy.

Some speculate that, as a doctor's office, the building probably was a way station for many souls at the ends of their lives. "I don't think we have really identified anyone [as being the ghost]," she said. When a New Mexico ghost study group spent most of one night studying the two restaurants, a server's tray unfolded itself in front of the team and strange knocking was heard in the building.

Hortencia says it's an honor to own two of Valencia County's most historic buildings. The great thing about them is that people who love history or ghosts – or both – can explore the interiors of the Luna Mansion and Teofilo's at the same time they enjoy a delightful meal.

Our Lady of Refuge Chapel

Our Lady of Refuge (Baldwin G. Burr)

Ten miles to the south, another of the Rio Abajo's most beautiful and historic buildings stands amid alfalfa fields and a garden of old-fashioned flowers, the scent of lilacs filling the air. Educators Michael and June Romero live in the historic home of José Felipe Castillo and his wife María Guadalupe Romero Castillo, built in 1878 and 1879. Guadalupe is Michael's great-great-aunt, the sister of his great-grandfather.

Our Lady of Refuge Chapel is part of the home and, today, is the site of events ranging from historical society meetings to weddings. The chapel was consecrated in 1850 as a mission of Our Lady of Belen at another location, then was sited at a couple of other spots and finally moved into the Castillos' welcoming adobe home. It continued as a mission of Our Lady of Belen until 1912 when it was deconsecrated and became a private place of worship.

It has stood watch over so much history through the years – one former resident recalled sitting on the porch early one morning and witnessing what she later discovered was the first atomic bomb detonating at the Trinity site 90-some miles to the south. When the Romeros bought the house in 1989, they had a bit of a forewarning that a non-corporeal part of the past would come along with the thick adobe walls and brick floor.

Although the original residents of the house have no recollection of ghosts, that seems to have changed when the home changed hands in the 1950s. During the talking stage in preparation to the purchase of the house, Michael recalls sitting in the living room with the former owners. "I don't believe in ghosts and neither does June," he said, "but certain things have happened. Out of the clear blue, I said, 'I suppose there are ghosts in this house' and he looked at me and said, 'As a matter of fact, there are.'"

"He went on and identified the two ghosts by name – one is a black man named Raul who walks around in *pecheros* – overalls. He always has one side snapped and one side open. … He was supposed to work for the family." A friend later told Michael that he remembered Raul, that he was a real person.

The second ghost, the former owner told the Romeros, he'd encountered while shaving one morning when he saw a figure in black go by the open door. Thinking it was his wife, he stepped into their bedroom and found her still in bed – in a white nightgown. Returning to the bathroom, he said, he saw her again, a short woman in a black dress with buttons running from the neck to the floor.

Romero said he was astonished to hear the story because it fit in so neatly with a tale he'd been told by two other observers. He and his father had owned the property across the street and had been working there. They hired two men to help for a couple of days and told them they could stay in the adobe house on the property. It had been home to Francisquita, the wife of Ruperto, one of the Castillos's sixteen children.

"After the first night, I came to the house early and they were already outside working. As soon as I got there they asked me in Spanish if there were spirits in the house and I said, '*Hay ratas, gatos* (there are rats and cats) but no spirits.'"

After the second night, the two men rushed outside when Michael arrived, telling him they'd seen a small lady wearing a long black dress buttoned down the front walking through the house, sometimes straight through the walls. It sounded like the same ghost.

The former owner of the Castillo house told the Romeros that, soon after the old house where the two workmen had had their experience was torn down, he could tell that another presence had moved in. "It blew my mind. I didn't believe a single word until [he] described her," Michael said.

The Romeros have also had their experiences with Raul. "I was standing at the kitchen counter making a salad, and June was sitting at the table. Through the doorway, I saw someone standing looking at the Christmas tree. … I was talking to him … and said 'Rick's in there.' I came around the counter and there was nobody here. Rick (a visitor) was in the back of the house, nowhere near the tree."

The ghosts of the Romero home must be among the most helpful in the world. One day, Michael's daughter reported that she awakened after sleeping late the morning of a high school track meet. She saw a black hand pointing to the alarm clock; she arrived at school just in time to catch the bus to the meet. Raul was being helpful.

"When she got home that night, she asked me if I had awakened her. I said I hadn't. She said, 'I knew you would say that and I worried about it all day,'" Michael said.

Another time, June was saying goodbye to some friends after a visit. Michael walked into the kitchen, glancing through a door at the laundry room, where someone he assumed was June was standing by the washing machine. "The ladies were saying goodbye and I called out to them, 'Let me get June for you.' And her voice came from that direction, saying she was there saying goodbye to the ladies. … She came back in and we found my undershirts, shorts and socks folded and piled neatly on the dryer," he said. June hadn't touched the laundry since putting it in the dryer.

One cold, snowy day, Michael was late coming home from work. It was dark already and he knew the main part of the house would be freezing since it was heated with wood rather than a thermostat-based system. When he walked in the door, a well-stoked fire was merrily blazing in the living room and the house was "toasty warm," Michael said. "I called my father to thank him for lighting the fire, but he didn't know what I was talking about." No one else had access to the house.

June says she often hears the sound of people talking in the house. "I've spoken – and there's no one here," she said. Once, she heard the strings of her guitar being plucked, even though there was no one in the room.

One of the ghosts has also exhibited a playful streak. When Michael was sanding the kitchen floor, he got an ice cold drink from the refrigerator, popped it open and set it on the cabinet. A while later, when he went back for it, it was nowhere to be seen. "I opened another and started sanding. The same thing happened: it had disappeared. It happened three times. Finally, I went to the sink to get some water and looked out the window and there were the three Pepsis sitting on the wall [around the yard]. It was a very hot day, and they were all still ice cold. That was so weird," he said.

Despite their experiences, the Romeros love their home – and feel quite comfortable sharing it with people from its past. "There's nothing frightening here. It's a very welcoming place," June said.

The Felipe Chávez House

The Felipe Chávez House (Valencia County Historical Society)

Less than a mile to the south, just off Belen's historic Main Street, another old adobe – beautiful and serene with a shady courtyard – that once belonged to Felipe Chávez, better known as *El Millonario*. Legendary in Valencia County, Chávez was one of New Mexico's most successful businessmen and merchants of the nineteenth century. He traded in everything from sheep to boots to building supplies, and his contacts in the world of business spanned the continent and even crossed the Atlantic Ocean. He was a member of the New York Stock Exchange. He remained loyal to his home town, staying there in the sprawling adobe he'd built in 1860. He was a judge for some time, even building a small jail at the rear of his property.

Ymelda and Leroy Baca and their daughter Gretta Aguilar bought the house – on the State and National registers of historic places since 1980 – and have worked diligently and with loving kindness to restore it. At the same time, Ymelda is collecting decades of ghost stories that are told about the hacienda. A longtime teacher specializing in bilingual education, she is also translating documents about the building from Spanish to English.

Speculation is that the main haunter of this historic spot is Felipe's daughter Margarita, basically cut out of her father's will with a scant $3. "She is said to haunt the place," Ymelda said. "You hear doors open and close, and you feel the presence of a white cloud that comes through. It's like a fine white mist. But I'm not at all frightened – I'm not scared there. "We've renovated it back to the feel of the era. … It's not a negative ghost, it's a positive one. They seem to be very happy, to be at peace here. Maybe they feel the sense of being at home, as it was in the past."

Being the daughter of a wealthy man, perhaps Margarita loves beautiful things. "There was a doll that was missing. Someone gave me a little house made of adobe and I had a little doll, a storyteller, in front of it. It was gone for about three weeks, and then they returned it facing the other way," Ymelda said. A *santo* – an image of a saint – is still missing and has never been returned, whether taken by ghostly or corporeal hands, it will probably never be known.

When the family first bought the property, they were faced with thick dirt of seven years' making while the hacienda stood vacant. "I didn't even know it had brick floors, it was so dirty. We worked really hard and, when we finished cleaning, we left for a while. When we came back, there were footprints leading out – small ones, a woman's," Ymelda said. Other times they hear a sound of footsteps on the roof – but whether they're produced by a ghost or neighborhood cats Ymelda isn't sure. The tenants in one of the apartments in the back of the house has heard them, too.

They've also heard the voices of children at times when youngsters would normally be in school. Years ago, when the beautiful home had been converted into apartments, at least one child died in one of the rooms, the victim of an epidemic, someone who had lived in the house told the Bacas.

Some say Felipe Chávez was cheated by the Confederate Army, which bivouacked nearby, soldiers helping themselves to his merchandise. "One lady said she'd seen the ghosts of soldiers walking in the courtyard," Ymelda said. When the Baca family bought the hacienda, they had it blessed and created a small chapel in one of the rooms. It's part of the spiritual feeling that love and family give a building. It's exactly what the Bacas hoped to restore along with the floors and doors and walls.

The Belen Harvey House

D ┌┌ ┌ ┐ // ∩ ∂\/┌\/ //∩//┌┌

The Belen Harvey House (Belen Harvey House Museum)

Our Lady of Refuge Chapel and the Felipe Chávez Hacienda aren't the only haunted spots in Belen. Take Main Street south, turn left at historic Reinken Avenue leading to the railroad yard overpass, make a short jog south again at First Street, and you'll find the Harvey House Museum. Belen has long been one of the largest rail centers on the old Santa Fe Railway lines. Sitting on what are now the BNSF tracks with the sounds of trains going in and out all day, the museum houses a substantial collection of railroad and city-related memorabilia. In addition, it hosts everything from art and quilt shows to displays by the local model railroad club to traveling shows from the Smithsonian.

Dozens of visitors enter its doors every week and volunteer docents tell them stories about the Harvey Girls who once worked in the restaurant and how they lived in the smaller room upstairs. They know the history of the Hub City, set almost smack dab in the center of New Mexico, and the colorful characters who played their roles in the history of the area, beginning in the 1700s when Belen was first settled.

Those docents sometimes feel as if they aren't quite alone, even if there are no visitors exploring the various rooms of the museum. Laura Anderson, who has been a docent for more than 11 years, remembers that things began heating up when meetings stopped being held in the building and the chairs were moved into one of the storage rooms. "They say when things get moved, it stirs up the ghosts," she said.

Sure enough, one day she saw one – a man wearing a yellow-and-black plaid shirt, sitting with his elbows on his knees. "I knew he was there and I saw him clearly from the corner of my eye," she said. The docents have speculated that, once upon a time, the Harvey House was used as a reading room, housing railroaders waiting for their next shifts on the trains. "I think he's older because his arms and hands look like he's older," she said. "You mainly see the shirt and jeans. I'll see him once in a while, walking, out of the corner of my eye.

"I've never had a feeling of fright. But one of the other docents got scared. She was upstairs on the south side of the hallway and she saw a man crossing the hall from the left to the right. She said it was like a shadow; she wouldn't have noticed the clothing." She's heard someone coughing in the building, thinking maybe it was one of the model railroaders but, upon exploring, finds she's alone.

The ghost apparently likes her. "If I'm here on Christmas Eve or the last day before a holiday, I always wish him a Merry Christmas or a happy holiday," Laura said.

Recently another docent was showing her some gemstones that she'd purchased when one of them rolled off onto the floor. "We looked for it for an hour. I swept the floor four times. She used a yard stick to reach under the furniture to try to find it. ... She took the broom outside to shake it in case the stone had gotten caught inside. I decided to talk to the ghost. I said, 'You can get into places we can't and this gem is really important to her. Can you help me find it?' She came back inside and sat in her chair ... and I saw it right there. I said, 'Look between your feet' and there it was. I think it was my friend [the ghost] who found it. It could have gone between one of the [floor] boards."

Laura said there have been tales of another ghost at the Harvey House as well. "I think there's a female, but she doesn't come around very much. I haven't really seen her – she's more of a white glare. A couple of times there has been a brightly lit area where there shouldn't have been one," she said. She doesn't believe the ghosts are out to scare people at the Harvey House. "There's just a feeling in here of happiness; that's why those two people are still here – they were happy here," she said.

The Agustín Archuleta Building

Another historic building, this one in Los Lunas, also serves as a museum. The old Agustín Archuleta building has been many things – a private home, a police and fire station, and a library before being remodeled as the Los Lunas Museum of Heritage and Art. Cynthia Shetter, village librarian and director of the museum, says she's heard tales that the floor boards have always creaked as if someone is walking on them. And, on February 29, 2008, when the museum opened, Cynthia arrived early to make sure everything was ready and her key wouldn't work – on any of the doors. "I couldn't get it to open at all. I was so frustrated. We'd also had this thing with the bathroom doors locking from the inside on us. I sat and said, 'This isn't funny. I need to get in there.' I walked back to the door and it opened – right away," she said. Another time, during a musical performance, someone tried to get into the bathroom and it was locked. She went to get a key and found the door open.

"I haven't seen a ghost but ... one young patron wanted to do EVP (electronic voice phenomena) work and talk to the ghosts, an employee and a volunteer were there and the kid set up a tape recorder and put it on a bench. He started asking questions and the tape recorder went flying off the bench. His face got white and he got sick to his stomach," Cynthia recalled. Because the Luna family gave its name to Los Lunas, one of the museum's first exhibits featured facts about them. One of the items on display, borrowed from the Luna Mansion, was the rocking chair of Josefita Manderfield Otero, the very one said to rock by itself. One of the patrons detected a cold spot around it, Cynthia said.

The Los Lunas Library

Cross the street and walk a few blocks east and you'll come to the site of the old White Hotel, now the Los Lunas Public Library. Doctors' offices had also been there. Some say a legendary hanging tree once grew there, its limbs hanging over what was Cynthia's office. "You could see where it had rope marks on it," she said. "I haven't seen anything here, but, when you're alone, you hear books moving around. My staff doesn't like the teen room, and that's where the tree was. When they're working at the front desk, they say they will see someone walking by – and there's no one there. ... The workers also feel cold spots."

254

Recently, a library worker "was sitting in the break room and something hit the trash can lid hard and it was rocking back and forth. She just sat there watching it rock," Cynthia continued. "The only thing I've ever see was when … I saw these guys come in dressed in long dusters – one had long hair. … It was in the middle of July and it was hot. I thought 'why did they have coats on in July?' I kept an eye on them and they were sitting on the floor, looking at books in the reference section. They went into the other room – and then they weren't there. I asked everyone else if they had seen them and they hadn't a clue to what I was talking about."

The Central Hotel

Central Hotel (Matt and Carl Baca)

If many stories can be recounted about old buildings that once served as jails or doctors' offices, there must be as many stories as there are rooms in old hotels. Matt Baca's son, Carl, was the former owner of the historic Central Hotel near the railroad depot in Belen. The Bacas took a photograph of it once and were surprised to see something that looked "like a ghost floating high up on the outside of the building." They definitely hadn't seen it when they took the picture. A ghost hunter made a midnight visit to the hotel and took images of orbs floating in mid-air. And Matt, who did a lot of upkeep on the building, had one frustrating mystery happen every now and then. "I used to go in quite often because the roof was leaking, and we'd set up buckets to catch the rain. When I'd go back, those buckets had been moved away and some of the doors were open and some were not.

"I once went there with an individual [and] when, he walked in, the hair on the back of his head stood up. He said he's very sensitive to things like that. He was almost very reluctant to go in. He could sense the presence of something. I never sensed it but, once in a while, especially when I'd go to the second floor, I'd had this sensation. I can't quite describe it – a sensation," Matt said.

A sensation. A feeling of being watched. The sound of footsteps where no one human walks. Ghosts somehow seem to belong in historic buildings – so much has happened there. So much emotion. So many people. So many stories.

A Maze of Unfriendly Stones: How Three Women Tourists Survived the Badlands, 1938

by Richard Melzer

We sometimes forget that Valencia County was nearly four times its current size. Extending to the California border in the west, the county once included the town of Grants and several natural wonders, including Mount Taylor, the Ice Cave, and the desolate lava badlands. Many residents and tourists enjoyed exploring Valencia County's vast landscape in the days before Cibola County was created in 1981. Most people have fond memories of hiking, fishing, and camping in various parts of that largely unsettled terrain.

Postcard of The Badlands (Richard Melzer)

Unfortunately, other visitors to western Valencia County had less pleasant experiences to recall. Some encountered harsh conditions and rugged landscape, resulting in tragic outcomes. With help often miles away, many suffered tragic accidents. Others suffered agonizing deaths.

A Trip West

Three out-of-state visitors gave little thought to danger when they set out from the El Fidel Hotel in Albuquerque on Tuesday, July 19, 1938. Two of these travelers, Irene Piedalue and Marie Antoinette de Lafarest, had left their homes in Kentucky on July 14. They had met Laura Piedalue, Irene's sister, in St. Louis, Missouri, before continuing their trek without incident.

Irene, a 45-year-old state extension service worker, and Laura, a 47-year-old New York welfare worker, had planned a grand Western tour with their friend Marie before Marie was scheduled to return to her native France after a two-year stay in the United States. The young French woman had supported herself in the U.S. by teaching French at the University of Kentucky. The trio had planned their month-long itinerary to include stops at the Grand Canyon in Arizona and Yellowstone National Park in Wyoming before visiting Irene and Laura's relatives in Montana. The excursionists planned to drive the entire route by themselves, quite a feat in an era when few women drove cars, much less traveled long distances through largely-isolated areas without male companions along for protection.

Irene, Laura, and Marie were clearly independent, brave individuals who preferred vacations filled with challenges and adventure to those filled with luxury and leisure. They had no way of knowing just how challenging—and dangerous—this particular vacation was about to become.

Tuesday, July 19, started uneventfully for the Piedalue sisters and their French companion. The three women left the El Fidel Hotel at about 7:00 a.m., mailing a postcard to a relative in Montana and proceeding west on old Route 66. Irene, Laura, and Marie drove from Albuquerque, over Nine Mile Hill towards Grants. Once in Grants, a gas station attendant told them about the Ice Cave and suggested that they take a detour to see this remarkable, but seldom-visited, site. Their curiosity piqued, the women turned off Route 66 and followed the attendant's directions by heading south along an unimproved dirt road.

Located twenty-seven miles southwest of Grants, the Ice Cave was famous for its twenty-foot deep floor of permanent ice made possible by a temperature that never rose above thirty-one degrees Fahrenheit. Visitors in the 1930s entered the main cave by climbing down a long, steep, crude ladder. Unlike today, there was no visitor center, no sturdy stairway, and no map to locate the cave in the midst of miles of inhospitable dried lava. Irene, Laura, and Marie arrived at the Ice Cave about 11:00 a.m. Parking their Chevy sedan, they ate some sandwiches and eagerly ventured out to find and explore the cave.

Hopelessly Lost

Not familiar with the area, the women walked within a hundred yards of their destination, but the cave's unmarked entrance was only visible from a short distance, and the women overlooked it. The stranded tourists became disoriented, and within hours they were hopelessly lost. The three women did their best not to panic, but they soon began to "scramble madly over the rocks, with no idea which way we were going," according to Irene. Time sped by and, after hours of futile searching, waning daylight, and fading hope, the women realized that they would have to spend at least one night in their barren surroundings.

Conditions only grew worse the following day. The travelers had had no food since the previous noon. Eating leaves and twigs proved useless. Laura saw a lizard, but couldn't bring herself to capture, much less eat it. Marie saw a rabbit, but said, "I was so surprised to see any living thing I did not think to eat him until he was gone." Luckily, they never encountered more dangerous animals, like snakes, wolves, or coyotes. Water was nearly as scarce as food, with thirst a major concern in the sweltering summer heat. Fortunately, it rained at night. The rain was "like a gift from heaven," in Marie's words.

With only an aspirin tin to catch the precious liquid, the women resorted to lying on their backs to swallow as much rain as they could with their open mouths. Irene complained of "how hard it is to get water that way. The rain will hit you in the eye, ear, and everywhere but your mouth!"

Unfortunately, the cold rain also drenched the shelterless women, leaving them chilled each night. As Marie put it, "If it hadn't been for the rain, we'd have died, but it chilled us through." Marie and her friends lit small campfires with the few matches Laura carried to light cigarettes.

For once, Laura's harmful habit had proven beneficial.

By day, the badlands' dark lava absorbed the scorching heat, while shredding the women's footwear and injuring their feet. Ironically, Marie's $1.98 shoes held up better than Irene and Laura's more expensive $8.00 footwear. Travel was precarious over the sharp, jagged lava rocks where a person could easily slip, be cut, or suffer sprains or broken bones. Although no bones were broken, the lost women were soon covered with cuts and bruises. To make matters worse, no one knew that the women had decided to stop at the Ice Cave before proceeding in their travels. Irene and Laura's relatives in Montana would probably not miss them for several days—or until it was too late.

Panic began to set in after days of wandering aimlessly through what Marie described as "a maze of unfriendly stones.... The sun beat down on us and burned our flesh almost unbearably." At one point Irene grew so hysterical that Laura told her to "hush up or I would slap her face" to settle her down.

The women stayed together most of the time, although Marie was once separated from her companions when she ventured up a small hill for a better vantage point. The French teacher spent an entire night alone before her American friends miraculously met up with her the following morning. Nonplussed, Marie claimed that her sleeping place was actually more comfortable than her friends' had been on that otherwise dreadful night.

The castaways observed several TWA passenger planes flying high above them. After a few days, they noted the time of day when these flights went by. At those moments, they frantically waved their hands and yelled as loudly as they could, but to no avail. "They either didn't see us, or may have thought we were Indians," said Marie. "No one but an Indian could exist for long in such country."

After three days in the wilderness, the exhausted women could not even yell. In fact, they were less and less able to speak to each other through their increasingly parched lips. But with time the women began to think more rationally about how to deal with their plight and, hopefully, survive. More composed and assertive than her companions, Laura became the group's leader. They now hiked from one isolated small tree to the next, resting in the welcomed shade to conserve their dwindling energy.

Just as wisely, they left torn pieces of paper along their route so they were able to retrace their steps, if necessary, or determine if they had already traversed the otherwise unmarked terrain. And the women talked while they were still able. "We kept up our morale because we had each other to talk to, and we could encourage each other," said Marie. "One person, left there alone, would be almost certain to perish."

Most importantly, the women usually kept their heads and remained optimistic that they would either find their way out or be rescued before too long. Devout Catholics, they prayed often and left their fate in God's hands. Their faith was well-founded.

The Search

W.E. Martin, the owner of Grant's Craige Hotel, was headed home to his large sheep ranch south of town on Tuesday, July 19, 1938, when he spotted an abandoned Chevy sedan about 1:00 p.m. It was the same vehicle that Irene Piedalue, her sister Laura Piedalue, and their French friend Marie Antoinette de Lafarest had left about an hour earlier to go looking for the Ice Cave. Seeing an abandoned car along this stretch of isolated road was unusual. But this particular vehicle was especially memorable because of its distinctive license plate number, G777. Irene Piedalue had prudently requested this plate number so it could be easily remembered in just such an emergency. Irene's strategy worked. W.E. Martin made a mental note of the car's location and its unique number.

Heading back to town two days later, the rancher spotted the same car parked at the same place. Seeing no sign of human life in or near the sedan, Martin sped to Grants to spread the news and recruit help for an urgent search. Dozens readily volunteered, especially when they traced the license plate number and learned that the missing travelers were three women who had not been seen for four days. Clearly, there was no time to waste. Many groups and individuals volunteered to assist. State policemen, Forest Service personnel, highway department workers, Civilian Conservation Corps enrollees, businessmen, clerks, ranchers, cowhands, and sheep herders offered their time, labor, and knowledge of the rugged terrain. Their small army soon numbered 150 eager soldiers.

From eastern Valencia County, Sheriff Henry Jaramillo called Deputy Sheriff Jerry Baca in Grants. Jaramillo instructed his deputy to quickly gather some men and join the search party. Baca recruited Toney Romero and Casimiro Tafoya. In Santa Fe, Governor Clyde Tingley heard of the crisis and hurried to the scene to help organize and direct the hunt with all the resources and authority at his command.

Searchers arrived on Friday afternoon. State policemen, equipped with a heavy rope, checked the Ice Cave, but no one was found in the frigid, isolated cavern. With little sunlight left, the difficult decision was made to postpone a wider search until Saturday morning. If the women were still alive, they would have to spend yet another night in the wilderness.

Gathering again on early Saturday morning, the anxious searchers formed a long line and set off across the dismal landscape with twenty yards between each man. Progress was slow and brutal. The volunteers faced the same hazards of heat, dryness, and sharp lava rocks that had plagued Laura, Irene, and Marie for days. According to an *Albuquerque Journal* reporter, the searchers slipped "at almost every step on the jumbled masses of sharp rock as [they] carefully searched deep crevices in which the women might have slipped and examined for footprints on occasional patches of soil among the rocks." Moving forward, the searchers had no idea if they would ever find the lost women, no less what condition they would be in if they had somehow survived their long ordeal.

Found at Last

Finally, searchers came across a broken heel from a woman's shoe. Within moments they also discovered bits of paper that the women had left behind to mark their path. Spirits began to lift. Maybe it was not too late after all. Suddenly, about noon, a young cowboy named Jimmy Helton spotted the lost women in the distance, about three miles from the Ice Cave they had first set out to explore. Rather than go directly to the women, Helton rushed back to recruit additional help and grab a canteen of water for the undoubtedly thirsty survivors.

Accompanied by Toney Romero, Louis Díaz, Tony Díaz, and Stan Sánchez, Helton returned to the small crater where he had seen the lost tourists. Thrilled that the trio was alive and seemingly well, the men used a hand mirror to flash signals and alert all other searchers of their apparent success.

From their perspective, Laura, Irene, and Marie later recalled the glorious moment when they saw Jimmy Helton and his fellow rescuers. Just moments before, Laura had wandered into yet another dead end in their seemingly endless search for a way back to the road and safety. Laura recalled, "I scarcely dared tell the others [of the dead end], but as I turned I saw the men coming toward us."

In Marie's words, the sight of other human beings was the "most beautiful thing we've ever seen and we've traveled to many interesting places and seen many beautiful things." Given an orange to split three ways, Marie was equally effusive in declaring her first bite of food "the most wonderful orange I have ever tasted."

Jimmy Helton and his friends carried Laura, Irene, and Marie on makeshift litters made of pine boughs. At the road, they were greeted by a joyous crowd and Governor Tingley, who insisted that they rest in his car. A Grants doctor and two nurses gave the three survivors quick examinations and emergency treatment. The women suffered from rather serious cases of exhaustion, hunger, and exposure. Concerned that they not eat or drink too much too soon, the doctor told them each to drink no more than half a glass of milk on their ride back to Albuquerque.

Tingley's Guests

Tingley accompanied the women to Albuquerque. As grateful as they were for his generous assistance, they later remembered the soft cushions of his expensive car as much as they remembered anything he said on the trip east on Route 66. Once back in Albuquerque, the women checked into El Fidel, the same hotel they had stayed at the night before their harrowing ordeal had begun. Still weak, Laura and Marie walked shakily to their rooms, while Irene required the assistance of two state policemen.

Eating their first solid food the following day at noon, the grateful women rested and regained their energy over the next several days. Meanwhile, front page headlines announced the happy ending to the tourists' long ordeal. Reporters noted that Governor Tingley invited the "plucky" women to dine with him at the Governor's Mansion in Santa Fe when their health returned and his own bruises, suffered in the search, had healed.

The much-anticipated lunch at the Governor's Mansion took place as promised. Given the royal treatment by Tingley and his staff, the women expressed their gratitude to the governor and everyone who had helped in their hour of need. According to Marie, "We are already forgetting the hardships of being lost." Displaying remarkable resiliency, the French tourist added that "the things we will remember [about New Mexico] are the amusing things and the beautiful blue sky and the stars at night." If Governor Tingley's intent was to counter the negative news of female tourists getting lost in New Mexico's badlands, he had clearly succeeded. In Marie's words, "New Mexico has adopted us, and we have adopted New Mexico."

Proving their enduring courage, Laura, Irene, and Marie vowed to continue their western tour, with Arizona's Grand Canyon as their next destination. Their only concession was that they promised to simply gaze into the famous canyon, rather than attempt to climb down its steep trails. And the women were sure that they would not be exploring any more caves, at least for the balance of their western trip!

As Irene Piedalue, Laura Piedalue, and Marie Antoinette de Lafarest headed west on Route 66, Governor Tingley bid them farewell and praised the 150 men and women who had helped in the successful search and rescue mission, calling them "the most efficient posse I ever saw." No one could dispute the governor's assertion. Valencia County residents had answered an urgent call for help and had responded with all the determination and courage they were known to offer travelers on this and many other occasions in the long history of the Rio Abajo.

Lonnie Zamora and the
Socorro UFO Incident, 1964

by Paul Harden

Sightings of Unidentified Flying Objects (UFOs) reached epidemic proportions in the 1960s. Project Blue Book had been formed in 1951 to scientifically explain these strange occurrences and determine if they presented a threat to U.S. national security. When sightings occurred, government personnel arrived at the scene to begin the "official" investigation. In some cases, their job was to keep the story low-profile, discouraging local newspapers from reporting the incident in detail.

Keeping the story low-profile did not happen in Socorro on April 24, 1964. The basic story was reported in Socorro's *El Defensor Chieftain* three days later:

> What appears to be substantial evidence of an unidentified flying object landing and taking off in Socorro has been observed.
>
> City Policeman Lonnie Zamora, a highly reliable source, saw a four-legged, egg-shaped object, and two persons in a gully a mile south of the courthouse shortly before 6:00 p.m. Friday. He saw the object rise straight up and take off, and disappear beyond Six-Mile Canyon to the west. Some of the evidence of the landing and take-off remained in the gully. There were four shallow holes where the object apparently landed on its legs; there were burned greasewood and seared clumps of green grass; there were two round, very slight depressions. No footprints were found.
>
> At least one other person—an unidentified tourist traveling north on US 85—saw the UFO just before it landed in the gully. Opal Grinder, manager of Whiting Brother's Service Station on 85 north, said the man stopped at the station and remarked that aircraft flew

low around here. Grinder replied there were many helicopters in this vicinity.

The tourist said it was a "funny looking helicopter, if that's what it was." The man said further the object had flown over his car. It actually was headed straight for the gully where it landed moments later. The tourist also commented that he had seen a police car heading up the hill. This was Zamora's car.

Grinder did not know of the object at that time, and did not attach importance to the traveler's remarks.

Zamora doesn't know what the object was, but for those who desire to speculate, there are three possibilities. First, it may have been a top-secret U.S. aircraft in an advanced stage of development. Second, it may have been an advanced type of aircraft or space ship of another power. Third, it may have been a space scout ship from another planet.

[Policeman Zamora] was patrolling Park Street, where he had begun pursuit of a fast-traveling car several blocks ahead of him. He was almost on the old road when he heard what he described as a blast or a roar. [The "old road" was old US 85, today's west Frontage Road to the Luis Lopez overpass. In 1964, I-25 had just opened from Albuquerque to San Antonio.] His first thought was that an aluminum building used to store explosives had blown up. He forgot about the speeding car and headed up a very rocky dirt road toward the building. On the third try, driving very slowly, he managed to get up the road which lead to the top of the mesa overlooking the gully where the UFO had landed. [This is the steep dirt road and mesa just to the west of Raychester's Jewelry.]

The policeman said he first saw the object at an estimated distance of 150 yards, and he thought it was an overturned car. He was looking out of his car window as he drove towards the top of the mesa. Zamora said one of two persons at the UFO, whose back was to him, turned his head and looked straight at him. The two persons standing by the object appeared to be dressed in white overalls, and, and from the distance Zamora saw them, they appeared to be "child-like," that is, small.

When he stopped his car on the top of the mesa and directly opposite the place in the gully where the UFO had landed, he saw it again, but the persons were not outside the object on which the sun gleamed brightly. He got out of his car and started toward the UFO. [With his car facing southwest, Zamora walked southward into the gully.] Then he again heard the roar or blast that had brought him to the scene and saw flames. Dust was flying around the object.

The policeman believed the object was about to explode. He was about 50 feet from the UFO, and for protection he dropped to the ground and covered his face with an arm.

No explosion occurred and Zamora also realized the object was not heading in his direction. He raised his head slightly. He saw the UFO, which seemed to be heading south on landing, rise straight up for an estimated twenty feet, which brought it about on a level with the police car on the mesa top. The object appeared to maintain this altitude beyond the explosives building and due west in a straight line for about two miles to the perlite mill. On the other side of the mill the UFO gained altitude very rapidly, passed over Six-Mile Canyon, became a speck in the sky, and disappeared.

Zamora radioed the sheriff's office immediately after the object had taken off. [The radio dispatcher on duty was Nep López.] State Police Sergeant Sam Chávez, State Policeman Ted Jordan, and Under Sheriff James Luckie responded. Chávez and Luckie said the burned clumps of green grass and the greasewood were still hot when they arrived. The military later took samples of the burned earth for analysis.

An inspection of the scene Saturday morning showed the object landed astride a narrow, rock-strewn dry wash in the gully. Officers earlier had circled with stones the four places where the legs of the object had touched earth. The holes were shallow, about a foot long by six inches wide. They did not appear to have been made by an object striking the earth with great force, but by an object of considerable weight settling to earth at slow speed and not moving after touching the ground.

The clumps of green grass and two greasewood bushes seem to have been seared all at once by an extremely hot flame. There were also broken branches on one greasewood.

After Captain Richard Holder was apprised of the UFO occurrence, he made a report of it to the proper agencies at White Sands Missile Range. Investigations of the incident will be conducted by designated government agencies.

By Sunday afternoon, hundreds of curious persons had trampled the scene and there was virtually no evidence left of the landing marks.

This now-famous Socorro UFO landing occurred early Friday evening, April 24, 1964. By Saturday, the trek to Socorro by military and Project Blue Book personnel had begun. Also by Saturday, half the town of Socorro had heard of the sighting. Many had gone searching for the landing site. Lewis Reddell, publisher of the *Chieftain*, and editor Ted Raynor, were escorted to the site early Saturday morning by Sergeant Chávez. Raynor took numerous photographs of the depressions left in the sand by the landing legs, the burned greasewood plants, and of publisher Reddell and patrolman Chávez inspecting the site. With the *Defensor Chieftain* photographs of the depressions from the landing legs and the burned bushes, this incident also remains one of the few UFO landings with evidence that was captured on film.

Officer Lonnie Zamora (Socorro Police Department)

Later interviews with Patrolman Zamora and the tourists added more details to the mysterious event. Zamora was worried that the explosion that he first heard had come from a dynamite storage building on the mesa top. The ovoid did not appear to have any doors or windows and there was a strange red insignia on the side. As the object lifted off from its position in the gully, Zamora reported that the roaring noise changed to a high-pitched whine. The tourists, two men from Iowa, reported seeing a silvery object rising out of black smoke. One also said he saw portholes and a Z-shaped red insignia.

The dispatcher that took Zamora's radio call was Nep López, accompanied that evening by his 20-year-old son, Pablo. As Under Sheriff James Luckie dashed out of the office, he asked Pablo if he wanted to go along. Minutes later, Luckie and Pablo López met Zamora at the site. Sergeant Chávez was already there. Moments later, State Patrolman Ted Jordan arrived. All of these individuals saw the landing depressions and the still smoldering bushes within ten minutes following the incident.

The principal investigator for Project Blue Book, astronomer Dr. J. Allen Hynek, arrived in Socorro on Wednesday, April 29. As reported in the Thursday, April 30, *Chieftain*,

> Dr. J. Allen Hynek, special consultant to the Air Force
> on unidentified flying objects, was here Wednesday at
> the request of the Air Force. He visited the site with

Zamora, talked to him at length there, and interviewed others. He found the site so trampled by the curious that little of scientific value could be obtained.

In a follow-up visit a few months later, Hynek reported,
The Air Force is very much interested in the case and there has been nothing to discredit the investigation. But an acceptable answer concerning the object observed by City Policeman Lonnie Zamora has not yet been found.

One amusing story came several weeks after the UFO sighting. Motorists driving from Magdalena to Socorro noticed "shadowy figures with mysterious round lights seen roaming around the desert." This was promptly reported to the state patrol, who found the strange alien creatures roaming the desert west of Socorro to be members of a Bureau of Land Management (BLM) survey crew.

In 1968, a report issued by the congressional Condon Committee concluded that further studies of UFOs were unlikely to yield any further scientific discoveries. The Air Force testified that UFOs did not pose a threat to national security. As a result, Project Blue Book was disbanded in January 1970. During its 19-year lifespan, Blue Book investigated 12,618 UFO sightings, determining 701 of them to be "unexplainable." The Socorro sighting remains one of the top ten unexplained sightings.

Blue Book's director, Major Hector Quintanilla, wrote, "There is no doubt that Lonnie Zamora saw an object which left quite an impression on him. There is also no question about Zamora's reliability. He is a serious police officer, a pillar of his church, and a man well-versed in recognizing airborne vehicles in his area. He is puzzled by what he saw, and, frankly, so are we. This is the best documented case on record."

Early skeptics of the Socorro UFO considered it to be a colossal gimmick to promote tourism. Others claimed the entire affair was a hoax, based on the fact that the landing occurred on land owned by Holm O. Bursum, Jr., the mayor of Socorro at the time. However, a careful document search revealed that Bursum never owned this parcel of land. Historical research cannot prove what policeman Zamora did or did not see that April evening. That is for the reader to decide.

In 1966, Chamber of Commerce president Paul Ridings proposed building up the site to promote tourism. The Chamber and volunteers built stone walkways and steps into the arroyo from the mesa top, a rock walkway circling the landing site, and some wooden benches. Much of this rock work remains at the site today. Driving up the steep hill west of Raychester's Jewelry, this site is several hundred yards beyond the houses to the south in the arroyo bottom. Unfortunately, this is not the correct site. Since vegetation at the real site had not yet grown back, many people were spooked that the area might be radioactive. As a result, the "Chamber site" was built in the proper gully but closer to old US 85. It remains an interesting historical site in itself.

About a month after the landing, Socorro Junior High student Rick Baca drew a sketch of the craft based on Zamora's description. It has since found its way into numerous books and UFO web sites. Baca still lives in Socorro and still has his original sketch.

A Sketch by Rick Baca of the UFO based on Lonnie Zamora's recollections (Rick Baca)

Aside from the obvious suggestion of a visit from the far beyond, there have been claims that the object was a prototype lunar test vehicle flown in secret from the northern reaches of White Sands Missile Range or that it was a hoax perpetrated by clever students from New Mexico Tech with too much time on their hands. The latter theory was given some impetus when some 1968 correspondence between Linus Pauling, the Nobel laureate, and Dr. Stirling Colgate, then-president of New Mexico Tech, was uncovered in the Linus Pauling archives at Oregon State University. In this letter, Colgate told Pauling that the event was a hoax. Further investigation by UFO skeptics revealed that there was no love lost between Zamora and the students at Tech where Zamora had worked as a mechanic before joining the Socorro police force. In fact, it was stated that Zamora had a reputation for "hounding" Techies and that the speeding car had been a decoy to get Zamora to the scene where he could be the subject of their prank.

Following the 1964 UFO landing, Lonnie Zamora remained with the Socorro Police Department and worked for the City of Socorro in other capacities until his retirement. Zamora has seldom talked of the incident nor ever sought attention before his death in 2009. Yet, though never his intent, Zamora remains one of the world's best known Socorroans.

Before She Was First Lady: The Disappearance of Ida Jo Cargo and Her Children, 1966

by Richard Melzer

Ida Jo Cargo shivered in the crisp night air on Sunday, March 19, 1966. The frightened young mother clutched her two small children to give them warmth and reassure them that they were safe. But Ida Jo was justifiably concerned. She and her children, 3-year-old Veronica Ann and 1-year-old David Anthony, had been out on the desolate mesa west of Belen since before sunset. They had not eaten for hours and were hardly dressed for the cold night temperature.

Roots in Belen

But at least Ida Jo could see the lights of Belen in the distant Rio Grande Valley. Belen was Ida Jo's hometown. Born to Trinidad and Margarita Anaya in 1941, she was the fourth of eight children in her large family. Christened Adelida (after her maternal grandmother) Josephine (after St. Joseph because she was born on his feast day), she was always known simply as Ida Jo. As children, Ida Jo and her siblings had learned to work hard and take responsibility without complaint. They took turns working in their grandfather's grocery store on the corner of Aragón and North Main streets in Belen. The children did everything from running the cash register to pumping gas for customers at the gasoline pumps out front.

The children also helped on the Anaya family farm on Mesa Road. Trinidad Anaya worked for the Santa Fe Railway, but always grew crops and raised livestock to help feed his large family. When not working, Ida Jo enjoyed many pastimes, including going to the Oñate Theatre to see her favorite actress, the beautiful and talented Carmen Miranda.

More seriously, as a deeply spiritual person, Ida Jo prayed often and looked forward to events at Our Lady of Belen Catholic Church. She felt a special devotion to St. Anthony, ironically the patron saint of travelers, lost items, and seemingly lost causes. But most of all, Ida Jo enjoyed her family. Her siblings remember that family members did everything together, especially eating dinner at their kitchen table each evening. Trinidad and Margarita Anaya encouraged their children to express their opinions, think independently, and be resourceful, no matter what circumstances they faced.

Ida Jo Cargo (Anaya family)

Ida Jo had gone to school in Belen, graduating from Belen High School in 1959. She'd been a popular student with an early interest in politics and her Spanish heritage. *El Aguila*, Belen's high school annual, listed her membership in the school's government and Spanish clubs. In addition, she played the clarinet in the school's marching band.

Ida Jo's family had deep roots in Spanish history. Her sister, Pauline, has traced the family's genealogy to Christopher Columbus himself. Family ancestors arrived with Don Juan de Oñate and the original Spanish settlers of New Mexico in 1598. Other ancestors returned with Don Diego de Vargas in the resettlement of 1693.

More recently, Ida Jo's grandfathers were both heavily involved in politics. Her maternal grandfather, Ignacio Aragón y García, had been elected as Valencia County's sheriff (1929-31) and had served on the Belen school board for twenty-five years. Both sides of Ida Jo's family had been active in the Democratic Party since the 1930s.

Stuck

But politics were the last thing on Ida Jo's mind on that cold Sunday night in March 1966. She had driven with Veronica and David to meet her family for a picnic to be held at a favorite family spot near the Rio Puerco. Pauline, who had originally planned to go on the picnic with Ida Jo, had had to change her plans, so Ida Jo had gone ahead with her two children, driving Pauline's yellow convertible Volkswagen "bug."

Ida Jo knew the way, but had taken a wrong turn on an unmarked, unpaved road. To make matters worse, her car had gotten stuck in the sandy bottom of a box canyon. Finding no shovel in the VW's trunk, she tried to dig out with only her hands. Despite her best efforts, the tires only spun deeper in the sand.

After two hours, Ida Jo realized it was no use. Searchers could not see her if she stayed with the car at the bottom of a canyon. She and the children would have to start walking before it grew any later. Ida Jo wondered how long it would be until her family came looking for her on the mesa. Or they might not look at all, assuming that she had had to skip the picnic because something had come up regarding her husband's political campaign.

Ida Jo had met her husband, David Cargo, after she had attended the Western School for Secretaries in Albuquerque and had been hired as a legal secretary in Cargo's law firm, located in the Sunshine Building in downtown Albuquerque. Cargo was new to New Mexico, having only arrived in the state in 1957, after graduating from law school at the University of Michigan. Ten years Ida Jo's senior, Cargo had been taken by Ida Jo's striking beauty, good heart, and clear intelligence. The couple fell in love and was married in Albuquerque on September 2, 1960, just six months after they first met.

Although a relative unknown in New Mexico state politics, Dave Cargo had great political ambitions. A Republican in a heavily Democratic state, he had already served two terms in the New Mexico state legislature when he announced his candidacy for governor in 1966. Cargo ran a strong campaign for the highest political office in the state. He became well known and admired for his independent, low-key, populist style. Traveling throughout New Mexico in his old green Ford, Cargo was soon called—and is forever remembered as—"Lonesome Dave."

Ida Jo did her share of traveling during her husband's unorthodox campaign for governor. She supported David's political ambitions and often walked door-to-door, meeting people, distributing campaign literature, and soliciting votes. Ida Jo's sister, Pauline, remembers one such walking tour in Las Cruces. Going from one neighborhood to the next, Pauline wore out the only pair of shoes she had brought along on the three-day trip.

By all accounts, Ida Jo proved to be one of Dave Cargo's main political assets. Young, personable, graceful, and beautiful, she reminded many New Mexicans of a Hispanic Jacqueline Kennedy. According to one newspaper report, a woman at a political rally in Lovington told Ida Jo, "I'm going to vote for your husband because you are so pretty." Ida Jo's fluent Spanish made her especially appealing to her Hispanic admirers. David Cargo remembers large crowds of up to 8,000 in Las Vegas and 12,000 in Tierra Amarilla. Ida Jo frequently spoke at these political rallies, making brief remarks in both Spanish and English.

With her family's interest in the Atrisco land grant, there were even rumors that she was a "card-carrying" member of *La Alianza*, the radical land grants organization led by Reies López Tijerina. David Cargo recently confirmed these rumors, adding that Ida Jo sympathized with *La Alianza*'s goals, but could hardly be counted as a militant member of the group. Ida Jo was expected to help Cargo carry several counties with large Hispanic populations, including Valencia. According to Cargo, when a political rival declared that the only voters supporting Cargo in Valencia County were railroad workers and Ida Jo's family, Democratic leader Filo Sedillo declared, "That's the whole county!"

Ida Jo's Trek

But Ida Jo's trek on that cold March night in 1966 was far more difficult than any campaign trip she had ever taken. As time passed, it was apparent that Ida Jo lacked the strength to carry both Veronica and David. Rather than simply wait for help, which may or may not arrive soon, she had to do something to ensure her children's safety. As resourceful as ever, Ida Jo devised a logical plan of action. She would leave one child along the road and carry the other a short distance. She would then place the second child beside the road and back track to retrieve the first. She hated to leave either child alone, but there had been no traffic and she hoped that there were no rattlesnakes or other dangerous animals in the vicinity.

The going was exceedingly slow. With no moonlight, it was pitch dark. Her only hope was to keep moving and remain optimistic that she and her children would persevere. She undoubtedly prayed, especially to St. Anthony. It seemed that Ida Jo's prayers had been answered when she came across a corral. If there was a horse in the corral she could ride it to Belen and get help. But the corral was empty. She had to continue on foot.

Fortunately, Ida Jo was optimistic and determined by nature. Once, when she lived with her sister, María, in an apartment near Central Avenue in Albuquerque and briefly worked at Bataan Memorial Hospital (later the Lovelace Medical Center), she was about to board a city bus when she realized that she lacked the change for bus fare. Never considering giving up and turning back, Ida Jo simply walked the entire distance to work—in high-heeled shoes. Pauline remembers another occasion when two friends from Las Cruces were staying with Ida Jo and Dave on the night before the friends were scheduled to run a marathon race in Albuquerque. The pair talked about the upcoming race and where they hoped to finish the next day. Ida Jo enjoyed the conversation, but could not understand why the runners were planning to finish anywhere other than first place. Their "defeatism" made no sense in her way of thinking about a race or any other challenge in life.

And so Ida Jo remained optimistic that she and her children would survive and eventually be rescued. They had to be. It was, after all, Ida Jo's twenty-fifth birthday, and she was, after all, pregnant with her third child.

Meanwhile, Dave Cargo had spent the weekend on the campaign trail. He'd been glad that Ida Jo and their children had plans for an outing with her parents, leaving him to focus on pressing political matters in northern New Mexico. Cargo had not heard from Ida Jo, but had had no reason to be alarmed. His wife was undoubtedly having a wonderful time, as she always did when the Anayas gathered as a family.

Search and Rescue

But the Anayas became worried when they returned home from their picnic and discovered that Ida Jo and her children had left for the event but had never returned. The family alerted the sheriff's office, starting a search that lasted well into the night. As many as seventy volunteers and police officers joined the search party. Learning that his family was missing, Dave Cargo joined the group about 10:00 p.m.

But no one found Ida Jo and her kids on the mesa that night. Instead, Ida Jo, carrying little David, finally came across an isolated radio command station manned by Sandia Army Base soldiers on the west mesa. Soldiers at the outpost listened in amazement as she told them of her experience and asked them to call for assistance. The police arrived in moments.

Ida Jo and young David were safe, but they still needed to find Veronica, hopefully at the spot where Ida Jo had last left her. Anxiously retracing Ida Jo's route, under sheriff Frank Sedillo and Ida Jo finally found the girl, safely awakening from a peaceful sleep on the side of the dirt road. Taken to her parents' home in Belen, Ida Jo, Veronica, and David rested the best they could while reporters gathered to learn the details of their long ordeal. When asked how she felt, Ida Jo said she was fine, except for soreness in her legs, understandable after her estimated seventeen-mile, ten-hour trek.

The story of Ida Jo and her children's journey made front page news on Monday morning, March 20, although some political opponents suggested that the whole drama had been staged by the Cargos to gain publicity and political support. David Cargo still laughs at the thought.

First Lady

Cargo went on to win his race for the governor's office, beating Democrat T. E. Lusk with 52 percent of the vote. Election results show that "Lonesome Dave" easily carried Valencia County and other largely Hispanic counties, thanks in part to Ida Jo's campaign work, popularity, and valuable genealogical ties. By all reports, Ida Jo made a fine First Lady. At 26, she was New Mexico's youngest First Lady. She was also the state's first Hispanic First Lady since María García Larrazolo, Governor Octaviano A. Larrazolo's wife, in 1920.

While her husband served as the state's chief executive for two terms (1967-69 and 1969-71), Ida Jo promoted the arts, encouraging Hispanic and Native American artists in particular. She opened the Governor's Mansion to the public every Friday afternoon from May to September, with Spanish food and entertainment provided. Still close to her family and friends in Belen, she hosted her Belen High School class reunion at the Governor's Mansion in 1969. Fifty-three couples attended, with four couples coming from as far away as California and one couple from as far as Illinois.

Accompanying her husband to meetings and conventions across the country and into Mexico, Ida Jo was enormously popular among the national and international leaders she met. Dining at the White House three times, she was especially admired by President Lyndon B. Johnson, Senator Daniel Patrick Moynihan of New York, and Henry Kissinger, Secretary of State during much of the Richard Nixon administration. Ida Jo counted LBJ's wife, Lady Bird, as a personal friend.

Despite all this attention and activity, Ida Jo managed to raise her growing family. She gave birth to her son, Patrick Michael, on September 20, 1966. A healthy infant, Patrick was no worse for his mother's traumatic experience six months prior to his birth. A year later, on September 11, Ida Jo gave birth to María Elena Christina, the first baby born to a New Mexico state governor and his wife while in office. A fifth child, Eamon Francis, was born in 1973.

Dave Cargo left office in 1971 and decided to move his family to Oregon, where they remained from 1974 to 1985. Returning to New Mexico, the Cargos divorced in 1985. Ida Jo remarried in August 1990. Always creative, Ida Jo studied art, painted, and wrote poetry, including poems about her family, their farm, the railroad, and Belen. Tragically, she died of cancer while living with her second husband, Dennis Robson, in Midland, Texas. She was only 55.

Ida Jo's finest moment was not on a political stage at a campaign rally, in the Governor's Mansion in Santa Fe, or even in the White House in Washington, D.C. Her finest moment was protecting her children on the lonely mesa west of the place she loved the most and where she had been most happy, her hometown of Belen.

Valencia County's Most Famous Cold Case: Tara Calico's Disappearance, 1988-present

by John Taylor

A parent's worst nightmare is to lose a child, especially in a violent crime. Before Patty Doel died, she still had hopes that her daughter, Tara Calico, was alive. After more than twenty-five years of searching and praying, Tara's family still has no answer to the mystery of what happened to their bright, beautiful daughter who vanished in broad daylight on September 20, 1988.

Tara Calico (www.taracalico.com)

Tara Leigh Calico, a freckle-faced brunette, was 19-years-old. She was a sophomore, maintaining a 3.9 GPA at the University of New Mexico's Valencia Campus, worked at a local bank, and had plans to become a psychologist. Those who knew her described her as a very intelligent young woman who was athletic and outgoing, with many friends.

A Fateful Bicycle Ride

On that September morning, Tara left her Rio Communities house at about 9:30 a.m. to go on her daily thirty-seven-mile bike ride. Her normal route was an "out-and-back" on N.M. Route 6 toward the intersection with Route 60. This particular day she was a bit worried that she might not make a 12:30 p.m. tennis date with her boyfriend. She took her mother's pink Huffy bicycle because her own bike had developed a flat a day or two before.

Tara was last seen at about 11:45 a.m., heading north on Route 6, about two miles from her home. When Tara failed to return home, Patty went out looking for her, thinking that she would find her walking home with a disabled bike. Tara wasn't there. In fact, she wasn't anywhere.

"I was fifteen, a sophomore in high school," her sister, Michele, remembered. "I remember one of my sister's best friends and her boyfriend came to get me from school. They picked me up, and when we got home, there was a bunch of cops." Michele remembers being briefly told that Tara hadn't come home from her bike ride and that people were out looking for her. The house was in chaos with people going in and out. "I didn't understand what was going on," she said. "I just assumed that she maybe had gone a different way and that we were going to find her. I didn't think that she was missing until later on that evening when I started to realize how serious it was. But I just kept thinking that she was going to come back."

The Search

Valencia County Sheriff Lawrence Romero was in charge of the search for Tara, which soon got national attention. A cassette from her Sony walkman was found a few miles south of her last known location, and a broken piece of the cassette player itself was recovered from the John F. Kennedy campground, several miles east of Route 6 in the foothills of the Manzano Mountains. Rain and wind on the night of her disappearance obscured any other evidence of what might have happened. However, witnesses reported that she may have been being followed by a dirty white or light grey 1950s Ford pickup with a homemade camper shell. Police released a composite sketch of the driver, based on the witnesses' recollections.

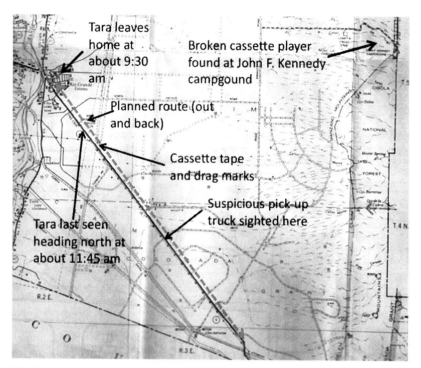

Tara leaves home at about 9:30 am

Broken cassette player found at John F. Kennedy campgound

Planned route (out and back)

Cassette tape and drag marks

Suspicious pick-up truck sighted here

Tara last seen heading north at about 11:45 am

The Search (John Taylor

In the days, months, and years following Tara's disappearance, her family never gave up working on finding out what happened to her. They pleaded for any kind of information, appearing on national television and investigating the case themselves. "We were both deputized after Tara's disappearance and were able to investigate the case," John Doel said of himself and Patty. "It allowed us to carry weapons and also to be able to contact any other law enforcement agency on behalf of the sheriff's department regarding the case. We were both commissioned as auxiliary deputies. It's been a rough twenty years, especially on Patty. It was extremely hard on her, but she never gave up hope; she never quit."

Police Composite Sketch of Suspect (Valencia County News-Bulletin)

Another person who has never given up trying to find answers in the case is former Valencia County Sheriff Rene Rivera, who assumed responsibility for the cold case when he was elected in 2007. While he wasn't on the force when Tara initially disappeared, he began his law-enforcement career the next year and began receiving information about the disappearance. "I've actually been working on this case ever since I started with the sheriff's department in 1989," Rivera said. "People would come up to me and give me information, and I would write a report and turn it over to the detective who was working the case. Once I got into detectives in 1996, the case was given to me."

A Polaroid Photo

In the years since the disappearance, Rivera and other investigators have been following up on any leads they've received, including a Polaroid photo of an unidentified female discovered in Port St. Joe, Florida, in June 1989. The photo was discovered on the ground in a convenience store's parking lot where a white Toyota van had been parked. The picture depicts a long-legged young woman and a smaller boy lying on some sheets and a blue striped pillow. Their mouths were covered with duct tape and their hands were tied behind their backs.

Possible Image of Tara Calico (www.taracalico.com)

Some people at first believed that the boy in the picture was Michael Henley, a 9-year-old boy who vanished in April 1988 in northern New Mexico. But Henley's remains were found in the Zuni Mountains in 1990. Patty and John Doel believed that the girl in the photo was their daughter. However, the Federal Bureau of Investigation examined the photo and couldn't determine whether the girl was Calico, a conclusion confirmed by experts at the Los Alamos National Laboratory. "I don't think it's her," Rivera said of the picture. "It does resemble her quite a bit, but I don't think it's her. And if the picture is of her, it could have been taken here and then transported somewhere else."

Other leads Rivera has followed up on over the years included another possible sighting in Florida, as well as several alleged burial locations throughout Valencia County. Rivera has obtained search warrants for various properties where someone said Tara's body had been buried. "We've dug both by hand and with backhoes," the former sheriff said. "Any lead that we got, we followed through with it, because we didn't want to leave anything out."

A Waiting Game

Rivera claims that he knows what happened to Tara that day and who is responsible. While he won't say who the suspects are, he did say that he's received information that two men, who were teenagers at the time of Tara's disappearance, abducted her after finding her riding her bike, and had help afterwards disposing of her body. But locating her body is that one piece of evidence that is keeping the sheriff from making an arrest. He said he hopes that the people responsible, or those who know what happened that day, will lead them to her remains so they can finally close the case.

"We do have a case put together, but we want to make sure that this case is a concrete case to where we'll be able to effectively do our jobs," he said. "We're just waiting to get a little more evidence--her bicycle, her clothing, or Tara herself." Rivera said several people have told him that, while riding her bike, Tara was approached by two individuals in an older model Ford pickup truck. He said these two people had been following her, grabbing at her, trying to talk to her. "The information I have is that the truck accidentally ended up hitting her," Rivera said. "I believe the truck bumped her bike, at which time she fell to the side of the road. From there, the individuals took her."

The sheriff thinks that the two men knew Tara, and she may have threatened to call law enforcement. He says the two men panicked, took her, and killed her. Rivera said two other people may have become involved in the situation afterwards and may have knowledge of what happened to her and where she may be buried. "If Tara was killed, I would say her body is still within the county," he added. "I think that she's still in the same general area that she was taken."

Closure?

After nearly twenty-five years, Rivera hopes that these suspects, or even anyone who they told what happened that day, will come forward and finally put an end to the mystery. "I'm hoping that this time around, these people will finally realize that it's time to talk and time to put her to rest," the former sheriff said. "Enough is enough. At this point, I'd like to recover her body. I wanted to do it before her mother died [in May 2006], but she still has family and they want and need answers."

When John Doel learned through the media that Rivera had two suspects in mind, he said he would hope that arrests would be made regardless of whether the sheriff's department was waiting for more evidence. "I thought it was silly when I heard it," Doel said. "There's such a thing as circumstantial evidence, and I know, in other places, they've gotten a conviction on strong circumstantial evidence. It should have never been said unless they're [the sheriff's department] is willing to make an arrest and go forward with it."

Tara's stepfather and sister said they're always hoping someone will relent and come forward, so that one day the family will find closure. "We have, to an extent, moved on with our lives, but it's always in the back of my mind," said Michele, who is now a mother herself. "I've learned to appreciate people more and things that people normally take for granted. I just want to express how grateful my family is for everyone who has done anything during this process for us," she added. "We're eternally grateful for those who helped, and I want them to know that we sure do think about them."

Section III—Accidents and Disasters

"The Most Terrible Accident in All of Aviation:" Mount Taylor, 1929

by Richard Melzer

Aviation was still new and exciting in the 1920s. Only two decades after Wilbur and Orville Wright's first flight on December 17, 1903, airplanes had demonstrated their value in warfare during World War I and in peacetime pursuits, including the first flight in New Mexico in early 1911.

News of daring, record-setting flights filled the newspapers and kindled admiration for early airplanes and their intrepid pilots. In the most famous flight of this kind, Charles Lindbergh astonished the world by flying the first solo flight across the Atlantic Ocean in the spring of 1927. Belen's own Art Goebel captured national attention when he won the coveted $25,000 Dole Prize for completing the first successful flight from the mainland of the United States to Hawaii, just three months after Lindbergh's celebrated landing in Europe.

Even the 1929 University of New Mexico's football team traveled by air, becoming the nation's first team to use this most modern form of transportation to travel to an away game. Enthusiastic but cautious, Coach Roy Johnson sent his second-string players by plane, while sending his first-string team (and himself) by train to play Occidental College in Pasadena, California. Nothing seemed impossible by the late 1920s. Aviation captured the public's imagination as America's exciting new frontier.

In small, tentative efforts, even passenger lines had been established by forward-thinking entrepreneurs. Wealthy, adventuresome men and women braved travel on these earliest commercial flights. There were, of course, those who cautioned against attempting too much too soon. A May 15, 1924, editorial in the *Alamogordo News* warned of "the hazards and number of fatalities" that made stunt flying, no less commercial flights, a risky business.

But the number of skeptics grew smaller as the attraction of commercial flying, with its speed, comfort, and relative safety, grew more and more appealing to modern travelers. Transcontinental Air Transport (T.A.T.) provided the most ambitious early passenger service in the United States. Beginning in July 1929, T.A.T. offered travelers coast-to-coast service, with air travel during the day and railroad travel at night, since planes still lacked adequate facilities for night flights. Crossing New Mexico, for example, westbound T.A.T. flights landed in Clovis where passengers touched down in the early evening and traveled in Pullman cars by train overnight to Albuquerque. The following morning, travelers boarded a waiting T.A.T. plane that flew them on to Winslow, Arizona, over hundreds of miles of what was then western Valencia County. Similar train/plane relays through Arizona brought passengers to their final destination in Los Angeles. The total coast-to-coast trip took just forty-eight hours, reducing travel time by a full-day-and-a-half.

The Flight

One such Albuquerque-to-Winslow leg of T.A.T.'s coast-to-coast service took off on schedule at 10:20 a.m. on Tuesday, September 3, 1929, less than two months after the new route's initial flight in Albuquerque on July 8.

Piloted by 29-year-old Captain J.B. Stowe of Long Beach, California, the plane's manifest listed two additional crewmembers. Twenty-three-year-old co-pilot E.A. Dietel hailed from Los Angeles, while 22-year-old steward C.F. Canfield came from Peekskill, New York. With Army flight training and several years experience, Captain Stowe was considered one of T.A.T.'s best pilots. Young C.F. Canfield had just graduated from Harvard University and had taken the job of steward to learn the new airline business from the bottom up, hoping to eventually advance to higher levels of authority in the new industry.

In addition to the three-man crew, five passengers flew on that fateful morning. The only female passenger, Corina Raymond of Glendale,

California, had many ties to the airline business: her husband George was a T.A.T. clerk and her father, A.W. Horton, was the airport manager in Winslow. Passenger William Henry Beers of New York was the editor of *Golf Illustrated* magazine. Beers was en route to Pebble Beach, California, to attend the 1929 national amateur golf championship. The press described passenger Harris Livermore of Boston as a "prominent shipping man." M.M. Campbell was identified as the sales manager of a paper company based in Cincinnati. Finally, passenger Amasa B. McGaffey was a well-known, highly-respected citizen of New Mexico. He was, in fact, the founder of the small community of McGaffey, sixteen miles southeast of Gallup.

Headed into stormy weather on September 3, 1929, the T.A.T. plane, known as the "City of San Francisco," was last seen near Grants, not far from Mount Taylor, thirty miles to the northeast. And then the T.A.T. plane disappeared.

Transcontinental Air Transport's "City of San Francisco" (Historical Aviation Studies and Research)

Ground crew members in Winslow grew concerned when Captain Stowe failed to land at his scheduled time. Inclement weather could explain a short delay, but passenger Corina Raymond's dad and his men became increasingly anxious as minutes turned into hours with no sign of the "City of San Francisco." Although no distress signal had been received, the passenger plane was clearly in distress.

Several cowhands, sheepherders, railroad workers, and Navajo residents reported seeing the "City of San Francisco" flying in the skies near Gallup about 11:30 a.m. Using these initial leads, search planes took off from Winslow and concentrated their efforts on western New Mexico and eastern Arizona. The greatest airplane search in Southwest history had begun.

The Search

T.A.T. sent every available plane in its fleet to conduct as quick and as thorough a search as possible. Planes, pilots, and ground crews arrived in Winslow from Albuquerque, Clovis, Phoenix, and Amarillo. Other airlines sent planes and crews of their own. Military planes rushed to the scene as well. Army and Navy officials in Washington, D.C., dispatched every available military search craft at their disposal. Military planes soon arrived from as far south as El Paso and as far west as San Diego.

Forming what the press called an "aerial armada," seventy planes slowly circled mile after mile of desert terrain in search of any clue that might solve the mystery of what had happened to Captain Stowe, his small crew, and five passengers. Each search craft carried a supply of food and water to drop to possible survivors on the ground.

Other groups offered their assistance. National Forest officials provided search personnel and equipment. Telegraph operators along the Santa Fe Railway between Albuquerque and Kingman, Arizona, stood ready to relay information about the missing plane as quickly as it might be received. Indian scouts familiar with the rugged terrain accompanied several pilots to lend their expertise. Many planes carried high-powered field glasses, although continued bad weather hampered visibility, especially in the first days of the hunt.

On foot and in the air, searchers scoured the earth's surface for a plane with a wing span of 74 feet, a length of 49 feet, 10 inches, a weight, when empty, of 6,100 pounds, and a payload of 3,900 pounds. The missing craft could accommodate a maximum of ten passengers. Powered by three 425-horsepower engines, the "City of San Francisco" could cruise at ninety-five miles-per-hour and reach a top speed of about 130 miles-per-hour. One of ten aircrafts of its kind in the T.A.T. fleet, the plane's fleet number was A19. It bore the wing number 9649.

Unfortunately, the plane was designed so that no exit from the craft was possible while in flight. As a result, neither passengers nor crew wore parachutes. To make matters worse, the plane carried only enough food and water for two light meals, hardly enough to sustain life in the desert for more than a day. The plane did have radio equipment on board, but Captain Stowe could only receive radio messages, not send them.

News of the missing plane and its eight people on board spread quickly throughout the United States. Eager to learn all they could about the search, Americans from coast to coast listened intently to their radios, while carefully following each newspaper report wired from the Southwest. In response to the demand for information about every detail regarding the search, the *Gallup Independent* printed the first extra edition in its 18-year history. According to the *Independent*, "No event in many years has caused such a storm of excitement in Gallup." The same could be said of Winslow in Arizona, of Grants in western Valencia County, and of most other large and small communities in the region.

Residents of Gallup and western Valencia County were particularly anxious about the flight and its fate because the five passengers aboard the "City of San Francisco" included A.B. McGaffey. McGaffey had founded a successful lumber company in western Valencia County in 1910. Based in a small settlement in the Zuni Mountains, the company's sawmill employed an ethnic mixture of European immigrants, Hispanic residents, and Navajo Indians. With a population of 650 by 1929, the village of McGaffey was long known—and later remembered—for its beautiful setting, Saturday night dances, and elaborate Fourth of July celebrations. Its founder was known as one of the most generous, most admired men in the region.

A.B. McGaffey was a sportsman as well as a businessman. For years, McGaffey and several of his friends had met each fall to hunt wild game in locations as distant as Alaska. In 1929, their plan was to hunt game in northern California. Although McGaffey had previously traveled to his hunting destinations by car and train, in 1929, one of his three sons had convinced him to try modern plane travel for the first time in his life. Family members and friends now regretted McGaffey's decision to add more adventure to his already-adventuresome annual trip. Many gathered in Winslow, anxious for the slightest bit of good news. They hoped that if his plane crashed, McGaffey, described in the press as "a rigorous, athletic man," could lead survivors over a countryside that he knew as well as most natives.

Friends and business associates from the Gallup area were so concerned about McGaffey's safety that they organized a search party of their own soon after the "City of San Francisco" disappeared. Led by McKinley County Sheriff Dee Roberts and Horace Moses of the Gallup-American Coal Company, a caravan of cars and ambulances headed south toward Zuni to pursue a report that the T.A.T. plane had been sighted somewhere in the pueblo's vicinity.

A terrible thunderstorm, combined with a torrent of rain and strong winds, made progress on the road to Zuni almost impossible. Telephone poles blew down. Several vehicles got stuck hub-deep in mud. Night fell, making progress even more difficult. The search party finally arrived in Zuni past midnight after a five-hour journey. The weather cleared the following day, but not a trace of the lost plane was found, despite the best efforts of McGaffey's loyal friends.

Not willing to give up, Horace Moses assigned nearly every member of his coal company's work force to join the extended search. Indian trading post operators were alerted to be on the lookout. Search parties even entered the Grand Canyon on a wild hunch that the "City of San Francisco" might have been blown off course and crashed in that most rugged section of northwestern Arizona.

T.A.T. was so eager to find its lost plane (and repair its damaged safety reputation) that it offered a reward of $5,000 for information leading to the discovery of the airline's lost plane and the eight people on board. The parents of C.F. Canfield, the youngest crewmember aboard, offered an additional $5,000 in reward money.

Over five hundred Navajos, Zunis, local settlers, lawmen, and ranch hands scoured the countryside on horseback, in trucks, and on foot. Famed distance runner Andrew Chimoney and a group of his fellow Zunis "scoured the country in rabbit-hunting fashion, spread out over a wide formation through the piñon undergrowth of their mesa and mountain terrain," according to a *New York Times* reporter. The reporter added that "the Zunis are noted for their ability to race over their rocky

294

terrain for days at a stretch without fatigue." Wise to the ways of nature, many Westerners searched the sky for circling buzzards to help locate the plane and its possible victims.

Hearing of the "City of San Francisco's" disappearance, the nation's foremost aviator made plans to join the search in person. Charles Lindbergh had been instrumental in T.A.T.'s creation, recruiting skilled pilots and serving as the company's technical director since May 1929. Although he normally shunned publicity, Lindbergh granted interviews and made speeches to promote T.A.T. and instill public confidence in its safety. It was no surprise that many Americans referred to T.A.T. as the Lindbergh Line. Few Americans realized that Lindbergh also had a large vested interest in T.A.T. and its success. The famous airman drew a handsome annual salary and owned no less than $250,000 in T.A.T. stock.

The Lone Eagle was no stranger to New Mexico. Flying in his famous "Spirit of St. Louis," Lindbergh had visited New Mexico as part of a national tour within months of his triumphant return from Europe in 1927. He returned to New Mexico in 1928 to help shoot over a hundred aerial photos of ancient archeological ruins. He had also visited the region while helping to establish T.A.T.'s air and rail routes to the West Coast.

To help in the search for the "City of San Francisco," Lindbergh and his newlywed bride, Anne Morrow Lindbergh, quickly packed their supplies and took off from Roosevelt Field in New York at 2:05 p.m. on Friday, September 6. The couple flew in a plane that had just broken the coast-to-coast speed record. Making short stops in Columbus, Ohio, and St. Louis, Missouri, the Lindberghs hurried west. Charles and Anne arrived in Winslow at 3:50 p.m. on Saturday, September 7. Just as their plane neared the Winslow airport, their motor suddenly sputtered and died, having run out of gas. Displaying his famous flying skills, Charles made a dead-stick landing and brought his ship to a safe, dramatic stop.

But even after their quick trip and emergency landing, Anne Lindbergh was not overly confident that she and Charles—or anyone else—could be of help in the search for the "City of San Francisco." Anne wrote to her mother, "There is still some hope, but it is desolate country and [if there are survivors] they have no food with them and only a little water....and it [would] take them days to get back to civilization." Others quietly agreed, although every rumor, including sightings as far off as northern Mexico and southern California, was pursued in earnest.

But then the searchers' luck suddenly seemed to have changed. On Friday, September 6, search plane pilot D. W. Tomlinson delivered promising news after returning from a flight to an area about a hundred miles north of Winslow. Tomlinson reported that he had spotted four men on a high, isolated mesa. Seeing Tomlinson's plane, the men had rushed to a nearby Navajo hogan, had grabbed white shirts, and had waved the garments in what appeared to be a distress signal. Tomlinson optimistically concluded that the men he had seen were survivors from the T.A.T. flight. If there were four survivors, maybe there were others in the hogan, including some in need of immediate medical attention. With his fuel running low and no place to land safely, Tomlinson hurried back to Winslow to report his discovery and dispatch rescuers on horseback to aid the stranded party.

But Tomlinson's optimism was premature. Closer inspection showed that the men he had seen were not flight survivors, but simply enthusiastic rural residents who had probably never seen a plane before, or at least not one in the vicinity of their isolated home.

Finally Found

Finding nothing in the region near Gallup and Winslow, pilots broadened their search area toward more eastern parts of Valencia County. And that's where searchers finally met success, of a kind, about 11:00 a.m. on Saturday, September 7.

Asked to be on the lookout around Mount Taylor on his regular flight east from California to Albuquerque, pilot George K. Rice of the Western Air Express Company searched the southern slopes of the largest volcanic mountain in New Mexico, located about thirty miles northeast of Grants. Flying as low as he dared, Rice spotted the remains of an airplane wing near Mount Taylor's peak, over 11,000 feet above sea level. Resting upside down, the number on the plane's wing was clearly visible: 9649. "The City of San Francisco" had been found at last.

Several hundred yards further on, the aviator found what everyone had been looking for, but all had dreaded they might ultimately find: a crash scene with the cabin and remainder of the plane in shambles. Worse yet, there was no sign of life. All on board had apparently perished during or shortly after the terrible crash. Rice took aerial photos to confirm his gruesome discovery. The pilot rushed to Albuquerque to relay his news to a waiting world.

Hearing Rice's report, A.M. McGaffey's friends in Gallup were now as determined to get to the crash site as they had been to find the previously missing plane. The group drove through Saturday afternoon and began their accent of Mount Taylor at 4:45 p.m. But, as Rice had reported, "no trail or road led to the immediate vicinity of the wrecked plane." Anyone venturing to the crash site would have to travel most of the way by foot over incredibly rugged terrain.

Wreckage of the "City of San Francisco" (Museum of New Mexico, #166109)

The Gallup party finally suspended its search about 10:30 p.m., making camp at 9,000 feet altitude. Many in the group could not sleep in the bitterly cold overnight temperatures. Eager to move on, the men continued their trek early the next morning. Shouldering stretchers to remove all eight bodies, they proceeded ten miles through deep canyons and dense woods. Their search for the downed plane was futile until two planes circled the crash site to reveal the targeted destination. Charles Lindbergh, piloting the high-speed craft he had flown from New York, swooped particularly low over the crash site to aid those on the ground.

The men from Gallup claimed that they were the first to arrive at the crash site by land, although local ranchers and a Valencia County deputy sheriff were not far behind. One pack team included Tom Palmer, the most famous Mount Taylor guide and mountain lion hunter of his generation. By 9:00 a.m., no fewer than seventy-five men had arrived on the mountain. The scene they found "resembled nothing so much as a city dump," according to one newspaper report. "Metal was strung in hundreds of places over a wide territory." As feared, all eight on board were dead. Suffering severe burns from the fire that had engulfed the plane on impact, few of the passengers or crew members were easily recognizable.

Corina Raymond's body was the first to be identified, thanks to the rings and other jewelry she wore. A.B. McGaffey was also identified by a piece of jewelry: a Masonic ring recognized by O.L. Gray, the Santa Fe Railway trainmaster at Gallup and one of McGaffey's closest friends. The bodies of T.A.T. officers Stowe, Dietel, and Canfield were identified by the gold buttons on their uniforms, although the buttons were blackened with soot from the fire. Stowe and Dietel were found in the ship's cockpit "with their left hands up before their faces as if warding off a blow," in the words of a reporter who had arrived at the crash scene.

The badly burned bodies of passengers M.M. Campbell, William Henry Beers, and Harris Livermore were the last to be identified, by process of elimination. Valencia County lawmen insisted that the bodies of A.M. McGaffey and his fellow crash victims could not be removed until an official inquest was held. All present had to wait another two hours before District Attorney Fred Nicholas arrived, held an inquest, and finally released the bodies for removal off the mountain. Led by undertaker Dominic Rollie, the Gallup party struggled to carry the victims' remains on horseback to the Canyon Lobo ranger station where ambulances waited to transport them either to Gallup or to Albuquerque.

According to one story, the first searchers on the scene had waited for the district attorney and others to arrive by sitting on some steel boxes found among the plane's scattered cargo. They later learned that the boxes contained $50,000 that was being transported by air to the federal mint in San Francisco.

Reporters used a portable telephone, set up at an isolated surveyor's camp and connected to a switchboard in Grants, to relay news of the dramatic developments. Marcel Marsalis, the lone telephone operator in Grants, connected reporters on the remote phone to their newspaper offices across the country. Rescue workers and reporters praised Marcel for her untiring, efficient work from Saturday, when the crash site was identified, to late Sunday, when the victims' bodies were successfully removed from Mount Taylor. Although she had refused to stop to eat or rest for over thirty-six hours, Marcel was as calm, courteous, and helpful on Sunday night as she had been at Saturday noon. Identifying Marcel as the hero of the day, newspapermen offered her gifts of money for her exceptional work. Like all true heroes, she humbly refused the reporters' generous offers.

Search pilot Rice also refused to accept any of the $10,000 offered as reward money for the person who first discovered the missing plane. He did, however, accept an Associated Press check for exclusive use of his aerial photos of the plane wreckage.

The T.A.T. crash, search and discovery made a powerful impact on people and places, far and wide. Friends and relatives mourned their losses. Captain Stowe's young wife, who had bravely insisted throughout the ordeal that her husband would eventually be found alive, sadly returned to the small house that the couple had just recently purchased in Clovis. The community of McGaffey was never the same after its founding father perished. McGaffey's sawmill soon closed and most families moved away.

T.A.T. had changed as well. In the days and weeks following the crash, T.A.T. canceled its east-west flights more readily when inclement weather threatened western New Mexico or eastern Arizona. But the Mount Taylor crash, plus another tragic T.A.T. crash in January 1930 that cost sixteen lives near Pleasanton, California, left the young company close to bankruptcy at the start of a far different crash: the Great Depression of the 1930s. To its credit, T.A.T. weathered the economic storm, changed its name to Trans World Airlines, or T.W.A., and flew not one, but two transcontinental flights through Albuquerque en route to Los Angeles each day by mid-1934.

Investigation

An investigation into the causes of the plane crash on Mount Taylor followed in 1929. Most investigators agreed with search pilot Rice's assessment that that the tragic crash "appeared to have been an unavoidable accident," caused by poor visibility in terrible weather conditions. Rice told reporters that it was "almost impossible to predict weather conditions in that section, they develop so suddenly."

Rice and other observers believed that Captain Stowe had encountered an ominous storm and had crashed into Mount Taylor while attempting to turn back to Albuquerque, rather than continue on. There seemed to be no other plausible explanation for the "City of San Francisco" to have been anywhere near Mount Taylor, a rough area that experienced pilots avoided whenever possible.

Investigators concluded that the crash had occurred on Tuesday, September 3, at 11:01 a.m.; the wrist watches of four crash victims had stopped at that exact moment. In Anne Lindbergh's, and undoubtedly her husband's, opinion, it was "just one of those un-understandable, hideous accidents." Privately, Anne confided, "It seems to me the most terrible accident in all of aviation."

Despite this tragedy in Valencia County, most aviators were not about to abandon their exciting new pursuits. Ironically, on September 7, just as the search for the "City of San Francisco" had ended, the press announced that England's H. R .D. Waghorn had broken the world speed record, racing his plane at 329 miles per hour during a flying competition in Europe.

Despite the tragic events on Mount Taylor in 1929, the world continued its fascination with flying. Other heart-wrenching disasters would follow, but far greater advances were yet to come.

The Isleta Bus Crash Tragedy of 1930

by Richard Melzer

Friday, April 11, 1930, started as an exceptionally clear spring day in Isleta. Pueblo Indians greeted the day in prayer, just as their ancestors had done for hundreds of years. By 9:00 a.m., local residents were hard at work. Two seventeen-year-olds, Joe Olguin and Sam Jojola, were busy in their fields not far from where the Santa Fe Railway crossed a major new highway called Route 66. Route 66 connected Chicago in the distant east to Los Angeles in the distant west. Opened in 1926, Route 66 was destined to become one of the most traveled, storied highways in American history.

In New Mexico, Route 66 originally ran through Valencia County, coming south from Albuquerque, running through Isleta, then Peralta, and finally Los Lunas before heading northwest to Grants along today's State Road 6. As Route 66 meandered through Valencia County, it crossed the Santa Fe's tracks twice: once in Isleta and again in Los Lunas. Neither crossing was considered particularly dangerous, especially compared to several more hazardous crossings identified by New Mexico State Highway Department officials.

The Isleta crossing looking west along Old Route 66 (John Taylor)

Traffic on Route 66 was regular, but not heavy in 1930. Cars, trucks, and buses traversed the major artery, competing with the Santa Fe for the business of transporting passengers and goods through the Southwest. Two vehicles from these competing forms of transportation were headed for Isleta from different directions on Friday, April 11. From the north, Train No. 7 had left Albuquerque at 9:10 a.m. with its regular mail delivery to points south. C. C. Davis was at the throttle. A veteran engineer, Davis was described in the press as "one of the crack railroaders of the Santa Fe system."

From the east, a Pickwick Company bus en route from Los Angeles to Denver traveled through Isleta, having just gone through Los Lunas and Peralta. Twenty-four-year-old Forrest D. Williams was behind the wheel. Williams was rated an excellent driver, with an unblemished accident record in his five-year career as a Pickwick Company employee. He had a well-earned reputation as a careful driver who never drove a bus unless he was sure that all of its equipment was in perfect working order. Williams was said to have been well-rested and alert when he took the wheel that Friday morning. It had been over twelve hours since his last driving assignment.

But both Davis's train and Williams's bus were running behind schedule on April 11. For an unexplained reason, Train No. 7 had been twenty minutes late leaving Albuquerque. Meanwhile, muddy roads outside Flagstaff, Arizona, had delayed the Pickwick bus before Williams had taken over as its driver in Gallup. Due in Albuquerque at 10:00 a.m., Williams had carefully stopped at every railroad crossing along the way while doing all he could to make up time and arrive at his destination as close to schedule as possible.

On any other Friday, the engineer on Train No. 7 and the driver of the Pickwick bus would have never seen each other, no less crossed paths. But this was no ordinary Friday.

Bus Passengers

The twenty-six passengers on board the Pickwick bus had been comfortable and relaxed during most of their trip east. Many talked or joked with their traveling companions, most of whom they had first met after boarding the bus at one stop or another. Other passengers gazed out their windows, admiring New Mexico's passing landscape. At least one man played solitaire. Another slept. Passenger Frank L. Meyers later recalled that he and his fellow travelers thought driver Williams "was a fine fellow. We all liked him."

Like most bus loads of passengers, this was a mixed group, with backgrounds as varied as their destinations. Ellis Huff, a furniture salesman from Los Angeles, was traveling with his wife and eight-year-old son, Kenneth, to Oklahoma City. Two young California mothers, Katherine Dufner and Mona Utter, had boarded at Los Angeles with their infant children. Little Betty Dufner was said to have "won the hearts of all on board." Thelma Luft was en route to a new teaching job in Steamboat Springs, Colorado.

Corporal Roland Anderson, recently returned from duty in the Philippines, was heading home to Iowa on furlough. Perhaps on impulse, he had purchased a $5,000 travel insurance policy shortly before departing from Los Angeles. An older veteran, Richard C. Childers, had caught the bus in California, but had nearly missed reloading at two stops along the way. In each instance, fellow passengers had called out for the bus driver to stop so Childers could climb on board and continue his trip. The old Indian scout's family had tried in vain to convince him to stay home that morning, but he had been determined to make the journey.

Pete Tortelato and his friend Tom Nieto of Santo Domingo pueblo

A 1930 Pickwick bus similar to that involved in the Isleta bus accident (photo from GMC Truck and Coach Division)

were returning from the Navajo reservation, having traded their turquoise jewelry for Navajo blankets, as they did most every year. Tortelato was considered to be one of the best silversmiths in Santo Domingo. Unbeknownst to his fellow passengers, C. E. Mallory was a convicted felon who had recently been released from California's Folsom state prison. Free just two days, Mallory was en route to his hometown of Seneca, Missouri.

Train Crash

Train No. 7 was experiencing an equally uneventful trip from Albuquerque as it approached Isleta. Engineer Davis remembered nothing unusual about the trip until he approached the road crossing near the north end of the pueblo. Then everything changed in an instant. There was something wrong—very wrong—at the crossing. A Pickwick bus was attempting to cross the tracks in front of Davis's oncoming train. A crewmember shouted, "The big hole! The big hole!" railroad slang meaning that Davis should throw his brakes as quickly and as hard as possible.

Blasting his train whistle, Davis applied his brakes, but knew that it was already too late to stop in time to avert a collision. He could only hope to reduce his speed to from forty-five to thirty-five miles per hour before the inevitable crash occurred. As Davis sped toward the crossing bus, he saw the panicked expression of a bus passenger who anticipated what was about to happen. The passenger fumbled with his window in a desperate effort to escape. The man's face was frozen in terror. Then the crash came, and the man's face disappeared.

Survivors and witnesses recalled the incredible sound as the mail train plowed into the smaller vehicle in its path. The train pushed the bus down the track for hundreds of yards, causing multiple explosions, and splitting the bus in two. Baggage and human bodies were hurled through the air as if weightless. Davis, his train crew, Indians from Isleta, and passing motorists rushed to lend assistance. No one could have anticipated the gruesome scene they found. Small fires were everywhere. Bodies, luggage, and debris were strewn up and down the tracks. Some passengers were pinned below the bus's crushed chaise. All were black and charred. Most victims were beyond help. Others cried out in anguish and pain. Ellis Huff staggered about in shock, searching for his wife and young son. He threw himself on the ground in grief when he discovered that his wife was dead and his son was fatally injured.

Deputy Sheriff Harold Hubbell sped to the crash scene at sixty-five miles-per-hour. Hubbell later described his mostly futile efforts to help the injured. Kneeling by one passenger, Hubbell had barely asked the victim his name when the man suddenly "slumped down and died." Ten feet away a girl cried for water, but died before Hubbell could bring it to her. Nearby a man lying on the ground asked if someone could place something under his head. Hubbell rolled up some rags and put it under the man's head, but "in a moment he was dead."

Hearing the crash from his home, Isleta police officer Esquipula Jojola rushed to the local schoolhouse and retrieved five fire extinguishers. At the crash scene, he used the extinguishers to put out as many fires as he could. Arriving about the same time, Marcelino Zuni bandaged the head of a bleeding passenger. Sam Jojola and Joe Olguin ran from their field with buckets full of water that they used to give drinks, wash blackened faces, and put out more fires. Cruz Abeita helped in every way he could. Pueblo children ran home in fright. Recalling the damage and carnage, one eyewitness later declared, "It was a miracle that any passengers escaped alive."

News of the disaster spread quickly. Within minutes more help and six ambulances (provided by local mortuaries) arrived from Albuquerque. Albuquerque Mayor Clyde Tingley and his wife, Carrie, were among those who did all they could to assist. Other arrivals were far less helpful. In fact, the road from Albuquerque was soon so crowded with curiosity seekers that rescue and clean-up operations were hampered and delayed.

Rescuers discovered that driver Williams and eighteen of his passengers were dead at the scene. Three more passengers would die in the coming week, making this the worst transportation disaster in New Mexico history. Victims included all three children and their mothers, school teacher Thelma Luft, Corporal Roland Anderson, Pete Tortelato, Tom Nieto, former Indian scout Richard Childers, and ex-convict C. E. Mallory.

Many bodies were so damaged in the crash that it would take days before they were identified. With no passenger list to assist them, authorities had to rely on evidence found at the scene or provided by anxious friends and relatives in distant states. R. C. Stevens of Illinois was identified by the business cards found in a card case on his remains. Schoolteacher Thelma Luft was identified by her unique gold wedding ring. Katherine Dofner was identified by an abdominal scar from a recent operation. Six Santo Domingo friends identified Pete Tortelato by his clothing.

A fortunate few survivors required only minimal treatment and were released after several hours or a few days. Somehow, M. R. Perkins, the man engineer Davis had seen frozen in terror in a bus window, was among the living.

An inquest, heard before Justice of the Peace C. L. Ritt, was held at 10:00 a.m. the following Monday. The courtroom was packed throughout the daylong session. Testimony by at least two passengers revealed that bus driver Williams had looked to his left (south) but not to his right (north) before proceeding onto the tracks. An Indian youth who had been waiting near the crossing to catch a bus ride to Albuquerque testified that the bus had slowed down, but had not stopped before going over the tracks. Mrs. P. R. Olguin, an Isleta jeweler who had been working in her garden and had watched the bus go by, was sure that Williams had, in fact, stopped, however briefly. Given this mixed testimony and inconclusive evidence, the official inquest closed without fixing specific blame for the tragedy.

Aftermath

Several families, left destitute by the loss of their loved ones, contacted the Pickwick Bus Company in hope of receiving financial assistance in paying funeral expenses or transporting bodies home for burial. Company officials responded by calling the accident a "lamentable tragedy," but offered no monetary compensation. The company even refused to pay refunds for the tickets of those who survived. At least one newspaper declared these refusals "cold-blooded," "baffling," and "disgraceful."

But there was some good news among all the bad. One small miracle involved driver Williams's wife. When the 21-year-old widow was unable to pay the $15.50 she owed in rent for her Albuquerque apartment, her landlady confiscated her few belongings. A benevolent local attorney saved the day by paying the widow's debt, allowing Mrs. Williams to retrieve her property and leave for Nebraska with her 8-month-old baby and her husband's remains.

News of a far greater miracle soon appeared in the press. According to newspaper reports, Mr. and Mrs. H. W. Coffin and their son had been onboard the ill-fated Pickwick bus, but had gotten off at a stop in Needles, California, and had missed the bus when it departed. Only their luggage, already on the bus, was lost in the wreckage. Mrs. W.R. Smith was equally fortunate. Acting on what she called a hunch, Mrs. Smith had left the bus in Flagstaff, opting to complete her journey to Kansas City by train. She later read of the disaster from the safety of her home.

Banner headlines had first announced the crash in a rare extra edition of the *Albuquerque Morning Journal*. Press coverage in Albuquerque, Santa Fe, and throughout the region continued for many days. Outraged by the disaster, several editorials offered suggestions to prevent similar crises in the future. The *Morning Journal* asserted that bus drivers should be reminded of the law that required them to make complete stops before proceeding over tracks. The *Journal* also suggested that "stop, look, listen" signs be placed at every railroad crossing in the state.

Other newspapers called for more radical measures. On April 12, the *New Mexico State Tribune* (later the *Albuquerque Tribune*) urged that every bus be staffed with two employees, one to drive and the other to disembark and check up and down the tracks at each railroad crossing. "That's a lot slower," admitted the *Tribune*, "but it's [much] safer." By May 1 the *Tribune* went further, urging the construction of overpasses or tunnels over or under every major railroad crossing. The *Tribune* deemed the cost of such construction to be necessary "to protect motorists from their own folly [and] from the imperfections of powerful [railroad] machinery."

Today, those who pass the disaster scene at the intersection of routes 147 and 314 will notice that a crossing gate has been installed. Traffic is still regular, if not heavy, but the crossing is now safer than it was in April 1930. However, there are many other railroad crossings in New Mexico that still lack crossing gates. And there are still motorists who try to avoid long waits by racing across tracks as trains approach and crossing gates come down. The consequences are sadly predictable.

In short, despite much progress, tragic accidents still occur and needless deaths still follow. Drivers must be continually vigilant. History only repeats itself when we refuse to heed its clearest warnings.

Piper Cherokee Down: The Torres Family Airplane Tragedy, 1969

by Richard Melzer

A single-engine Piper Cherokee (N5752W) took off from Mid-Valley Air Park at 6:55 a.m. on Thursday, October 23, 1969. A pilot and two passengers were on board the small white plane that fateful day over forty years ago. All three men thought of their planned three-and-a-half hour trip to Denver as an adventure. They had no idea how much of an adventure lay ahead as they peered into the morning sky.

The rented Piper Cherokee was piloted by 18-year-old Albert Stacy Torres. The second oldest in a family of seven children, Stacy had started flying in June 1968, and had received his private pilot's license on June 15, 1969. According to his flight instructor, Jerry Arnold, Stacy "caught on quickly, was very sharp, and was a really confident" young pilot. By October 1969, he had logged one hundred hours of flight time.

Stacy had just recently graduated in the class of 1969 at Belen High School. His senior yearbook noted that he had won awards in math and science, had belonged to the school's rocket club, and had served as the president of the local chapter of Vocational Industrial Clubs of America (VICA) for two years. Reflecting his interest in math and science, Stacy was a freshman majoring in engineering at the University of New Mexico in the fall of 1969. His dream was to combine what he loved most: to own a ranch in Canada with an airstrip so that he could fly to distant places to work as an engineer.

Passengers

Stacy was accompanied by his 43-year-old father, Alfonso "Al" Torres, as the Piper lifted off the runway on that October morning in 1969. Al was a native of Tomé, the youngest of five brothers. After serving in World War II, he was honorably discharged from the Navy. Al had returned to New Mexico to open a car repair business in Tomé. Three years later, Al married Charlotte Ulibarri of Jarales and soon moved his business to River Road outside Belen. An active community leader, he belonged to the Knights of Columbus at Our

Lady of Belen Catholic Church and served as a volunteer fireman for many years.

Stacy Torres and the Piper Cherokee (Torres family)

Charlotte Torres remembers that Al loved outdoor adventures, including hunting, boating, skiing, swimming, and flying. Al flew every chance he got when he was young. Respected as an excellent mechanic, he enjoyed working with machines and building his own vehicles. He built a small tractor for yard work, as well as a recreational vehicle for trips as far away as California.

Al and Stacy had recently designed a mercury switch that could warn truck drivers when their heavy equipment vehicles were in danger of overheating. In fact, Al and Stacy were en route to Denver to meet with a lawyer who was doing research to see if a patent for their invention already existed. Typically, Al was less interested in the patent and potential profits for himself and more interested in giving Stacy the experience of seeing how patents worked for his future career in engineering.

The second passenger on the Piper Cherokee was Al Torres's friend, 38-year-old Orlindo "Lindy" García. Lindy was a Belen native and a Korean War veteran with a degree in business from the University of New Mexico. A bachelor, he ran his own bookkeeping business in Belen. Al was one of Lindy's many clients. Like Al, Lindy was active in the Belen community, especially in the local Lions Club and at Our Lady of Belen Catholic Church. Lindy was "along for the ride" on October 23.

He had looked forward to the trip and apparently had little fear for his safety. When Charlotte Torres asked him if he had any trepidation about the flight, he reminded her that he was taking survival classes and felt confident that all would go well with Stacy in the pilot's seat and Al close by. Lindy had survived a vacation in the jungles of Mazatlán, Mexico. Why shouldn't he survive a plane trip to Denver?

Stacy, Al, and Lindy's flight went well as they flew north into Albuquerque. There, at Coronado Airport, they landed to pick up another passenger, Tom Mayhew. Stacy had met Tom at UNM where Tom was a fine arts major in his third year at the university. Born in Pueblo, Colorado, Tom had grown up in Farmington, New Mexico, where his dad worked as a geologist for Shell Oil Company. Friends recall that Tom was eager to go to Denver to see his girlfriend and make amends after a recent fight. Tom had a fellow student from his UNM dorm take him to the airport to meet Stacy's plane. Clearly anxious to get going, Tom had gotten up at 4:30 a.m. and had arrived at the airport by 5:30 a.m. At least one airport worker saw the Piper Cherokee land and Tom climb on board.

But there were increasingly difficult conditions to contend with as the Piper headed further north. The weather was growing worse. Falling snow and dense fog made flying extremely hazardous. Stacy and his passengers could not have known how bad things were ahead.

With no word from Stacy or his passengers by late morning when they were due to arrive in Denver, people began to fear for their safety. Charlotte, who worked in the office at her husband's business, recalls having a "weird feeling" at work that morning. Lindy's sister, Dylia Castillo, recalls having a similar "really uneasy" feeling at about the same time at her job with the Belen schools. Worried, Charlotte called the airport to check on her husband's and son's safety.

By 1:00 p.m., airport officials called Charlotte to report that they were concerned that the Piper Cherokee might be lost or, worse, might have crashed somewhere in the wilderness of northern New Mexico. The men had not arrived for their late-morning appointment in Denver, and their five-hour supply of fuel would have been used up by about noon. It was time to alert the authorities and launch a search. If the plane had crashed, time was of the essence in rescuing the possibly injured men on board.

310

The Search Begins

As word spread of the apparent disaster, dozens of friends, relatives, and complete strangers volunteered to help in any way they could. In the next few days, search and rescue teams covered large areas on the ground while seventeen search planes scoured the surface from the sky. Fires and any suspicious-looking white objects seen from a distance were checked out on land or from the air.

Teams of three to five men traveled in four-wheel-drive vehicles, on horseback, and by foot over the rough terrain. One five-man crew from Belen entered the Pecos Wilderness. Led by seasoned outdoorsman David Chávez, the search team headed for Santa Bárbara Canyon. The men feared that Stacy's small plane might have had difficulty climbing out over the canyon's steep walls in an emergency.

At first, the local Forest Ranger would not permit Chávez and his fellow searchers to enter Santa Bárbara Canyon in such poor weather conditions. The ranger only allowed the men to proceed when they convinced him that Chávez know the terrain like the back of his hand, having gone on countless hunting trips in the Pecos Wilderness.

David Chávez recalls that the going was rough from the start. One man turned back almost immediately. Two others could go no further after a rough night sleeping in freezing temperatures in snow up to eighteen inches deep. Of the original five men, only Chávez and his friend, Arsenio Baldonado, remained to search through the canyon and climb far up Truchas Peak. It was a true test of endurance, but no trace of the lost plane or its pilot and passengers could be found.

Not discouraged, Baldonado returned to northern New Mexico to continue the search over many weeks. A contractor who had built Al Torres's garage on River Road, Baldonado even brought his young son, Arsenio, Jr., to help search. Baldonado recalls several exciting moments, including once when he came across two wild dogs and another time when he faced a wild bear. Baldonado joined Al Torres's oldest son, Nolbert, and Nolbert's uncles, Richard Ulibarri, Terry Ulibarri, and Serafico Carrillo, in a search effort along the ridge of the Rio Grande Gorge. Searching in vain, the five-man team almost froze to death before finally being picked up by a truck. Other groups had similarly harrowing experiences. But Nolbert and the others kept going back, time after time.

Exhausted searchers ate when they could and slept on floors, in trucks, and wherever they could find room, giving little thought to their own comfort or convenience. Rural residents of northern New Mexico were consistently generous and sympathetic.

When not hiking or climbing, volunteers questioned local people along the Piper Cherokee's planned flight path. Some reports were encouraging. A veteran pilot said he had heard a plane flying at low altitude with what sounded like a "troubled" engine near Peñasco about 10:00 a.m. on October 23. Thirteen-year-old Mary Ann Brown had seen a similar plane near Llano at about the same time. A deer hunter in the area saw a small, frightened basset hound and wondered if it could have belonged to someone on the plane and had somehow survived a crash. Four days after the plane's disappearance, a Pan American pilot flying over the area reported seeing plane wreckage just north of the Colorado border.

Family members and friends remained generally optimistic through the first weeks of the search for the four men and their plane. Alvarado Torres, Al's brother, confirmed that the four travelers had warm clothing and were well prepared for cold weather conditions. Charlotte Torres had faith in her husband's and son's ability to deal with crises. Charlotte recalled Lindy's confidence in his survival skills. News circulated that Tom Mayhew was a well-trained Eagle Scout.

Many groups and hundreds of individuals helped in valuable ways. Countless prayers were offered at Our Lady of Belen and other community churches. State Senator Tibo J. Chávez secured the use of a search helicopter and called Governor Dave Cargo to enlist additional help. Los Lunas School Superintendent Bernard Baca also secured the use of a plane which he flew to aid in the search. The New Mexico and Colorado Civil Air Patrols, the U.S. Forest Service, the U.S. Game and Fish Department, the New Mexico State Police, and the U.S. Marshall's office were similarly generous with their time and resources.

Reward money was offered as well. The First National Bank of Belen, led by John C. Johnson, offered a $1,000 reward for information that might lead to finding the lost aircraft and its passengers. An account to help fund the search was also opened at the bank. The Farm Bureau added a hundred dollars to the offered reward. Dylia Castillo and her husband, Ralph, placed hundreds of handbills announcing the reward money in post offices throughout northern New Mexico and southern Colorado.

Despite these many efforts, nothing of the Piper Cherokee, its young pilot, or its three passengers was discovered in late October or early November 1969. The search continued, but the odds of a successful rescue declined as the weeks passed and winter weather made traveling impossible much of the time.

To make matters worse, none of the earlier leads had borne fruit. After some investigation, searchers discovered that Tom Mayhew had recently purchased a dog, but it was a spaniel rather than a basset hound. The crash site reported by the Pan American pilot was never found. And white objects seen in the distance consistently turned out to be other things.

Frustrated, the Civil Air Patrol suspended its search in the first week of November. With most of the northern mountains blanketed in snow, any crash site would be covered until the following spring or summer. It was a trying period for everyone who waited for news. Therese, Al Torres's oldest daughter, remembers that she and other members of her family "held our breath every time the phone rang." As Dylia Castillo recalls, the victims' families were left in limbo in what seemed like an endless nightmare. Prayers for the lost men continued through the winter, but the chances of their survival grew dimmer with each passing day.

The Following Year

Fast-forward to May 1970, the following year. Al Torres's brother-in-law, Abelicio Ulibarri, has decided to take time off from work to search for the missing plane on his own. After studying maps, Abelicio drives his truck to an area just north of the New Mexico-Colorado border to survey several sites. The last place he visits is the Bear Lake Campground in the South Cuchara Mountain Range of the San Isabel National Forest.

As soon as he arrives at the campground, Abelicio experiences a powerful sense that this is the place that he and so many others have been looking for. Looking up to La Veta Pass, he feels sure that the pass is where the downed Cherokee and its passengers will be found. But Abelicio does not attempt to climb to the pass that day because the trail is still snow-packed and treacherous. He marks the location on his map and vows to return later that spring when more snow has melted.

Excited about his search, Abelicio returns to Belen to visit his sister, Charlotte. Abelicio takes Charlotte aside and tells her of his travels and of his conviction that he knows exactly where Al, Stacy, Lindy, and Tom can be found. Abelicio tells Charlotte of his plans to climb La Veta Pass as soon as conditions allow. But Abelicio never has a chance to return to La Veta Pass and climb the mountain to confirm his strong belief. Tragically, Abelicio died of a sudden heart attack on May 16, 1970. Unknown to the Torres and Ulibarri families, total strangers are destined to do what Abelicio had been so determined to achieve, but could not.

Four young men from Garden City, Kansas, decided to hike in the San Isabel National Forest in late May. Two, Craig Letourneau and Tim Larson, are schoolmates about to enter high school later that year. Tim's older brother, Greg, and his friend Rob Rupp, are already out of high school. At least one of them is familiar with this hiking area and, with school just out, the older boys have agreed to take Craig and Tim along on a three- to four-day outing.

The day is Friday, May 29. The boys have planned to hike to the top of a 12,000-foot high mountain, a climb of some three or four hours. Tim and his brother argue as to which route is best to take. Finally, Greg gives in to Tim's preference. As Craig later recalls, it was as though something drew the boys in that particular direction that morning. The four young hikers follow a stream for quite a distance until it disappears into the mountain. Then they hike on snow that is still frozen but relatively easy to walk on. The younger boys tolerate the thin mountain air better and are soon far ahead of Greg and Ron.

Success at Last

Craig is in the lead as he and Tim approach the top of the mountain. Suddenly, Craig sees a downed Piper Cherokee near the edge of a ridge. Assuming it's an old crash scene, he calls to Tim and the two friends approach the site for a look. On closer inspection, Craig and Tim realize that they are the first to discover a relatively recent crash site. Three bodies are found outside the plane. A fourth, the pilot's, is found inside.

The fuselage is in remarkably good condition. Most of the damage is to the front end, as if it had been in a head-on collision. The plane's tail had suffered hardly any damage. The aircraft's large-letter identification number is clearly visible: N5752W. Once the older boys arrived, the four hikers gathered items that might help identify the crash victims and their aircraft. They take the plane's logbook, two maps, a camera, and a checkbook belonging to Tom Mayhew

The Torres crash site (Torres family)

Noting the plane's identification number, the teenagers hurry down the mountain to share their news with authorities as soon as possible. Craig, Tim, Greg, and Ron report their startling discovery to Forest Ranger Ralph Hickey at nearby La Veta, Colorado. The ranger recalls that he had reported hearing a plane in trouble the previous fall. But his information was dismissed because no one thought that the lost Piper Cherokee had traveled this far north.

News of the discovery of the Piper Cherokee, its pilot, and its passengers spreads quickly. Officials at the First National Bank in Belen, which had offered a cash reward, are alerted within hours. Marion Herlihy at the bank calls Charlotte Torres. The Torres family is preparing to attend a May procession in honor of the Virgin Mary when the phone rings with the long-awaited news. The family's prayers have been answered. At least they now know their loved ones' fates. The García and Mayhew families are notified as well.

Robert Torres, his uncles, Richard and Serafico, and Arsine Badland leave immediately for the crash site in southern Colorado. Driving through the night, they arrive early the next morning. While his companions rest, Arsine forges ahead. Finding the crash site, Arsine returns to escort Norbert, Richard, and Serafico up the mountain to the very place where Abelicio Ulibarri had planned to search. Soon, a helicopter attempts to reach the crash site, but is unable to land on the rough ground. Hours later, a twenty-man team of expert mountain climbers is sent in. They are able to transport the bodies down from the mountain without mishap.

The bodies of Stacy, Al, and Lindy are returned to Belen. On June 2, a funeral service for all three men is held at Our Lady of Belen, where so many fervent prayers for their return had been offered. So many friends and relatives attend the funeral service that cars are parked down Church Street all the way east to South Main. The three local crash victims are buried in the Catholic cemetery. Tom Mayhew is buried in Farmington, his home town.

Learning of the reward money from the forest ranger they had spoken to in Colorado, Craig Letourneau and his friends claim their reward of $1,100. Craig recalls that he spent his share on a down payment for his car, a Plymouth Duster. He doesn't recall how the other boys spent their shares of the reward.

Fast-forward two years to 1972. Norbert Torres, his cousin Lorraine, and Lorraine's husband Gilbert García make a pilgrimage to the crash site high in the Colorado mountains. Gilbert has constructed a five-foot wrought-iron memorial cross with a small plaque bearing the names of Stacy, Al, Lindy, and Tom plus the date of their tragic crash. The visitors erect their *descanso* in a pile of rocks mixed with small pieces of the wreckage. It is a fitting mounment to the four talented, respected New Mexicans who died there. The monument was still standing when Craig Letourneau revisited the site some twenty years later.

What Happened?

So, what happened on the morning of October 23, 1969?

Although those events will forever remain a mystery, it is apparent that Stacy and his passengers flew into the first heavy snowstorm of the 1969 winter season. Stacy was probably flying at a high enough altitude, but visibility was no doubt marginal at best. Suddenly seeing a ridge as they attempted to clear a 12,000-foot high mountain, Stacy was probably unable to make the Cherokee gain altitude fast enough to avoid colliding with the rugged terrain. The plane crashed. Al, Lindy, and Tom were apparently thrown from the plane on impact. Stacy remained pinned in the pilot's seat. The travelers had done the best they could under horrible circumstances. But no amount of flying skills, survival methods, or emergency supplies could help them in such terrible flying conditions.

Family and friends still miss Stacy, Al, Lindy, and Tom. Their deaths were tragic because they were all so young and had so much more to live for and contribute to their communities. But if there is a lasting lesson to be learned from this tragedy, it is the lesson learned by Charlotte Torres and her family in the weeks and months following Al's and Stacy's crash. Charlotte says she was overwhelmed by the outpouring of love and support that so many offered to her family in their time of need. Charlotte's daughter, Therese, later wrote, "As ironic as it may seem, our hope in finding my father and brother alive never came true, but we did gain hope for the future through the caring of our community."

The people of Valencia County are like that. It is a wonderful truism for all to remember when we think of those long-ago events when four good men were finally found and brought home to rest at last.

Michael Todd
and the "Unlucky" Liz, 1958

by Richard Melzer

Michael Todd was at the top of his personal and professional world in 1958. Born Avrom Hirsch Goldenbogen in 1909, Mike Todd had weathered several business failures and personal tragedies in his life, but he had always landed on his feet and had always gone on to greater successes. Appropriately, when his friend, Art Cohn, wrote Todd's biography, Cohn named the book, *The Nine Lives of Michael Todd*.

On his ninth life in 1958, Todd was the consummate showman of his day. He had just produced two blockbuster movies, the Academy Award winning hits *Around the World in Eighty Days* in 1956 and *South Pacific* in 1957. He had married the beautiful movie star, Elizabeth Taylor, in February 1957. Taylor gave birth to the couple's first child, a daughter, the following August.

But Mike Todd's ninth life suddenly ended on March 22, 1958, when his private plane crashed in a desolate spot in the Zuni Mountains of what was then Valencia County. Todd's plane, en route from Burbank, California, to New York City, was utterly destroyed. All four men on board, including Todd, Art Cohn, the pilot, and co-pilot, were killed.

Michael Todd and Elizabeth Taylor (London Telegraph)

Michael Todd in New Mexico

Michael Todd had flown to New Mexico several times before March 22, 1958. He had filmed a rocket-launching scene for *Around the World in Eighty Days* at the White Sands Missile Range in 1955. More recently, Todd, Cohn, and a press agent had flown to Albuquerque to help promote past and future film projects.

Todd and his friends had visited Albuquerque for five hours on Wednesday, March 19, 1958. On landing, a convertible had carried them from the airport to downtown. Banners displayed on each side of the sporty vehicle read, "Welcome, Mike Todd." The same words on the Sunshine Theatre's marquee had greeted them as they traveled down Central Avenue. Todd had spent his time in Albuquerque speaking to the Kiwanis Club, being interviewed by a KOB-TV newsman, conducting a press conference, and signing unreadable autographs. Described in the press as "dapper and cocky," Todd said he liked Albuquerque, calling it a "virile" city that needed to do more to advertise itself and its many assets. There was some talk about Todd's next big movie project, to be based on Miguel de Cervantes's *Don Quixote*, the most famous novel in Spanish literature. Art Cohn suggested that some of the movie might be shot in New Mexico.

As busy as Todd had been during his short stay in New Mexico, the showman had found time to phone his wife during a fifteen-minute break. Liz Taylor had told him that she had gotten a head cold and was not feeling well. His active day over, Todd had departed from Albuquerque at 4:00 p.m. He was home in time for dinner with his family in Southern California. The speed and convenience of modern airplane travel clearly fit Mike Todd's non-stop lifestyle.

Flight to New York

Todd was scheduled to fly on a much longer trip three days later. Chosen as the Showman of the Year, Todd was to be honored on March 22, at a Friars Club dinner before 1,200 guests at the Waldorf-Astoria Hotel in New York City. A ten-hour cross-country flight to New York City was planned, with refueling stops in Albuquerque, Tulsa, and other cities along the way. Todd did not look forward to his East Coast trip. It would take him away from his young family and his work in California.

Elizabeth Taylor, still suffering from her cold and finishing a new movie, *Cat on a Hot Tin Roof*, would not accompany him.

Hoping to make his trip as pleasant as possible, Todd had called several friends to see if they had time to join him. Singer Eddie Fisher, comedian Joe E. Lewis, director Richard Brooks, and movie star Kirk Douglas were among those Todd called. They all had other plans. Only Art Cohn would go along.

Liz Taylor remembers the day her husband left on his final journey. She recalls that Todd was so reluctant to leave that he returned upstairs to say goodbye a half dozen times. Worried because she had heard predictions of heavy thunderstorms, Taylor urged him to stay home. "Don't worry," he replied in his typically confident manner, "I can fly above any storm." He promised to call her at 6:00 the following morning, when his plane was scheduled to stop in Albuquerque to refuel.

Todd's plane took off from Burbank at 10:41 p.m. on Friday, March 21. The producer and Art Cohn were the only passengers, although the twin-engine Lockheed Lodestar 10 could accommodate as many as six, with room left for a newly remodeled section large enough for a king-size bed. Todd had spent $25,000 on the remodeling project, although it added dangerous extra weight to his aircraft.

Lockheed Lodestar 10 similar to "The Liz" (Lockheed-Martin)

Forty-five-year-old World War II veteran William S. "Bill" Verner piloted the $100,000 plane. Thirty-four-year-old Thomas Barclay served as co-pilot, filling in for the plane's regular co-pilot, who had failed to appear for work. All went well on the east-bound flight over California and most of Arizona. The plane and its crew had a good flight record. There was no indication that this trip should be any different from the countless others Todd had taken in the past. Todd had, in fact, named his plane "The Liz" in honor of his famous wife and because the craft had performed so well before, most recently on his flight to Albuquerque and back home on March 19.

Disaster

But "The Liz" was heading straight for disaster on the night of March 21-22, 1958. The plane encountered increasingly inclement weather as it entered air space over eastern Arizona and western New Mexico. Rain and scattered snow caused freezing conditions. About 2:15 a.m. pilot Bill Verner radioed the air traffic controller in Winslow, Arizona, that he was experiencing "moderate" icing on his wings. To alleviate the problem, Verner requested permission to raise his altitude from 11,000 up to 13,000 feet. Permission was granted. Moments later Verner confirmed that he had reached his new altitude, but that he was experiencing increased icing and was heading into a storm front. And that was the last anyone heard from "The Liz."

At 2:30 a.m., while working the night shift as air traffic controller at the Grants Airport, John Johnson spotted something ominous in the night sky to the southwest. A bright flash indicated that either lightning had struck or something far more troublesome had occurred. Johnson reported the incident to Dick Lane, the airport's manager. Flying in his own plane, Lane had set off at daybreak to inspect what he feared might be a crash site. His worst fears were confirmed. About twenty-two miles southwest of Grants and one mile north of State Road 53, Lane saw smoke rising through the dense clouds below his plane.

Hurrying back to Grants, Lane notified the state police. Within minutes four local men were at the scene to investigate. The four included New Mexico state patrolman Bud Smith, Smith's brother-in-law Woodrow "Woody" Thigpen, who owned the local ambulance service,

Woody's brother Wilbur, and Jim Barber, editor of the *Grants Beacon*.

Wilbur Thigpen remembers the terrible scene like it was yesterday. From what he saw, it was clear that "The Liz" had plunged to earth in a perilous nosedive, creating a ten-foot deep, twenty-five-feet wide crater. Mangled debris was scattered over a quarter of an acre. And so were human body parts. At least one man on the scene thought he had stepped on a broken piece of the fallen plane. Instead, it turned out to be a human head. The plane's destruction was so complete that early observers could not determine exactly how many people had lost their lives in the crash. For several hours it seemed that there had been three persons on board, rather than four. Learning that the plane belonged to Mike Todd, some even feared that Liz Taylor was among the bodies charred beyond recognition.

Woody Thigpen performed the awful task of collecting body parts and depositing them in cardboard containers for transport. The job took most of the day. Those on the scene also collected debris, including a book entitled *The World's Greatest Religions*, a new movie script, the plane's flight log, cocktail napkins engraved with the names "Liz and Mike," a watch, some cash, and a plain gold wedding ring.

News Spreads Quickly

News of the crash spread quickly through Grants and its surrounding communities. At the peak of a uranium mining boom in 1958, Grants had many new residents, but not many forms of entertainment. The idea of seeing a crash site, however muddy the roads and bad the weather, appealed to hundreds of men, women, and children as a good Saturday morning excursion. Interest in the isolated site grew in appeal as reports spread that Mike Todd had been one of the passengers on board the doomed plane. It was also rumored that Todd had been wearing a $100,000 diamond ring and had been carrying a large sum of cash. Treasure hunters joined curiosity seekers, jamming the roads from Grants to the crash site.

Meanwhile, Dave Candelaria arrived at the site. Candelaria, who owned 5,000 acres of mostly wilderness land, had received news that a disaster had taken place on a section of his land in the eastern portion of the Zuni Mountains. Candelaria later realized that people descended on the site "like fiends," often getting stuck in the mud, damaging the road, and cutting fences in their frenzy. Candelaria stayed at the site all day, but he was unable to halt the flow of traffic, much less prevent the damage people were doing to his property. Police roadblocks and radio announcements urging people to stay at home made little difference.

News of the crash spread far beyond Grants. Reporters rushed to the scene or called for first-hand reports from editor Jim Barber and other local citizens. Dave Candelaria got a call from as far away as London, England. The *Albuquerque Journal* asserted that for a fleeting moment Grants had become "the center of world attention."

The four men who died in the crash could only be positively identified after an inquest was held and their remains were removed to the French-Fitzgerald mortuary in Albuquerque. Todd was identified by a money clip on his person and by dental records relayed west from his dentist in New York.

There are two stories of how Elizabeth Taylor learned of the disaster. According to one, the actress was watching television when the news flashed on the screen. Another story had her doctor and Todd's business assistant come to her house to break the news and comfort her as much as possible. In either case, Taylor was so shocked that she was said to have run from the house and into the street, screaming. Taylor spoke to a few callers, was given a sedative, and went so far as to call the Grants Police Department to confirm the awful truth she hated to admit.

Burial and Memories

Michael Todd was buried at the Waldheim Jewish Cemetery in Forest Park, a suburb of Chicago, on March 25, 1958. Liz Taylor attended, but so did thousands of unruly "fans." A friend recalls that as Taylor left her husband's gravesite, "the throng surged forward with a roar. Somebody ripped away Elizabeth's black veil; others attempted to tear off her hat and coat." Once in her waiting limousine, dozens "stormed the car and began pounding on the windows." In Liz Taylor's words, "They swarmed like insects all over the car so you couldn't see out the windows."

Elizabeth Taylor eventually sued the New Jersey company that had leased "The Liz" to Todd. Charging Ayer Lease Plan, Inc., with negligence, Taylor sought $5 million in damages. Instead, a federal court awarded her $40,000, suggesting that Todd may have helped cause his own fatal accident by overloading the leased plane with expensive interior remodeling.

Somehow, Liz Taylor recovered from the loss of her third husband who, along with Richard Burton, was said to be her favorite spouse—among many. According to her most recent biographer, Taylor believed that "Somewhere, [Michael Todd and Richard Burton] are probably having drinks, waiting for me to join them." She finally did on March 23, 2011.

What do the people of western Valencia County (now Cibola County) remember of this famous accident? Some have vague memories of what they saw that day or heard from others. Many confuse this 1958 crash with the disaster, involving a Transcontinental Air Transport (T.A.T.) flight that crashed on Mount Taylor in 1929. But men like Wilber Thigpen and Dave Candelaria know better. Thigpen will never forget the horror of finding dismembered bodies at the crash site on that rainy Saturday morning. And Candelaria never forgot the invasion of curiosity seekers and treasure hunters who did so much damage to his property on March 22, 1958, and in the years that followed. Frustrated, he finally hired a man to bulldoze the plane's debris into a large hole at the site.

Few people come by to ask Candelaria about the crash anymore. Two men from San Diego dropped by a few years ago. And a certain historian from Belen visited him with a notebook full of questions. Dave kindly took the time to answer the historian's questions and point out the crash site, but you get the impression he's had his share of attention and doesn't want much more.

And that's the feeling one has at the crash site itself. It is time to let the large, man-made scar in the earth heal and return to its former state of peace and beauty deep in the Zuni Mountains. The tragedy of 1958 should not be forgotten, but its site and all those who died there should be allowed to rest in peace at last.

Earthquakes
in the Rio Abajo, 1849-2004

by Paul Harden

Earthquake Swarms, 1849-1869

In the spring of 1855, a detachment of U.S. Dragoons were dispatched from Santa Fe to inspect Ft. Conrad south of Socorro and Ft. Fillmore north of Mesilla. One of the dragoons, Private James Bennett, recorded in his journal: "April 19. With Governor [David W.] Meriwether down the Rio Grande to Socorro where we stayed at Mr. Connor's house. About 10 o'clock P.M. a noise of distant thunder was heard for 4 or 5 minutes. The earth trembled. Houses shook. Our horses were frightened. It was a shock or an earthquake. 2 houses were nearly destroyed." This is the earliest documented report of an earthquake in New Mexico that recorded the date, time, and partial extent of the damage.

However, local oral history and Army reports of the mid-1800's document that Socorro was no stranger to earthquakes. In the "Surgeon's Report on Socorro, N.M., 1852," John Hammond recorded, "On the morning of the 29th of December, 1849, snow fell to the depth of two or three inches. ..... The day began and ended with an earthquake - there was a shock at 6 a.m., and one at 8 p.m." Between December 11, 1849, and February 14, 1851, Hammond recorded a total of twenty-eight earthquakes in the Socorro area. Two or three quakes were recorded on a single day, many being rather severe, although no specific description of damage was recorded.

The Assistant Surgeon also noted areas around Socorro where the snow melted much faster than other areas, suggesting the base of the mountain to Socorro hot springs was warmer than other areas, perhaps due to underlying magma. The quartermaster at Ft. Craig recorded another earthquake in 1869.

In geological terms, continuous quakes in an area are known as earthquake swarms. Evidently, Socorro experienced periods of such swarms during the 1840's and 1850's. After the 1869 quake, Socorro was apparently quiet for the next twenty-five years.

1904

In early 1904, Socorro was again struck with several earthquakes. The February 27 *Socorro Chieftain* reported: "Socorro has experienced more earthquakes. Sunday night at about 11 o'clock those of the city who go to bed at an honest hour were roused from their slumber by a prolonged subterranean rumbling, which was immediately followed by a rocking of the ground ... and an ominous swaying and creaking of walls and roofs. The unwelcome experience was repeated six or eight times during the night. Three or four shocks were felt Wednesday."

Reports of the Socorro quakes spread across the country. Socorro even made the front page of the *New York Times* with a highly exaggerated report of the earthquakes, painting Socorro as virtually destroyed and cutoff from the world by road or rail.

In the March 19 *Socorro Chieftain* editor K.A. Drake published a scathing attack against such irresponsible reporters, beginning with "An *El Paso Herald* man has strange visions probably resulting from too much Texas Booze. Drake states that Socorro has suffered 15 earthquakes in the past 6 weeks, but the town is not leveled nor are the spring waters boiling, as reported in the *El Paso Herald*."

This was a sensitive topic for the struggling town of Socorro. Its population had dropped from 5,000 people in the 1880's to a mere 1,500 in 1900 following the closings of the area's mines and smelters. Socorro could not afford further drops in business and employment due to fictitious stories of earthquake destruction.

Despite the rosy picture painted by *Socorro Chieftain* editor Ken Drake and Mayor Holm O. Bursum, Socorro continued to be plagued by numerous tremors. While damage was minimal, the townspeople were getting increasingly anxious over the constant rumblings.

On September 6, two fairly strong shocks again hit Socorro. As reported in the *Socorro Chieftain*, "Socorro has again been shaken Tuesday morning between eleven and twelve o'clock.... This shock was followed in about ten minutes by another fully as violent. The two shocks coming so near together put people who were at all nervously inclined into a state of unpleasant apprehension as to what would happen next." In fact, Socorroans became so fearful of future shocks and house damage that many began to move their household furnishings outside, literally sleeping in their beds in their front yards. This persisted until the weather turned cold and the earthquakes seemed to subside. There were only a few mild tremors during the rest of 1904.

1906

Three months after the 1906 San Francisco quake, a strong earthquake struck Socorro. The July 14, 1906, *Socorro Chieftain* reported, "at ten minutes past five o'clock Thursday morning a loud and ominous subterranean rumbling was immediately followed by a wave like movement of the ground that caused the buildings of the city to rock like ships in a storm and the frightened inhabitants to rush into the yards and streets for safety. ... Many of the city's inhabitants did not dare remain in their houses any length of time Thursday and many of them have slept out of doors since. Luckily nobody was hurt though the property loss was considerable." The article explained that the town had been struck with tremors nearly every hour since. This quake has been estimated at 5.5 on the Richter scale.

On July 16, the strongest quake yet, estimated at 5.8 on the Richter scale, struck Socorro. The *Socorro Chieftain* described the damage from these two quakes. "Abram Abeyta's two-story brick residence on Eaton Avenue was one of the buildings of the city most severely damaged ... hundreds of pounds of plastering fell from the ceilings of the Court House ... [the home] of the family of Chas. Sterling had to be abandoned.... Doctor Duncan's office was badly wracked and considerable repairs will be necessary.... The entire brick business block extending from the plaza along the north side of Manzanares avenue was greatly damaged. ... The Socorro Drug and Supply company suffered considerable loss.... In fact, a great majority of the buildings of the city give some indication of the severe shaking and wrenching they received."

The main railroad line through Socorro apparently received little damage. However, the spur line to Magdalena was closed for several days due to falling rocks onto the tracks through Blue Canyon and misaligned track around Water Canyon.

It is clear from these newspaper accounts that the quakes of July 2 and July 12, 1906, were not just scary tremors, but very damaging earthquakes to Socorro. The July 21 *Socorro Chieftain* listed reports of damage also experienced in San Marcial and San Antonio, where the Catholic church with its tall steeple collapsed. The earthquakes were felt as far away as Albuquerque and El Paso, and from Alamogordo to Datil. No reports of damage were reported in Magdalena, except to the railroad line already mentioned.

The Church in San Antonio collapsed during the 1906 earthquake (Henry Walt)

After these two quakes, many Socorroans again moved their household furnishings outside, sleeping in their front yards throughout the summer as they had in 1904. Fortunately, the summer months allowed the homes to be quickly repaired. In 1906, newspapers were printed by letterpress, or raised steel printing. It was an expensive process to engrave photographs onto steel plates for printing, using equipment available only to the largest newspapers in the country. As a result, there are unfortunately no photographs of the earthquake damage in these early *Socorro Chieftains*.

The Socorro earthquake swarm continued throughout 1906. Then about noon on November 15, another large earthquake struck Socorro. This quake was also estimated at magnitude 5.8 on the Richter scale. Oddly, there is little information on this earthquake in the November *Socorro Chieftains*. Perhaps the editor was as sick of writing about the quakes as Socorroans were of reading them!

One article found around this time announced that the Socorro

Hotel had been permanently abandoned due to irreparable earthquake damage. Another article was that submitted by Leon Dominian of the School of Mines. Obviously an attempt to calm the town, he explained that the Socorro caldera, an extinct volcano, was not likely to erupt like Mt. Vesuvius. He honestly explained that earthquakes, whether the cause of mountain formation, volcanic action, or global shrinking, were not yet understood.

Tremors continued to plague Socorro for another year, then seemed to finally stop. The 1904-1908 period of Socorro's quakes and tremors remains the longest earthquake swarm in U.S. history. The Socorro earthquakes of July 16 and November 15, 1906, remain the two largest earthquakes ever recorded in New Mexico. With few exceptions, Socorro's ground has been quiet since 1908.

Socorro Chieftain.

SOCORRO, NEW MEXICO, SATURDAY JULY 14, 1906

EARTHQUAKES AGAIN

Socorro Experiences the Severest Shocks in Half a Century

THURSDAY MORNING, JULY 12th.

Buildings Rock like Ships in the Storm, Walls Crack, Chimneys and Plastering Fall, Shelf Goods and Bric-a-brac Hurled to Floor.

A new record for earthquakes has been established at Socorro. For ten days immediately preceding Thursday of this week slight shocks had been felt at

owned by W. H. Byerts and occupied by the family of Chas. Sperling, had to be abandoned for repairs. Doctor C. G. Duncan's office was badly wracked

Headlines in the Socorro Chieftain (El Defensor Chieftain)

Later Swarms

There have been no damaging quakes in Socorro since November 1906. However, a small swarm of tremors struck Socorro from October

25, 1960, through July 3, 1961. These quakes were measured around 4.5 on the Richter scale by seismographs at the New Mexico Institute of Mining and Technology. By this time, the college had an elaborate network of seismographs and was becoming a respected leader in geology and seismic research. Dr. Allen Sanford, in charge of seismic research at New Mexico Tech, took advantage of Socorro's many quakes to map the ground under our feet. He discovered that seismic waves tended to consistently bounce off a smooth layer of magma underneath a large part of Socorro County. His continued research allowed him to advance the theory of the "Socorro Anomaly," a large body of magma, about twelve miles deep, slowly expanding upward about an inch every ten years. As the magma body expands, earthquakes are triggered. Dr. Sanford's research is now the accepted model of Socorro's volcanic and seismic activity.

Recent quakes that were felt by Socorroans occurred on November 29, 1989, and January 29, 1990. No damage from these quakes was reported in the *Socorro Chieftain*.

Just recently, on May 24, 2004, a small quake near Bernardo, due to the expanding magma cone, was felt by many in the northern part of Socorro County and into Belen.

Future Earthquakes

One can't help but ask, will the Rio Abajo experience damaging earthquakes in the future? At present there is no way to predict with any certainty when an earthquake might strike. Due to the expanding magma underneath Socorro, minor tremors occur almost daily and will continue to do so, though few are felt. Occasionally, one will be strong enough to be felt. Socorro's earthquakes are largely due to this magma cone, not a fault line building up pressure. As a result, future large earthquakes are not likely. However, Socorro is located in a very seismically active region, and an occasional earthquake producing damage can not be ruled out.

The strongest earthquakes in Socorro, and New Mexico, registered 5.8 on the Richter scale. With modern forms of construction, an earthquake of this magnitude would cause little damage today. Still, inspecting one's home for things that might fall or break if rattled by an earthquake is always a prudent measure, regardless of where one lives.

While many believe the San Francisco quake triggered the damaging

Socorro earthquakes of July 1906, geologists verify there was no connection between the San Andreas Fault and the Socorro magma feature. Still, if the "big one" does hit California, no one will blame New Mexicans if they batten down the hatches here in the Rio Abajo!

Church Bells Rang Day and Night: The Spanish Flu Epidemic of 1918

by Richard Melzer and Oswald G. Baca

Eighty years ago, the United States faced the worst epidemic in our nation's history. The Spanish flu epidemic of 1918 killed over half a million Americans and an estimated 20 million persons worldwide. More Americans died of the flu than in all the country's wars of the twentieth century combined, including the First and Second World Wars. No one was safe, regardless of where a person lived or how hard a person tried to avoid the dreaded disease. Not even the residents of far-off Belen were immune once the flu germ entered New Mexico in the fall of 1918.

Residents of New Mexico and Belen tried various measures to avoid the flu. Governor Washington E. Lindsey urged the closing of all schools, courts, churches, and other public gathering places. Health officials warned people to avoid excessive eating, too much work, unventilated rooms, coughing or sneezing without handkerchiefs, spitting on the ground, and drinking whiskey. Despite the latter advice, some locals believed that drinking moonshine liquor was a good way to prevent, or even cure, the flu. Martín Quintana recalled that his father preferred this method, although his mother did not; true ladies didn't drink in those days, no matter what the emergency. Other homemade remedies were attempted, but to no avail. Some turned to *curanderas*, but not even traditional herbs and treatment helped in this crisis.

Belen, like all towns along major railroad routes, was especially vulnerable. Railroad workers and passengers could easily bring the flu germ from places across the state and, in fact, the nation. Belen's odd policy of allowing fellow Belenites, but not strangers, to debark from trains did nothing to stem the tide in this disaster.

Dozens in Belen caught the disease, with a high percentage dying of influenza or pneumonia within hours. Eduardo Abeyta, a worker at Belen's roundhouse, died in the epidemic, leaving his wife a widow and five young children fatherless. Frank Barror, a locomotive engineer, survived the epidemic, but his wife, Lucy, died of the flu at their home on Third Street and Ross. Another railroad worker, Fred Hawkins, lost both his wife and son. On October 10, 1918, the *Belen News* printed a long list of stricken residents, including the bookkeeper and cashier at the John Becker Store, and so many employees at the First National Bank of Belen were ill that the bank was forced to temporarily close down. Transported by wagon, many flu victims were brought to the local grammar school to receive care. Healthy neighbors often brought soup to the sick in their homes, only to catch the flu themselves.

Coughs and Sneezes Spread Diseases

As Dangerous as Poison Gas Shells

SPREAD OF SPANISH INFLUENZA MENACES OUR WAR PRODUCTION

U. S. Public Health Service Begins Nation-wide Health Campaign.

Spanish Flu warning sign (US Public Health Service poster)

Even Dr. Samuel Wilkinson came down with the illness, leaving Dr. William Radcliffe as the only local physician well enough to handle the onslaught of patients in need of attention. Health personnel arrived from out of town to help in the crisis. The Santa Fe Railway brought Dr. Knapp of Santa Fe to look after railroad employees and assist Dr. Radcliffe as much as possible.

But a whole army of doctors and nurses could not have stopped the flu and its deadly assault. Often at least one member of every family caught the flu, increasing the odds that others in each family would grow ill, too. According to one estimate, more than half of Belen was sick. As many as ten residents on a block reportedly died on a single night. Everyone was susceptible, but, in an odd quirk of fate, those in the prime of their lives, in their 20s and 30s, fell victim and died most often. One of the authors, Oswald G. Baca, lost both his maternal grandmother, Rebecca Armijo Sánchez, 22, of Jarales, and his paternal grandmother, Luz Romero Baca, 30, of Los Trujillos. They died in October, the worst month of the epidemic.

Church bells rang day and night to announce the passing of more and more residents. Belen's two hearses, a car and a horse-drawn buggy, were kept busy, with the car reserved for the rich and the buggy used by the poor. Without enough coffins available, the dead were hurriedly buried in mass graves.

Belen and the surrounding settlements of Los Chávez, Los Trujillos, Jarales, Bosque, and Pueblitos were among the hardest hit areas of New Mexico. In October 1918, burial records at Our Lady of Belen Catholic parish show an astounding 122 burials, or an average of four per day. For comparison, in September 1918, there had been only nine interments at the Catholic cemetery, and in November there would be only nineteen. In the entire previous year, there had been sixty-seven burials; in the succeeding year, there would be only fifty-eight.

Given the unprecedented number of burials, it was only a matter of time before rumors spread that some victims of the flu had been buried prematurely. According to one such rumor, a local woman was buried, but her daughter insisted that her mother was still alive. When the mother's grave was dug up, the exhumed body was reportedly in a different position than when it was originally laid to rest. A 35-year-old man from Bosque was also supposedly buried alive during the epidemic.

While digging a grave for another flu victim, the Bosque man's coffin was accidentally dislodged. The grave diggers opened the disturbed coffin to find the confined body in a contorted, belly-down position, indicating that the poor man had suffocated after burial had taken place.

The flu was just as bad in other parts of the Rio Abajo. In Isleta, for example, Dr. D.A. Richardson found a "deplorable condition" where ten residents died on a single day. Young adults were most vulnerable, but no one was safe from death, especially if a person caught pneumonia after a bout with the flu. Eighty-nine Isletans died before the worst of the epidemic finally passed.

Thankfully, the flu subsided as quickly as it had begun. Much of the epidemic remains a mystery to this day. Not even its name, the Spanish flu, is understood because the epidemic did not originate in Spain or any other Spanish community. Evidence points to its origin in March 1918, at an Army camp in Fort Riley, Kansas, from which it spread in two terrible waves around the world. All we know for sure is that the epidemic hit with incredible force in the last days of the First World War, showing no mercy to a world already ravaged by four years of violence and death. Some, like the preacher Billy Sunday, believed that the epidemic had been caused by so much sin in the world. Others believed it was caused by the Germans as part of their hated germ warfare.

Regardless of how or why it had come about, all were relieved that the epidemic had largely passed by early 1919. Tragically, more than a thousand New Mexicans died of the flu and never enjoyed the new year or the post-war era of peace. The First World War thus ended in Belen and the United States, claiming the lives of innocent citizens living thousands of miles from a battlefield, but unprotected from an enemy so small that no microscope of that day was powerful enough to detect it.

"Left with Not Even One":
Other Epidemics in the Rio Abajo

by John Taylor

> *"11 hijos muertos. No le quedan ni uno."* (Eleven dead children. She is left with not even one.) Fr. J. B. Ralliere, Tomé, July 31, 1892.

This terse entry in the Tomé burial records captures the tragedy of epidemic disease in Valencia County in the years before vaccines, antibiotics, and the other miracles of modern medicine arrived in the Rio Abajo. Major epidemics swept through the area every four to six years, preferentially taking the very young (50 percent of the documented deaths in the eighteenth and early nineteenth centuries) and the very old. Commentators at the time noted that these scourges killed far more people than the Indian attacks that were so feared by local residents.

Most of the epidemics occurred in the wintertime, suggesting infectious airborne microbial infections such as influenza, smallpox, measles, pertussis (whooping cough), and diphtheria, exacerbated by spending most of the time indoors in close quarters. Particularly virulent epidemics occurred in 1793, 1846, 1883, 1888, 1898, 1908, 1909, 1911, and 1918.

Although the 1918 Spanish flu pandemic was the most infamous, most of the earlier epidemics in Valencia County killed far more individuals. In fact, the worst epidemic of all was the 1898 smallpox curse that killed 11 percent of the residents of Casa Colorada and between 5 and 6 percent of the people from Valencia south to Adelino. Father Jean Baptiste Ralliere of Tomé also noted that in 1911 measles killed twenty-two children.

Of course, death was not the only consequence of epidemic disease. Survivors were left weakened, orphaned, or childless. Non-fatal diseases such as malaria were also endemic in the area, particularly after major floods had inundated the low-lying areas, leaving behind fertile breeding grounds for insect vectors. Father Ralliere himself is said to have suffered from this debilitating disease.

336

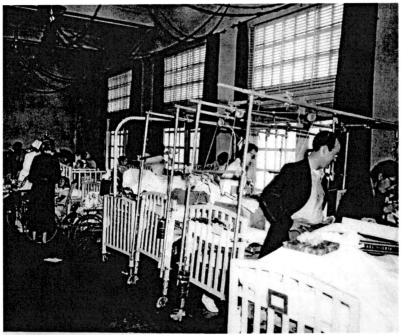

The Carrie Tingley Hospital in Truth or Consequences with a close-up of one of the polio wards (Carrie Tingley Hospital)

A terrible new epidemic struck the Rio Abajo and the United States as a whole in the early 1950s. Infantile paralysis, better known as polio, affected nearly 58,000 Americans, including forty-one residents (mostly children) of Valencia County in 1952 alone. Some local victims were sent to the Carrie Tingley Hospital in Truth or Consequences for special care. (The hospital relocated to Albuquerque in 1981 and continues to serve special-needs children under the auspices of the University of New Mexico Medical Center.)

Thanks to years of research and funding from March of Dimes campaigns, Dr. Jonas E. Salk developed a polio vaccine in 1955. Almost nine hundred children in Valencia County received the vaccine within a week after it was made available. Over nine thousand county residents took an oral vaccine developed in the 1960s, lining up at places across the county including five schools, the San Clemente Catholic Church, and the New Mexico Boys Ranch.

A Valley of Floods

by Richard Melzer

Water is life in a desert climate. For centuries, the Rio Grande has provided this precious resurce for the humans, crops, livestock, and wildlife of the Rio Abajo. But periodically and unpredictably the river has leapt from its banks, taking lives, destroying property, and devastating whole towns. Some of the worst flooding of the last 150 years occurred in 1855, 1884, 1929, 1937, and 1969. Each flood left great tragedy in its wake, but also stories of human kindness and hope.

The Flood of 1884

The flood of 1884 was so disastrous that it became the source of local legend and song. The flood was so bad that most residents of Tomé had to abandon their valley homes to seek refuge with friends and relatives who lived in *ranchitos* on higher ground. According to one legend, fleeing villagers emptied the Catholic church on their flooding plaza, carrying religious items to safety elsewhere in the village. Only one statue, an image of Christ, refused to go, making itself so heavy that not even several men could lift it. When the flood waters finally receded, much of the church had been destroyed, but not the corner where the Christ figure still stood. Parishioners were convinced that Christ had insisted on staying behind to protect his sacred home.

Further north, near Peralta, Don José Placido Romero encouraged his workers with drinks of bottled beer as they worked to dam the same flood of 1884. According to a humorous *corrido* (ballad) about the flood,

> Here comes Don Placido Romero
> Presuming his great wealth
> Hoping to dam the river
> With bottles of beer.

Having "inspired" his men to work hard, Don Placido is credited with saving his village—and his property—from the rushing waters of the Rio Grande.

Other floods are remembered for their far more divisive results. The flood of 1855 destroyed the Belen Catholic church at its original location dangerously near the Rio Grande. When the church was rebuilt, the bitter dispute over where it should be located divided the community for years.

San Marcial, 1929

The flood of August 13, 1929, was so devastating that it practically buried the small railroad community of San Marcial, thirty miles south of Socorro. The flood's force was so powerful that it pushed over locomotives and railroad cars. The water level became so high that some residents had to be rescued from second-floor windows with boats sent north from Elephant Butte.

San Marcial had been a thriving railroad town since the 1880s when the Atchison, Topeka and Santa Fe Railway designated it as a major division point on the Santa Fe's north-south train route through New Mexico. By the 1920s, San Marcial boasted a bank, a mercantile store, a drug store, an opera house, several churches, public schools and even a Harvey House. Only Socorro surpassed San Marcial in population and prosperity in Socorro County. San Marcial's 1,500 men, women and children were justifiably proud of their close-knit community where work was plentiful and nearly everyone got along.

But the bright skies over San Marcial suddenly darkened in August 1929. Unusually heavy rain caused the Rio Grande to rise so high and so quickly that the reservoir at Elephant Butte (built in 1916) could not handle the overflow. Despite heroic efforts, San Marcial's dike broke on Aug. 13.

Within hours the town was under as much as six feet of water. Many buildings, including a Protestant church, the opera house, and several adobe homes, were destroyed. Fortunately, no lives were lost. Outside assistance soon arrived and townspeople helped one another in every way possible. One family went so far as to move into a tent so that three families, left homeless in the flood, could move into their large, mostly undamaged home.

Downtown San Marcial after the floods of 1929 (Socorro Historical Society)

As floodwaters began to recede, businesses began to reopen. Families began to rebuild. Residents returned to work. Like a boxer who had been hit hard but tried to regain his balance, the citizens of San Marcial seemed determined to recover from the calamity of August 13.

And so Juliana "Judy" Serna returned to her job at the Harvey House by San Marcial's train tracks and depot. The 21-year-old San Marcial native truly enjoyed serving passengers and railroad workers at the Harvey House's large lunch counter. She and her friend Josephine Jojola made good money at the restaurant, especially with generous tips left by satisfied customers.

Travelers on the Santa Fe Railway knew that they could expect fresh food, efficient service, and reasonable prices at any Harvey House they visited. Built by the railroad and managed by the Fred Harvey Company, Harvey Houses could feed a trainload of passengers in thirty minutes without anyone feeling pressured or rushed.

Judy Serna, Josephine Jojola, and the rest of the Harvey House staff in San Marcial worked side-by-side in a well-run operation supervised by a house manager, respectfully known as Mr. Coverdale.

Judy and Josephine expected a normal work shift when they arrived at the San Marcial Harvey House on Tuesday, September 24. No one in San Marcial knew that the Rio Grande, the Rio Puerco, and the Rio Salado had all risen simultaneously, sending a wall of water downstream with San Marcial in its sights. Some five weeks after San Marcial's first inundation, this second flood struck and water had begun to enter the Harvey House's ground floor.

Mr. Coverdale ordered everyone to carry as much as they could up the stairs to the building's second floor. As the water rose, Judy and her fellow workers hauled everything possible, especially perishable foods. When the water rose as high as their chests, the crew realized that it was time to abandon their sinking ship. Mr. Coverdale and other men helped Judy, Josephine, and several Harvey Girls wade through the rising water to a waiting train.

But just as the castaways got to the train, someone yelled, "You might as well go back. The bridge is washed out!" It was too late to flee from San Marcial by train. Judy and her fellow employees waded back to the Harvey House and climbed its stairs to the still-dry second floor. As evening approached, they realized that they would be forced to stay the night, if not longer, until help arrived.

Taking charge, Mr. Coverdale reassured his staff that everything was under control and that they were safe. Years later, Judy recalled her manager's unruffled demeanor. "I'm going to take all of you out one way or another," he told them. "Don't worry. Everything is going to be O.K."

With faith in their manager and the optimism of youth, Judy and Josephine made the best of their dire circumstances. Sharing a hotel room, drinking free Cokes, and eating some of the food they had earlier helped carry upstairs, the friends began to forget their predicament and enjoy their adventure. Someone played music on a portable phonograph. The girls talked and even laughed through much of the night.

But the sounds outside could not be completely ignored, especially when Judy and Josephine tried to sleep. Water cascaded down the street. One building after another caved in. It seemed like only the Harvey House stood firm. At dawn the Harvey House staff awoke and some, including Judy, crawled out a second-floor window onto the roof to survey the damage to their surroundings. They gazed in amazement. All Judy could see was water. Startled, she sat down next to a window and simply stared.

As reassuring as ever, Mr. Coverdale told his staff, "A boat will come for us now that there is light. No need to worry. I will make sure that each of you will get out safely." True to the manager's promise, a large motor boat from Elephant Butte arrived to rescue those stranded on the rooftop. But how to lower people from the roof to the boat several feet below?

The train that had earlier failed to carry them to safety now played a key role. A long ladder was extended from the roof to the train, and each person slowly crawled across the makeshift bridge above the rushing water. Once at the train, the Harvey House workers climbed down into the waiting boat.

It was noon before everyone was safely aboard and traveling by boat through the flooded town. The scene was even more distressing than what they had seen from the Harvey House's roof. Calm as ever and eager to distract his workers, Mr. Coverdale promised a big lunch once they landed on "shore." The boat and its passengers finally reached higher ground where an anxious crowd awaited them. Judy spotted her brother, Felesino, standing knee-deep in water, eager to assist her and other flood victims. Carrying Judy on his shoulders, Felesino delivered his sister to dry land at last.

In another version of this story, a young cowboy (Judy's cousin) rescued Judy and her fellow refugees by riding his horse, Chapo, through the water to the hotel. The cowhand made many trips, each time carrying another grateful person to safety.

Once on dry land, Judy's brother Felesino urged her to hurry home to let her worried family know that she was safe. Their distraught mother had reportedly cried all night. Judy ran to her home, located on high ground west of town. Relieved to see her daughter alive, Judy's mother, Aurora, now wept tears of joy. After a brief reunion, Judy returned to her fellow workers to enjoy the lunch Mr. Coverdale had promised. The resourceful manager had somehow rescued food as well as people as he hurriedly abandoned his submerged restaurant.

The Harvey House staff and their San Marcial neighbors survived the terrible floods of 1929, but their community did not. Realizing that its offices and shops were beyond repair, the Santa Fe Railway abandoned all but its tracks that ran east of town. Without railroad employment and the income it brought, local residents faced the inevitable and began an exodus that took nearly a year to complete. Some Santa Fe employees took transfers to railroad towns as near as Belen or as far as San Bernardino, California.

Descendants still live in these and other towns, especially Socorro and Albuquerque.

And the floods destroyed thousands of acres of farmland up and down the valley. An estimated eight thousand farmers and their families joined railroad employees in a larger exodus from San Marcial and the surrounding area.

Judy soon moved to San Acacia where she met and married Joseph David García. The couple lived in Albuquerque and California before moving to Polvadera to own and operate a service station and bar. They raised three children, Joseph David Leroy, Mauricio Antonio, and María. When Joe García died at the age of 46, Judy ran the family businesses on her own before retiring to Albuquerque and, later, to Socorro. She died on January 22, 1993, at the age of 85. But Judy never lost her affection for San Marcial. She always remembered the friendly community and the fields where she loved to ride horses as a girl. She remembered the first plane to fly over San Marcial and how everyone stood outside and marveled at the strange machine in the sky above their town. Judy also remembered the first time she used a telephone and how her mother wept at the sight of young American soldiers passing by in trains en route to Europe during World War I. Judy remembered the horrors of the Spanish flu epidemic of 1918 when people died so quickly that they had to be buried in mass graves at the local cemetery.

And of course she remembered the floods of 1929. Judy's fellow residents of old San Marcial shared these memories and missed their lost town. More than a thousand attended a reunion held in Socorro's Sedillo Park on Saturday, August 26, 1995. Men and women laughed and cried and hugged and reminisced. Many wore specially produced T-shirts that read, "I survived the floods of 1929."

Several former residents have honored their little town in poems and a *corrido*, written by Ramón Luna and recorded by Eddie Benevidez. Translated by musicologist John Donald Robb, the *corrido's* lyrics read:

The [twenty-fourth of September],
I do not wish to remember,
For on that day the Rio Grande
Flooded the town of San Marcial....

The water was pretty high,
Houses were floating around,
And the people went weeping
To the top of the hills.

My poor people,
Oh, what luck befell them!
They all lost their houses,
Only the Harvey House remained....

Songs like Ramón Luna's *corrido* and stories like Judy Serna's personal history help us celebrate—and mourn—this proud little town in the heart of the Rio Abajo. This devastation is iconic because, prior to the damming of the river, flooding occurred periodically all along the Rio Grande. Villages like La Jollita, Sabino, Bosquecito, La Parida, and El Tajo were all destroyed by the capricious but vicious river, never to be reoccupied.

The Flood of 1937

The citizens of Belen were among the towns most affected by the valley's next disastrous flood, in mid-1937. Ironically, the valley had suffered a bad drought in 1936, with an adverse effect on crops and livestock in the area. Weather predictions were more favorable for 1937, with a "sufficient amount" of rain expected "to meet all needs," according to the *Belen News*. Few weather reports have been so wrong.

A deluge of rain fell on New Mexico in the last week of May 1937, inundating Belen and many other towns up and down the Rio Grande Valley. The valley suffered an estimated $1 million dollars worth of damage (equal to over $13 million in today's money). Roads north and south of Socorro were washed out, causing a postponement of the official opening of the Carrie Tingley Hospital for Crippled Children in Hot Springs (now Truth or Consequences). Flash floods killed six men in various parts of the state.

In Belen, at least twenty families were forced to abandon their vulnerable adobe homes. Eighteen of the stricken families lived in

Pueblitos, three miles south of Belen; other families fled from homes on or near North Main Street. Angie Chávez remembers so much water in her family's house on Cavalier Road that they loaded up their Model T truck with as much as they could carry and headed for higher ground in Casa Colorada. The family stayed with relatives until the water receded in Belen. When Geneva Gurulé did not arrive at work as a housekeeper and nanny at Dr. E.G. Brentari's home, the dentist hired a man to ride horseback to her flooded home to give her a ride to work.

According to Ken Gibson, the old Central School building (where Lowe's Grocery Store now stands) was so deep in water that the school's principal, Harriet Monroe, had to be rowed to the school in a rowboat. Bill Gore says that the water was up to his young waist in the lot across the street from his family's home at Sixth and Baca. Eleanor Love, living with her family on Mesa Road, remembers one of her older brothers having to swim across the flooded road to rescue their neighbor's endangered beehives.

J. F. Padilla's two-story Economy Cash store on North Main Street was the most damaged structure in town. The building's floors were ruined, and, with serious damage to the store's adobe walls, Padilla's glass display window cracked. Grateful that the damage was not worse, Padilla expressed his thanks to everyone who had offered their "splendid cooperation" in his hour of need. The storeowner's letter of appreciation appeared on the front page of the June 3, 1937, edition of the *Belen News*.

As a public health precaution, the Red Cross and the Valencia County Health Department scheduled times when local residents could receive inoculations against typhoid fever, a great danger for anyone who drank polluted flood water. One hundred and four men, women, and children were inoculated at the old city hall in Belen. Public health officials administered vaccines to dozens of other residents in Casa Colorada and Jarales on June 10. Meanwhile, residents found health-threatening debris, from garbage to sewage and dead animals, floating in the stagnant flood waters. Red Cross officials instructed all community members to boil their well water for at least ten minutes before using it.

The Belen flood of 1937 was terrible, but the editor of the *Belen News* asserted that it wasn't as bad as some Albuquerque newspapers would have their readers believe. In fact, Elfego C. Baca believed that the Duke

City's editors might have had an ulterior motive in exaggerating the damage done in Belen. According to Baca, "the Albuquerque papers are trying to give the impression that Belen was so badly situated that it was not safe to make investments here. Belen is as sound and safe as any other town along the Rio Grande."

The Flood of 1969

Belen was "as sound and safe" from floods as any other valley community for the next thirty-two years. But then everything changed in a single afternoon in June 1969, when Belen faced the worst deluge and destruction in its long history.

On Sunday, June 15, 1969, Joe L. Padilla and his family were about to sit down for a typical Sunday dinner in their home on South First Street. It was Father's Day, so the mood was particularly festive. The Padillas never got to enjoy their meal because the rain began to pour. Three inches of rain and golf ball-size hail drenched Belen in less than an hour. The Belen Drainage Ditch broke and overflowed. Water soon filled the streets and threatened many structures.

The Padillas and many families like them tried to keep the water out of their homes, but without success. It would be 1:00 a.m. the following morning before the Padillas found time to finally rest and eat the meal they had had to abandon the previous afternoon. In addition to the considerable damage to their home, the family's large chile and tomato garden was completely destroyed. All two hundred plants were lost in the flood. As luck would have it, the Padillas's house was in the worst hit part of Belen, west of the Santa Fe Railway tracks and south of Reinken Ave. An aerial view of the flood zone showed that Baca, Bernard, Castillo, Didier, Dillon, and Gilbert were among the streets that suffered the greatest losses in the flood zone.

Electrical power was disrupted, as was phone service until Monday morning. Fallen tree limbs and debris blocked roads and clogged irrigation ditches. Cars were so buried in mud or submerged under water that few could start. A visitor from Texas reportedly tried to free his car from the mud twenty times before he finally succeeded with the help of several Good Samaritans. Judy Márquez and two of her high school friends were driving to the Oñate Theatre for a matinee show when the floods struck

South Main Street. Suddenly their Volkswagen "bug" began to float! The girls thought this was great fun, especially when they saw a toilet floating down the main street of town.

More seriously, Matt and Theresa Baca had just begun building a new house on South Second Street while still living at their previous home on South Third. Standing at their place on South Third, they looked over at their new house. As the floodwaters swept in, the couple glanced at their first wall, but the wall had suddenly disappeared. In moments nearly everything they had built was either knocked over or under water.

Fortunately, emergency workers appeared shortly after the deluge began. City police, state police, and National Guardsmen were particularly quick to respond. Rupert Baca remembers that he and his fellow National Guardsmen had just completed drills when the crisis began. Not waiting for official orders from Santa Fe to call out the Guard, Baca and his men hurried to the flooded area to assist in any way they could. Most Guardsmen labored for the next twenty-four hours without rest. Even General John P. Jolly, the commander of the New Mexico National Guard, lent a hand when he arrived at the scene. Families from 145 houses were evacuated, along with as much of their furniture as they could carry with the assistance of National Guardsmen using large Army trucks. Salvaged goods from fifty households were stored at the National Guard Armory on South Main Street. Household damage totaled an estimated $380,000 ($2 million today).

Of the 145 evacuated structures, thirteen were completely destroyed, forty-seven suffered major damage, and another eighty-five needed minor repairs. Although no one was killed or injured, many residents had to be literally carried from their homes in the waist-deep water. At least one man called KARS radio station to ask for help in locating his wife. The station never learned if the woman was found, no less if her disappearance really had anything to do with the flood!

As many as twenty-five local businesses were damaged, including two beyond repair. Eppa Lake's well-digging equipment and two of his pickup trucks, including a new Dodge, were buried in silt. Herb Ellermeyer's F&E Store was flooded, with the greatest destruction to merchandise stored in the F&E building's basement. Water rushed in the back door of the Sugar Bowl Lanes on Dalies Avenue. Owner Marvin

"Sugar" Glidewell reported that the water had poured into the area of his pin-setting machines, but no further.

Sandy Battin, then a young reporter at the *Belen News*, recalls coming to work that Sunday to help prepare the paper's Monday edition. (The paper came out on Mondays and Thursdays in those days.) The newspaper's office was located on Baca Avenue, not far from the center of the worst flooded area. Determined to report on the flood and meet their deadline, editor Carter Waid and his staff worked through Sunday afternoon even as water covered their newsroom floor. Sandy remembers a fellow staff member sitting with her feet raised above the water level as she worked on an electric machine. If the woman had worked on her machine with her feet in water she may well have become the flood's first—and only—fatality.

A few blocks away, city hall lay in three feet of water. Files in the Valencia County Selective Service Board office, at Sixth and Baca, were soaked. Diligent office personnel salvaged the partially damaged files at the height of the Vietnam War.

On South Main Street, Donn and Marjorie Thompson remember water rising against both the front and back doors of the store they had purchased just four years earlier. They decided the best thing to do was simply open both doors and let the water rush straight through. Lorraine Romero says that the water was very high and caused great damage in her father's tavern on South Main and Didier, although the long bar and stools at Tommy's Lounge survived the disaster.

Local schools were affected as well, with damages estimated at half a million dollars, according to Belen School Superintendent John E. Aragón. Rio Grande Elementary, Jarales Elementary, and especially the old junior high school suffered roof damage, leakage, and the destruction of many supplies. The junior high school's playing field was so flooded that it resembled a formidable natural lake.

Although not in the center of the storm, other sections of Valencia County faced heavy damage, largely due to the hail that accompanied the heavy rain. In the Rio Grande Estates (now called Rio Communities) roofs, windows, gardens, and trees were destroyed. Nearly every house had at least one broken window. Residents even found dead birds in their yards, including three roadrunners that had gotten to be rather tame residents of the new neighborhood.

As in Belen's flood of 1937, the Red Cross arrived to assist with much needed emergency services and supplies. Headquartered at the local National Guard Armory, the Red Cross provided food, clothing, and shelter. With volunteer help, some 2,000 Belen residents received typhoid inoculations. As in 1937, residents were warned to boil their well water before using it. The situation may have been far worse if water sanitation workers had not acted quickly to shut down Belen's water supply before the flood had reached a crisis stage.

A helicopter sprayed insecticide to control flies and mosquitoes. Efforts were made to stop the spread of disease carried by rats and mice in the area. Cleanup and repair took months to complete. Thousands of gallons of water were pumped from homes, yards, and streets. A crew of forty-two city workers removed tons of sand, silt, and soil, laboring sixteen-hour days for more than a week after the flood. Belen Mayor Neel Alexander estimated that the total cost of damages and repairs equaled between $1.5 and $2 million (or about $9 million today).

Aftermath

Meanwhile, flood victims did the best they could to reconstruct their lives. Most families returned to their damaged, water-soaked homes to begin the difficult task of cleaning, drying, and restoring their possessions. A tour of the stricken area revealed many rugs, curtains, and clothes hung on fences to dry. Furniture, from sofas to mattresses, dried in the yards. Most families eventually moved back into their homes. Matt and Theresa Baca finished building their new home and have lived there ever since.

Others made the difficult decision to move to other parts of town, either because their homes were so damaged or because they did not want to face another storm in the same poorly drained area of Belen.

Most businesses also recovered. Fifty applied for emergency Small Business Association loans. Tommy's Lounge opened in about a month, but only after considerable remodeling. "Sugar" Glidewell opened the Sugar Bowl Lanes as soon as his pin-setting machines had a chance to dry. With continuous pumping, half of the water in the F&E Store's basement was emptied by Monday night; the other half was emptied by Tuesday evening. F&E owner Herb Ellermeyer began the equally hard labor of cleaning the mud-covered clothing that had been stored in his flooded basement. So much mud had to be cleaned from the merchandise that fire hoses were used to finish the task. Ruben Chávez and his cousin Larry Gurulé were among several teenagers hired to do the work.

On Sunday, June 29, two weeks after the flood, Ellermeyer held a huge sale in his store's parking lot. From 1:00 to 6:00 p.m. all items were offered at a fraction of their regular prices. So many Belenites arrived during the first hour of the sale that Ellermeyer later described it as "utter chaos." An estimated 1,500 customers filled the parking lot in search of bargains. The sale was so successful that old-timers refer to it as one of their few positive memories of the flood. Donn Thompson claims that he still wears some comfortable overalls that he bought at the sale, although he admits that they've seen their better days.

As often happens in the aftermath of a disaster, a small army of politicians soon descended on Belen to inspect the area, investigate what had caused the disaster, and promise funding to prevent the problem in the future. Unfortunately, few of these promises were kept, much to the dismay of sincere local leaders like Mayor Alexander, city manager Richard Aragón, and State Senator Tibo J. Chávez.

But somehow life went on after the flood. As reported in the *Belen News*, couples got married. Babies were born. Boy Scouts departed for the national Boy Scout jubilee in Idaho. Construction of I-25, with its anticipated Belen exits, continued with only slight delay. Authorities captured two escaped prisoners from the Los Lunas honor farm. Western artist Gordon Snidow announced that he had purchased the old Felipe Chávez mansion and intended to restore it to use as his home and studio.

The Father's Day flood of 1969 soon became a distant memory for most Belenites, only recalled as a point of reference when later flooding occurred. Tommy García "thought it was 1969 all over again" when his lounge on South Main Street was flooded after an inch of rain fell on Belen in half an hour in August 1974.

Most recently, residents of Belen were reminded of the tragedy of 1969 when several family homes were inundated with mud and water after heavy rainstorms struck the valley and the drainage ditch broke again in the summer of 2006. Driving through the stricken area, one had to be impressed by how courageously the affected families worked to dig out of the mess, clean up their homes, and somehow get on with their lives with the help of families, friends, neighbors, and even perfect strangers.

Generous help is the common theme in all the floods in Valencia County history. Residents opened their homes to flood victims in 1884, 1937, and in every other disaster. Businessmen helped fellow businessmen. Good Samaritans came to the aid of stranded motorists. National Guardsmen and city workers labored tirelessly.

The list goes on and on. In large and small ways, people helped people through each crisis. As *Belen News* editor Carter Waid put it in the aftermath of the flood of 1969, "we only see the true spirit of our people when there is a disaster." But that's exactly when we need the true spirit of our people most.

Bibliography

References

Baca, Oswald G. and Mary Ann Baca. *A Compilation of Burial Records of the Central New Mexico Villages of Tomé, San Fernando, Los Enlames, Valencia, Peralta, Casa Colorada, and Manzano: 1793-1795, 1809-1846.* University of New Mexico Southwest Hispanic Research Institute Research Report #005, Spring 1993.

_____. *A Compilation of Burial Records of Villages of Tomé, Valencia, Peralta, El Cerro, San Fernando, Los Enlames (Adelino), La Constancia, and Casa Colorada: 1847-1920.* University of New Mexico Southwest Hispanic Research Institute Research Report #006, Fall 1994.

_____. *Burial Records from New Mexico's Rio Abajo: Tomé and Associated Villages—1921-1956.* University of New Mexico Southwest Hispanic Research Institute Research Report #007, Summer 1995.

Ball, Larry D. *Desert Lawmen: The High Sheriffs of New Mexico and Arizona 1846-1912.* Albuquerque: University of New Mexico Press, 2011.

_____. *Elfego Baca in Life and Legend.* El Paso: Texas Western Press, 1992.

_____. *The United States Marshals of New Mexico and Arizona Territories, 1846-1912.* Albuquerque: University of New Mexico Press, 1978.

Bryan, Howard. *Incredible Elfego Baca: Good Man, Bad Man of the Old West.* Santa Fe: Clear Light Publishers, 1993.

_____. *Robbers, Rogues, and Ruffians: True Tales of the Wild West in New Mexico.* Santa Fe: Clear Light Publishers, 1991.

Bullis, Don. *New Mexico's Finest—Peace Officers Killed in the Line of Duty, 1847-2010.* Los Ranchos: Rio Grande Books, 2010.

_____. *Duels, Gunfights and Shootouts: Wild Tales from the Land of Enchantment.* Los Ranchos: Rio Grande Books, 2010.

_____. *Bloodville.* Chesterfield: Beachhouse Books, 2002.

353

_____. *New Mexico Historical Biographies*. Los Ranchos: Rio Grande
Books, 2011.

Deal, David Allen. *Discovery of Ancient America*. Irvine, California: Kherem La
Yah Press, 1984.

Fedewa, Marilyn H. *Maria Agreda: Mystical Lady in Blue*. Albuquerque:
University of New Mexico Press, 2009.

Fergusson, Erna. *Murder and Mystery in New Mexico*. Santa Fe: Lightning Tree
Press, 1991.

Gilbreath, West. *Death on the Gallows: The Story of Legal Hangings in New Mexico,
1847-1923*. Silver City: High-Lonesome Press, 2002.

Kutz, Jack. *More Mysteries and Miracles of New Mexico*. Corrales: Rhombus
Publishing, 1998.

_____. *Mysteries and Miracles of New Mexico*. Corrales: Rhombus
Publishing Company, 1988.

Lacy, Ann and Anne Valley-Fox, eds. *Outlaws and Desperados: A New Mexico
Federal Writers Project Book*. Santa Fe: Sunstone Press, 2008.

Marshall, Michael P. and Henry J. Walt. *Rio Abajo—Prehistory and History of a
Rio Grande Province*. New Mexico Historic Presevation Program, 1984.

Meketa, Jacqueline. *From Martyrs to Murderers: The Old Southwest's Saints,
Sinners and Scalawags*. Las Cruces: Yucca Tree Press, 1993.

Melzer, Richard. *Buried Treasures: Famous and Unusual Gravesites in New Mexico
History*. Santa Fe: Sunstone Press, 2007.

Morris, Roger. *The Devil's Butcher Shop: The New Mexico Prison Uprising*.
Albuquerque: University of New Mexico Press, 1983.

Perkins, Dixie, L. *The Meaning of the New Mexico Mystery Stone*. Albuquerque:
Sun Books, 1979.

Poldervaart, Arie W. *Black-Robed Justice*. Santa Fe: Historical Society of New
Mexico, 1948.

Saenz, Adolph. *Politics of a Prison Riot*. Corrales: Rhombus Publishing, 1986.

Sager, Stan. *Viva Elfego: The Case for Elfego Baca, Hispanic Hero*. Santa Fe:
Sunstone Press, 2008.

Simmons, Marc. *When Six-Guns Ruled: Outlaw Tales of the Southwest*. Santa Fe:
Ancient City Press, 1990.

Szasz, Ferenc Morton. *Great Mysteries of the West*. Golden, CO: Fulcrum
Publishing, 1993.

Tanner, Karen Holliday and John D. Tanner, Jr. *The Bronco Bill Gang*. Norman:
University of Oklahoma Press, 2011.

Tórrez, Robert J. *Myth of the Hanging Tree: Stories of Crime and Punishment in Territorial New Mexico*. Albuquerque: University of New Mexico Press, 2008.

ufocon.blogspot.com/2009/09/socorro-hoax-exposed-famous-1964.htm

Valencia County News-Bulletin: May 13-14, 1998; November 25, 1998; August 28-29, 1999; September 22-23, 1999; November 13-14, 1999; December 25-26, 1999; March 25-26, 2000; May 20, 2000; September 18, 2000; January 20-21, 2001; December 15, 2001; January 22, 2002; May 25, 2002; August 17, 2002; August 20, 2002; April 19, 2003; July 19, 2003; September 20, 2003; October 18, 2003; June 19, 2004; October 16, 2004; November 20, 2004; November 19, 2005; December 17, 2005; March 25, 2006; April 1, 2006; October 21, 2006; December 30, 2006; January 6, 2007; May 19, 2007; August 18, 2007; September 2007; November 17, 2007; December 15, 2007; June 30, 2007; January 19, 2008; July 26, 2008; August 2, 2008; February 7, 2009; March 21, 2009; August 21, 2009; September 19, 2009; December 12, 2009; February 27, 2010; March 6, 2010; January 15, 2011; May 21, 2011; June 18, 2011; August 27, 2011; September 3, 2011; November 19, 2011; November 26, 2011

Index

357

CPSIA information can be obtained
at www.ICGtesting.com
Printed in the USA
FSOW02n1929300717
36870FS